FROM THE TOP

First published in Australia in 2023 by TnF Press.

Email for correspondence: tomrobbtom@gmail.com

ISBN 9780645892604 (paperback)

ABOUT THE COVER

Sandy Cull, book cover designer extraordinaire, and I were working on the cover for this book and nothing seemed to grab me. Pictures of showgirls might have led potential readers to believe I was a drag queen, and feathers en masse seemed to be a touch too soft. A photo of me was out of the question. Poor uncomplaining Sandy must have been near the end of her tether when she lightly threw this left field design at me. I loved it instantly.

Two types of feathers are used in top class cabaret production. Yes, there is indeed a snobbery regarding feathers. Anything from a turkey is a no-no. Turkey feathers are relatively inexpensive for a reason, they shed constantly, and they break. Ostrich and pheasant feathers are the preferred go-to for durability and the all over wow factor. Both, however are extremely expensive.

Pheasant feathers, particularly the extra-long Reeve pheasant feathers, have been used in Chinese opera for centuries. Pheasants represented riches and were venerated. Once the tails of birds reared on pheasant farms in China reached a certain length (they grow up to two metres) they were then housed in tall cages with very little room for movement, the tail hanging out of a hole at the back to keep it off the ground. Twice daily these birds were exercised to keep them in top notch condition. One person, usually a child, walked in front with the lead and, a second child walked behind carrying the tail. A broken or dirty tail meant years of great care wasted. There are only two long tail feathers per bird.

T. L. W. ROBB

FROM THE TOP

TRAVELLER • OUTLAW • PRODUCER

CONTENTS

FOR THE TWO LOVES OF MY LIFE

LUIS AND POSSUM

The author, perhaps 12 years old, maybe in Ballarat.

INTRODUCTION

A tremendous thump overhead drew my eyes to the massive plate glass ceiling some ten metres above me, in time to witness soldiers in full battle dress sliding across it. The clatter of army boots on marble brought my attention back to the cavernous lobby two floors below. Soldiers, armed and ready, surrounded a tall figure with an oversized black moustache, unmistakable in his familiar black beret. A man with all too recognisable features whose face glared down from thousands of larger-than-life posters and banners adorning every public building, crossroad and monument in Baghdad. I was now looking down at the man himself, Saddam Hussein.

From Ballarat to Baghdad is quite a leap. Never had I dreamed as a young underprivileged boy from the sticks that it would be possible to find myself metres away from one of the world's most infamous tyrants. Maybe just as well, back then I was hardly the most stable of kids, and the looming largeness of it all might well have sent me into paroxysms of anxiety. My life became something even I couldn't believe sometimes. I was stopped in my tracks constantly by the breadth of it all. New countries, new problems, new adventures, times when life seemed to be a breakneck ride, and I was certainly a willing passenger. Naturally this would all seem a nonsense, of course, in the cold light of day. Each and every step along the way was taken with much thought to enable the next step, and the next. That's how we move forward in life, isn't it? Still, the wonder of it all was occasionally overwhelming, and at times, not just a little frightening.

Yes, tyrants were a part of the cast list of my life, along with movie stars, royalty, billionaires, assorted celebrities, and of course many wonderful showgirls. The backdrops, scenes and scenery supplied by many years of constant global travel and touring.

I do hope I've given a fair and honest account of the good times, and the bad. They were all extraordinary.

CHAPTER 1

A TRAVELLING CIRCUS

The story has it that on retrieving mother and me from Hamilton Hospital after my birth on September seventh, 1947, my father threw a pillow and a bundle of blankets into the boot of a borrowed car telling her, 'I've got the bedding stuff, where's the baby?' My mother's horrified expression told him all he needed to know: the baby was in the blankets. I was tiny, just a few pounds—so small I was taken back a few days later to spend some time in an incubator.

'Head like a lemon,' my father always said. He can't have been particularly fond of that citrus because by the time I was six, he'd headed for some far greener pastures, leaving my mother, my older sister Frances and me to fend for ourselves.

My mother, Olive Albina Rackham, was born in Ballarat, a Central Highlands city in the old 19th-century gold rush belt of Victoria. She had four older siblings, three girls and a boy. Her mother – my grandmother – was married off in her early twenties to a man nearly three times her age. I believe he was a police officer who, at some point in his career, stopped a runaway carriage and thus saved the female occupant from, at the very least, a fainting spell. For this brave action he received three things. A commendation from the brass, a writeup in a Melbourne paper, and a steel plate in his head from the kick in the skull he'd received from the horse. He died when my mother was two leaving a still-young widow and five children to eke out a living on his meagre police pension.

My father, Lindsey Wyatt Robb, had a very different start to life. He was born in Korumburra, a small town in Gippsland Victoria and had two older siblings, William and Alice. His father was a Victorian Railways employee who spent his weekends exhorting his fellow man to greater deeds in the name of his God. His mother was a looming, straitlaced Victorian woman who entered a room bosom first. These two chosen ones came into money at some point and by the time I first met them, any hint of the working class was imperiously shoved to the rear. They were very comfortably ensconced in a well-known mansion in Bendigo bearing the rather grand name of West End Hall.

As I was only five years old, West End Hall did not have the staggering effect on me it might have had on someone older. Someone already exposed to the indoctrination of 'wealth equals superiority'. It was for me, however, the most marvellous playground. There were the coach houses, stables and servants' quarters to be explored. The enormous fernery with its strange, dank smells to hide in. Enclosed by a high bluestone and brick wall, the front garden and the circular drive with its great spurting fountain were begging for a small boy to race around and soak himself. The cows in the paddock at the back were wonderful and warm, and one sloppy lick would cover my face in fresh grassy drool. The twin resting lions at the porticoed main entry positively beseeched me to sit on them. There was a photo floating about for many years of me doing exactly that.

Inside was another matter entirely, everything was forbidden. Grandmother wasn't one for allowing children to be seen or heard, the kitchen being the inside boundary limit to our freedom. The stairs are the only thing I remember about the interior of the house. Walking up those stairs to my cardiologist's rooms some sixty-five years later brought back instant flashes of my flight down those same stairs as a child, a maid wielding a vacuum cleaner in hot pursuit.

My parents met and married within a two-week period during WWII while both were stationed in Wodonga on the Victorian–New South Wales border.

Mother was in the Women's Auxiliary Australian Air Force (WAAAF), and Father in the Army. A fleeting romance followed by a rushed Registry Office marriage was quite common during those dark days when re-postings and death were uppermost in the minds of service personnel. There was no chance for true love to blossom and grow, no extended engagement period in which to fully get to know your chosen mate. Grab any shreds of happiness before the worst happens, cling onto the hope of survival and normality down the track. Father spent time in Pentridge Prison at HM's pleasure after his 'devil take the hindmost' two-day AWOL honeymoon. A month's confinement in peace time ensued for this little breach, I imagine a much sterner approach was taken in time of war. Probably the bravest, and possibly the only commitment the man ever made in his life.

Before war's end, father was posted 'overseas'—where exactly overseas was never mentioned. Three days before leaving for his posting, he and two others were returning to the barracks at night when all three were hit by an Army vehicle. A 'brownout' was implemented in Australia during WWII – not quite a full blackout – so headlights of vehicles were hooded, allowing just enough light to navigate. Father's two companions died in the accident, and he was hospitalised with a broken hip, other fractures and abrasions. This broken hip would be the cause of the removal of one of his legs from the hip down some 15 years later when bone cancer set in. I frankly cannot remember if it was his right or left leg. He'd been out of my life quite a while by the time the leg came off.

The Lindsey I later came to know was a tall man, around five feet eleven and well-built from many years spent on crutches. Just a hint of middle age spread, he was very German-looking with white skin that tanned well, blond hair and blue eyes. My sister Frances inherited her physical traits from him, skin colour (except she burns and peels, burns and peels) hair colour and eye colour and nothing from my mother at all. It's a strange world, genetics. A very physical man, my father never once let the loss of his leg impede him. Although a prosthetic limb had been fitted, it was cumbersome and drove him nuts. He moved more freely and was much nimbler on his crutches. He would swim, hike, drive, climb trees, and I once witnessed him carrying a large armchair on his head. Very brave in so many ways and yet, a complete coward in others. Responsibility terrified him. Shortly after they married, his mother told him, 'You've made your bed, now lie in it.' It was very apparent to her that Olive Albina had problems.

Although raised in poverty, mother held some strange class values. Quite unfathomable really. She despised her olive skin, equating it with being of the lower classes, and would never go out in the sun with bared arms. An excellent posture and a rigid carriage were deemed absolute musts, and this was drummed – and sometimes beaten – into us from a very early age. Until the day she died, although she was hampered by severe mental incapacity, she was never seen to slump in a chair or to lean against the back of one. She was always perched on the edge, ramrod straight.

She wasn't a tall woman, maybe five feet three or four, and thin with a large bust of which she was particularly proud. Her hair was dark brown and wavy, as was mine, and her dark eyes showed very little colour difference between pupil and iris. She was always very proud of her naturally wavy hair, and the fact she never went grey.

My skin was paler than hers and I tan if I even look at the sun. It was always suggested there was, shudder, Italian blood somewhere in the family past. I signed up for a DNA test 'on special' a few years ago and learned I was 'up to twenty percent' Arabic. What a huge shudder that would have sent down her rigid spine.

Never much of a doer, my mother preferred doing nothing at all, if the opportunity presented itself. She seemed to enjoy only two things really, knitting and reading murder mysteries—two things she was quite capable of doing simultaneously. Knitting intricate cable jumpers, patterns with a cowboy riding a bucking horse, nothing was out of reach. She would knit away at a furious needle-melting pace, racing through both sweater and book in no time at all. Very limited in social graces, mother would be completely lost among persons of even average intellect. Conversation, she felt, was best kept to two subjects, the weather and health. Especially hers.

Childhood memories are very strange things. Insignificant incidences might be recalled in high-definition detail while life-changing, meaningful occurrences fade or completely evaporate. Though consequences may be felt for a lifetime, the catalyst simply cannot be brought to mind. Not a single memory remains of the day my father left us. Surely the situation was explained to us somehow? 'Daddy's gone away', 'Daddy went to heaven', 'Daddy's pissed off with the chick down the road.' I was simply living my life.

One episode did, however, stay the course. Mother, my sister and I were on a train heading from Hamilton to Ballarat after the massive upheaval. Trains are fun when you are young, no matter what the reason for the trip. My sister and I were causing havoc in the passage, running up and down the length of the train when she spotted a man leaning on an open window ledge, staring into nowhere. 'Look,' she said to me, 'there's Daddy.' So it was, there was our father, large as life. Strangely we didn't rush up to him, running instead in the opposite direction to tell mother. That's where my recall of the event ends.

On our arrival into Ballarat, I could see Grandma, my mother's mother, waiting on the platform. In a burst of enthusiasm, I made a mighty kiddie leap from the train just before it stopped completely. I can close my eyes right now, see that monstrous iron wheel looming over me, smell the metallic dust of iron on iron from wheels constantly grinding on the tracks, and hear my grandmother screaming. I had fallen down the gap between the train and the platform. The wheels came to rest on my little winter coat. I have no idea whether the train was shunted back a little to free me or whether I was freed, leaving the coat behind.

Two of mother's four older siblings still lived in her hometown of Ballarat, some 175 kilometres from my birthplace. That train trip took us into a life of extreme poverty. After my father's desertion, my mother never recovered from what was then called a nervous breakdown. Her state of mental health, already shaky, left her unfit to care for us. She could be suffocatingly loving one moment, a dangerous outraged maniac the next. In her eighties, doctors discovered the poor woman was a dissociative with as many as three separate personalities. The diagnosis of this disorder was made far too late to be treated and she remained tormented until her death.

Our young lives became a painful travelling circus through orphanages, foster homes, relatives' homes (some kind, some incredibly unkind), tin sheds, boarding house rooms and attending a dozen schools across Victoria before I turned twelve. Hunger, cold, beatings and molestations of every description became our normal. Sounds quite Dickensian, doesn't it? No wonder that 'wandering gipsy' side of me developed, and always remained, so indelibly etched into my very soul.

CHAPTER 2

LOOKING FOR HOME

I've counted sixteen addresses for the first sixteen years of my life. After leaving Hamilton, our first stop was to stay at the Bond Street Ballarat home of Betty, Bob and son Arthur (not their real names because their son, my cousin, is not at fault and I don't intend him any grief. He is undoubtably a fine upstanding citizen.) Betty was my mother's sister, and I'm sure their little family was never thrilled to have us dropped on them.

Betty and my mother were alike enough to be twins and were often referred to as 'Billy and Betty', the terrible twins. Bob was a WWII pilot veteran, very quiet, and very much a loner. Fishing was his great love, and solo weekends away were the norm. It was often rumoured these fishing trips were a cover for his more furtive, clandestine operations—as a mafia bagman.

The story has it that after being posted to Italy, a friendship was struck with a 'mano nero' family which had a chapter in Victoria. I must say, for a humble mechanic, the family never seemed to want for anything. I was convinced that the story had legs due to the heavy presence of guns in their lives. Guns were everywhere. Under the beds, in the car, in the garage. They all knew how to shoot and were crack shots. There were new cars, furs, houses and garages and the best schools, university, and car for their son. Only a few months older than me, nothing was too much for him. No wonder Bob had a quiet side, concrete boots might be fitted to a more garrulous man.

Bob owned a garage outside of Ballarat, some fourteen kilometres away. The daily takings were brought home, and before it was counted and bagged up, my cousin would play with this cache on the floor. He usually made coin and banknote buildings for his Dinky toy cars to manoeuvre around. His cast-off school uniforms passed down to me were what I wore when I started school at the Ballarat School of Mines. Betty would proudly announce to all within earshot the pride she felt in the fact that her husband had never laid eyes on her naked body. That their son was conceived at all must surely have been a minor miracle. I can only presume Bob produced a nocturnal emission, and Betty rolled over in her sleep. The treasured son could do no wrong. A hand must never be lifted against Betty's precious gift to the world. From the moment we arrived there, every misdemeanour was transferred to me as the resident whipping boy, and all was well. On Bob's arrival home each day, he'd be given a vocal list of grievances from Betty. This would often be followed by me being picked up – usually by the hair – and thrown into the dirt-floored garage, where I would spend teary hours or even an entire night. Ballarat gets bloody cold; I can tell you from vast experience.

The Bond Street house was a small three-bedroom weatherboard. I don't know how the rooms were allocated before we arrived. Also in residence at the time was a man named Sam. I can't rightly say where Sam came from or how he fitted into the household, but I do know I was designated a place to sleep under the billiard table, on an army cot, between Sam and my cousin. My mother was on the floor behind the sofa in the living room, and where my sister slept, I have no idea. How long this arrangement went on for is lost in the memory maze of shunting and upheavals that followed.

How to tackle the many moves we made from that time on? There were four places we lived in at some stage in Bond Street alone. Opposite Betty's house lived the Sings, a Chinese family from Hong Kong—or someone in their past was. There was Jeanne, Wally and their two children, Kevin, and Pat. My sister and I lived there for a time, sleeping in shared beds with Kevin and Pat. Was my mother there? I don't recall. I do remember children calling me *Ching Chong Chinaman*, by association, I guess. Wally was a tight-fisted authoritarian, and food was always on short rations. I remember Kevin and me once locking poor Wally in the bathroom while we raided the pantry, escaping to the very top of the wood heap to stuff ourselves with our haul. We were given a good strapping for this, and painful though the small rebellion turned out to be, we thought it well and truly worth it. We then moved to a house further down Bond Street where we lived in a tin shed in someone's back yard. There was no furniture except a double bed on which all four of us slept. Four, because by this time we'd acquired a new family member. My grandmother, grandma, grannie – I've no actual recollection of what I called her – had been allocated to us to care for, reason unknown to this day. She was near to bedridden with Parkinson's disease and broken feet (don't ask).

Before we'd left Hamilton, I'd started going to school and continued all through this dislocated time once we moved to Ballarat. For me, being bullied began in kindergarten. Bullies start young and have a nose for it. We lived opposite the hospital, so to avoid the perilous walk home, I'd flag down an ambulance if one was passing, and hitch a ride. I guess they got to know me. The first time I did this, my mother nearly had a fit and thought the worst, I'm sure.

Although I never studied a day in my life, I was a good student with marks always near the top of the class. The Ballarat School of Mines required an entrance exam to determine which of six classes, A to F, a child's intellectual capacity placed them. My results installed me into the top fifteen percent, which meant I was placed at the lower level of the highest-class rating. I was what was called a bright student.

I can't have been more than eleven or twelve when I started suffering from Obsessive-Compulsive Disorder (OCD). Today it is a recognised mental disorder, but when I was still a kid, it meant you were just plain loony. The term is bandied about now, and to a considerable degree, has lost its kick. I continually hear people say, 'Oh she's/he's OCD, can't bear an unwashed dish in the sink, vacuums every day'. No, that's not OCD at all. OCD is crippling, totally and all-consumingly crippling. It is insidious, takes over your entire life, and puts a stop to any semblance of normal functioning. Because of it, other children (and some adults), teased me unmercifully. Teased and bullied, bullied and teased. The misery. There's nothing like difference to bring out the worst in people.

Breathing. Intakes of breath while having simultaneous thoughts of my mother, may cause her harm. Answer: Hold your breath.

Glimpsing pieces of rubbish, paper, ice cream sticks, bottle caps, anything while having thoughts of my mother may cause her harm. Answer: Pick them up and put them in your pocket.

Taking a step forward while having Mother thoughts may cause her harm. Answer: Go back and take them again … and again … and again … and again. While holding your breath even? Walk backwards. Yes, backwards is the go. I walk backwards for kilometres.

Turning lights off, on, off, on. Turning book pages, forward, backward, forward, backward. Blinking. Breathing. Walking. Counting. Scratching. Opening doors. Closing doors … Answer: Do it all again, over and over and over again. Touching anything while breathing? Answer: Hold your breath and do IT ALL OVER AGAIN.

An invisible string tied to my back may get tangled as I go through the day. Answer: Retrace ALL STEPS untangling the string.

Count EVERYTHING. The steps, the breaths, the cracks on the pavement the turning on and off of the light switch. Everything. Threes and fours were bad, fives and sevens' good.

And so on, and so on, and so on …

My life was at a standstill. I am insane. No, no, no, I'm not insane. I'm confused, bewildered, frightened, alone, so dreadfully alone.

I did have a session with a psychiatrist-type person, just the once. I was terrified. Was I going to be put away? I knew I wasn't crazy…or was I? Although I certainly can't lay claim to owning all the thoughts in my head at the time, I needed to stick by that one if I was going to get through it. I remained undiagnosed, which was probably a good thing because the term OCD wasn't a label then. I might have found myself locked away somewhere where I could no longer be an embarrassment.

Running parallel to this disorder was our constant moving from one place to the next. In no particular order, there was a room on the first floor of a brothel on the corner of Bond and Grant Streets. That little deal fell arse-over when mother declined to join the gals on the game, and we found ourselves locked out on the street. The police were called and a fab ride in the back of a 'Black Maria' followed. Police cars capable of transporting passengers were painted black before 'divvie vans' changed to blue. The name Black Maria has several origins; I like this one from Wikipedia:

> *'In a 1962 article in the Hackensack, New Jersey newspaper The Record, it claims the name Black Maria came from a 'large and riotous London woman. She was often picked up by the police for excessive drinking on Saturday nights. When the van went by, people would say 'There goes Black Maria again.' and the word stuck.'*

Another little room in Grant Street is on the list. Obviously, we hit the jackpot somewhere because we now had in our possession a tiny drop side table and two chairs. I remember this little stopover well because there was another resident there who took an extreme dislike to me. He would take supreme pleasure in tying me to the hills hoist clothesline and laying about me with whatever was handy. This prick was more than once the target of my sister's unbridled wrath, a thing to be witnessed only by the brave.

Then there was time spent with alcoholic George and his young son. Only me, I think on that occasion. George had accidentally killed his wife, throwing her about while performing over-exuberant dance moves. They were ballroom fanatics and had been practising in the kitchen. An enthusiastic swinging caught her head on the kitchen table, and that was that. George disappeared into the bottle. When sufficiently plastered, he would grab any of the vast array of instruments he kept and played exceptionally well and go off into a tear sodden blues set.

Later on, there was time spent at the Queenscliff orphanage, which I think was affiliated with the orphanage in Ballarat. Summer there was meant to be 'enjoyed' so it was off to the beach rain, hail or shine. The sleeping arrangements consisted of many double-decker bunk beds and the stench of vomit from several dozen children suffering sunstroke would be topped up nightly by a liberal dose of piss and shit from kids too sore and too sick to get out of bed. Never at any time was there a message from my Christian grandparents at West End Hall suggesting I should 'come and live with us in this enormous home and we'll take care of you'.

In comparison, the Ballarat orphanage sleeping quarters were huge dormitory rooms containing many single beds. Thin ex-army blankets were fiercely guarded and clutched all night long. The deeper sleepers would awake shivering without coverings. On weekends, you might be chosen to accompany some family or other on a day out. I'm sure there was no moral or criminal evaluation of these visitations. A gift might be bestowed by the kind folk and their privileged offspring but, it would have disappeared from your little bedside cupboard by morning. Older boys had to arise very early and were set to work on the adjoining farm before breakfast and school. Girls were set to scrubbing and polishing the floors of the long passages on hands and knees, in four rows. Front row scrubbed, the next row dried, third row applied the wax and the polishing row bought up the rear. Repeat.

The orphanage was demolished in 1968. When I heard about this in 2003, I drove to Ballarat to see the hole in the ground.

CHAPTER 3

BETWEEN THE BREWERY AND THE JAIL

In between the times I was being shunted around homes and orphanages, I was returned to my mother. My sister too, but rarely the both of us together. My mother's love for me was smothering and overwhelming. Reciprocation escaped me; I found her difficult to love.

Mother was not overly intelligent, never passed an opinion about anything, and, as mentioned, suffered severely from an undiagnosed multiple personalities disorder. I endured many beatings from her. As part of a family constantly shifting accommodation, the first thing I always did when we went to a new place was seek out a nook that I could get at least the top part of my body into, preparing for the rages and beatings I knew were to come. Whatever was at hand would do as a weapon, pieces of wood, kitchen utensils. I would hear my sister screaming, 'Stop, you'll kill him!' I asked her once why she was never beaten. She replied, 'I knew to start crying the moment she approached, which would instantly turn the frenzy into guilt and then a shared cry and cuddle. But you, you refused to cry, which absolutely enraged her.'

That is true. I have only recently, with the help of a psychologist, learned to cry. These days, I can instantly become a sodden mess; bursting into sobs at the slightest hint a hat might drop. I could never do it back then.

By the time I turned twelve, my mother would infrequently get into my bed and fondle my erect penis late at night. I became quite accustomed to this happening. The morning after, these episodes were always filled with her pathetic incessant begging denials of 'that didn't happen, did it?'. Her constant utterances regarding sex were 'It's filthy, dirty.' Or 'Never do anything to any girl that you wouldn't do to your sister.' I most certainly managed to follow that particular instruction.

Adding to the maelstrom of my home life, there was school, of course. There was always school. The collection of schools I attended have morphed into each other to become simply 'school'. They were either further advanced or remedial in their syllabus. I was either bored or hopelessly playing catchup. I could be in attendance for a few weeks or a few months. Making friends seemed pointless, and teachers were teachers.

Of all the schools in my collection, I vividly recall only one. The School of Mines in Ballarat (SMB) was established in 1870, the oldest school for technical education in Australia. I started attending SMB in 1959, at the age of twelve. The junior school, as it was known, was sandwiched in between the senior school – a small university-level establishment with which we shared many classrooms – the Ballarat Jail, and directly opposite on Lydiard Street, the Ballarat Brewery. Many parts of the school property still bore names adapted from the gold mining industry. The tennis courts were located in an area called The Battery.

The Ballarat Jail overlooked the school quadrangle. Morning assembly often involved an outraged headmaster desperately trying to be heard above prisoners shouting fabulous, loud obscenities that filled our ears. The brewery overwhelmingly jammed our nostrils with the stench of hydrogen sulphide, sulphur and mercaptan. Mercaptan is the chemical a skunk secretes when spraying. No wonder it took me so very long to enjoy the taste of beer. Now I'd suck it through a sock.

For the few years I spent at the SMB, I was mostly bored out of my brain and received almost daily punishment of 'the cuts' for arriving late. This came in the form of a decent strapping across the wrists, not the palms of your hands, the wrists. Deep welts in the wrists would swell to the point where I couldn't hold a pen. Why was I always late? Buses from the Wendouree West ghetto, some ten kilometres away, inevitably arrived late and then you had to add a good fifteen-minute walk to the SMB or a chest-heaving nine minutes if you ran. When I found a job cleaning out a nearby joinery business after school, I managed to save enough to buy a second-hand bike complete with butterfly handlebars sporting trailing, colourful, plastic streamers. My stylish bike allowed me to arrive on time, and at least this little act of brutality ceased.

During my time at the School of Mines and until leaving school, we lived in the Wendouree West ghetto which I remember very well. The following is from *The Age* newspaper August 28, 2011. Reading it took me straight back to 1960.

> *'They call it the ghetto. Nothing good comes out of Wendouree West, they reckon. In truth, few locals ever leave. Curtains are drawn down every street of this struggling suburb, five minutes' drive from Ballarat's grand facades. Broken windows are boarded up or covered over with corrugated iron.*
>
> *People here are poor and almost exclusively white, out of work and out of luck. But there's something confounding about this place they call home.*
>
> *Social dysfunction stalks the streets and with it, crime, busted-up families, mental illness and substance abuse. And yet the streets are named for flowers and the footpaths lined with pink blossoms in bloom. Kids play on scooters on the roads.*
>
> *Residents bear the tag 'Westies' with such pride it's spray-painted on the bitumen. Father Frank Smith says people are struggling but strong. 'Outsiders' see them as dole bludgers, no-hopers, drug addicts and thieves. Here they wear slander like a badge of honour.*
>
> *The people here are good but beset with many social challenges—there is a lot of poverty and family dysfunction, and then you have people trying to self-medicate through drugs and alcohol. Many people here must be in survival mode.'*

Streets were indeed named after flowers; we were living in Hyacinth Grove. I've often wondered how I came out of the ghetto without too much damage. Over the years and especially during the writing of this book, I've come to the conclusion that what saved me was being gay. As a gay boy, I didn't fit into the mould of the average ghetto teen. There were no gangs for me, no juvenile prison, no theft or vandalism. I had only one constant thought, a mantra—*I have to get out.*

I wish I could remember the name of my art teacher at the School of Mines. He was one person who showed me a way out. This teacher, recently married at the time, was a neighbour of mine in the ghetto. At school, he would often seek me out at lunchtime and take me to different art galleries in the centre of town. He took great care to point out each artist's intent and technique with their brush strokes and leaving areas of the canvas relatively blank, explaining how vital these negative spaces were. I was mesmerised once these concepts were described to me and more astonished that he would take the time to try and educate someone who consistently failed his class.

A grasp of mathematics completely eluded me, and science – although interesting enough – was not entirely up my street. English, I whizzed through, and a few of us, including my best friend Leigh Goldsmith, completed the year's course way ahead of the rest of the class. We asked for, and received permission to, start a class theatre project to fill in our time. Our little group of players took on such serious works as *The Glass Menagerie* and other works entirely out of our amateur reach. We were as happy as pigs in mud even though we understood nothing of the complex nuances of the plays we put on. Most of my other classes were of the technical variety but with a lean towards the artistic. Ironmongery I enjoyed. Forming white-hot metal into ornamental shapes was satisfyingly challenging. My clay sculpture class was fascinating. Oh, how I loved that room with its damp earthy smell and all the marvellous cold, clammy, red clay just waiting for me to squeeze and mould and get all over my clothes and in my hair. Wonderful stuff. Art, painting, drawing, I managed to fail dismally.

I did very well as academic averages go. In another time, if I could have pursued a longed- for higher education, I would have flung myself headlong into archaeology and Egyptology in particular. In the early sixties, higher learning was out of the question for the poor. Instead, I was pleased when a position in a factory was found for me.

CHAPTER 4

MOVE OVER MELBOURNE

Off I went to work in a factory of seven hundred men. In the days of junior (read slave) wages, I was working up to fifty hours a week for ten pounds (twenty dollars). Every penny of it went to my mother. I also worked eight hours every Sunday in a garage/milk-bar for two shillings (twenty cents), which I kept for myself. During the week, I would ride my bicycle the ten kilometres to get to work in the morning dark, and then back home at night. The four years of turning out thousands of nuts or bolts per day at Ballarat's M.B. Johns and Hattersley's valve manufacturing works instilled in me the lowest boredom threshold a human being can possess—and a lifelong loathing for the repetitive. Paradoxically, at age 70, I took up archery. A discipline which demands repetition of form sequence, shot after shot. I love it.

Even though I'd eventually grow to be six foot tall, I was then still relatively small and slight, the butt of many a practical joke. At the factory I remained the recipient of the bully boys' blows and tauntings, like those that had plagued me all my school life. Never mind, I was a tough little shit.

I often managed to escape from the mind-numbing repetitious work until the time I was found curled up sleeping in a packing box. The punishment was to make me the tea boy. Tea boy duty entailed hauling an enormous urn of steaming hot water around, pouring water into hundreds of waiting metal tea mugs held by rough, greasy, anxious hands. It gave me a chance to get my own back. Many a hand got an accidental scalding. I have news for you, Monsieur Talleyrand, revenge is not a dish best served cold; it is to be served as close to boiling point as possible.

Liberation from this gruelling fifty-hour week came when I was emboldened to take a sickie from the factory and hopped on a train to Melbourne. The visit to the city was in answer to a newspaper advertisement by Sportsgirl fashion store in Collins Street. They had a vacancy for the position of Trainee Window Dresser. What else?

Something this unsophisticated, unfashionable, weedy, country boy said or did in that interview must have struck a chord because I was hired on the spot. Within the week, I fled my shitty life of servitude to join an old school friend in a shared flat on Alma Road in St Kilda. Wondering how could I possibly mess off to Melbourne and leave my poor mother destitute? Easily.

A few months before my escape to the city, my absent father had reappeared. The injuries he had received during the car accident back in his army days led to him suffering dreadfully with bone cancer in his hip, and the eventual removal of his leg from the hip down. No doubt feeling he'd paid his dues, he came back to ask my mother's forgiveness and expected her to take him in, which she instantly did. I have recently learned that in doing this, he'd left another family to fend for itself. A short time ago, I found and met one of my two previously unknown half-brothers living in Brisbane. His story is as damaging to a child as mine was. Leopards and spots, I guess. So, you see, in taking off to the city way back then—I was free, free at last.

My little sojourn with Sportsgirl was liberating in more ways than one. The first exciting development was in my pay packet. I'd doubled my earnings from twenty dollars per week to forty, a whole heap of money in the sixties. Then, I began to revel in the freedom to come and go and do exactly as I pleased, with the entire fascinating city of Melbourne to explore. I could mingle with people with an artistic bent, explore my sexuality, discover I was as normal as the next camp man. It was overwhelming. I hit the ground running into that world and only stopped when I retired. I always wanted to see what was around the next corner.

Working in clean clothes without the grease, oil and ever-present smell of machined metal and coolant was otherworldly. Quiet working conditions with idle, witty banter drifting around the room was the stuff of dreams. Instead of hauling a heavy urn around on a cold concrete factory floor, morning tea meant a leisurely stroll up the arcade to Gibby's coffee shop in Carson Place for crumpets and honey or taking a few steps along Collins Street and descending the stairs to the subterranean Rumplemeyers for tea, and those exquisite little cream cakes.

Melbourne in winter was shrouded in eternal misty drizzle. Umbrella or not, you were going to get damp. I'd never seen a man carrying an umbrella before. Any gent wielding an umbrella back in Ballarat was setting himself up for ridicule at the very least. I bought myself a sturdy black brolly – no other colour would do for males in those days – and felt very smart as I parroted the distinct walk. Step, lift, swing, stab, chest out and the small flourish upon opening. I would exit the Flinders Street train station at Elizabeth Street and join the throng waiting for the lights to change, enjoying the audible plop as all umbrellas opened on the green light cue to make the dank crossing. I often wondered what that colourful little choreography must have looked like from above.

The '60s for me will forever be remembered as my first step into a society once so far out of reach, it might as well have been on the moon. I was surrounded by high fashion and the women who wore it. Sportsgirl's trendy staff were the cream of the fashion crop. Their long hair would be pulled back from the front then up and out into a cascade down the back, aided by the addition of at least a dozen hairpieces. Outrageously oversized bows held all of this in place at the crown. Lithe, long legged, miniskirted, runway-ready girls like the indomitable Sally Browne performed a series of meticulously rehearsed movements when alighting from low slung sports cars in front of Sportsgirl, me watching from the window I'd be working in that day. Nothing to see here, these clever young women certainly knew how to get out of a car with their modesty intact.

Guest artists were invited to entertain in the Sportsgirl store. I recall a very young Johnny Farnham belting out *Sadie the Cleaning Lady* as well-heeled, well-turned-out fashion plates picked up a little something for the coming weekends' 'happening'. There was always a whispering haunting me in the back of my mind: 'none of this is real'. A life so extraordinarily different to the one I'd known only a few short weeks before was unimaginable. Surely this is it, what more could there be?

Through friends of friends of friends, I was invited to the occasional après theatre soirees at the Toorak home of the outrageous Frank Thring. Anyone who knew him will tell you, Frank's presence filled a room to bursting. Not only his bulky height of six-foot two, but also his personality, his aura, completely dominated any space. For a soiree newbie such as me, it was riveting, exciting and completely overwhelming. He was kind, attentive and the perfect host. I often felt reduced to idiot level, but I must have held my own because the dreaded 'Pumpkin' moniker was instantly bestowed on me. *Pumpkin*, where the hell did that come from? The few times I was lucky enough to inhabit the rarefied atmosphere of the Thring throng doesn't give me the right to say I belonged. A more sophisticated me certainly could have made the cut. The opening was definitely there. Frank took a shine to me, but sadly due to my ignorant, unpolished state, I joined the league of the hesitant lost.

I tagged along with the arty crowd to drinks at the Australia Bar on Collins Street, meeting lots of talented and flamboyant theatrical persons and found myself fitting under the wing of the famous theatre designer Ann Church.

My association with Ann Church opened many doors. She was amazingly kind to me and smoothed the way to me seeing and working on sets for GTV Channel Nine's *In Melbourne Tonight* (IMT). IMT ran from 1957 to 1970. Hosted predominantly by Australian television royalty, Graham Kennedy, it became the top headlining show in that golden era of our television history. Further connections were made to the Victorian Ballet Guild, the National Theatre Ballet and the newly formed Australian Ballet. I could never stand children, even when I was one—always preferring the company of older people. After she decided I was to be her protégé, Ann introduced me to Rex Reid and Robert (Bobby, soon to be Sir Robert) Helpmann. Once I'd begun mingling with them, I found myself soaking up their wit and talent like a desiccated sponge.

Bobby and Rex were two gentlemen of a certain era and a certain cut, characters – some might say – eccentrics. I was lucky enough to get to know them well. Both had spent the de rigueur time required in London for Aussie men in the performing arts. They both danced and acted—actors called them dancers and dancers called them actors.

To be accepted in the London of those days, there was a need to don a certain cloak, a manufactured persona, one that would allow you to be viewed and accepted as sophisticated and belonging. A case of 'time for a touch up, your antipodean roots are showing'. Along with this came the habit of speaking in an odd faux British accent. An accent still slightly discernible as Southern Hemisphere colonial, but with the harsh vowels rounded out, and devoid of the nasal twang. I am occasionally guilty of this affected veneer myself. Why? Apart from acquiring the façade necessary to pass as theatre people in London, Bobby and Rex both possessed a razor wit which cannot be acquired—you are born with it or you're not. Bobby had it in spades, along with a look capable of turning any human being into a quivering, jellied mess. Their wit was most definitely what drew me towards them and anybody else who possesses such quickness, such cleverness. I lived in hope that some it would rub off.

CHAPTER 5

MY AUNTIE MAME

My father's older brother William lived in Sydney. Known as Will, he was married to Jessie, a blonde, wild-haired violinist with the Sydney Symphony Orchestra. They were both highly intelligent, well-educated people. The only University graduate in the family, Will was a counsellor for the City of Marrickville. He scandalised the family during the Second World War by refusing to join up and faced a court hearing as a conscientious objector. After his trial, Jessie told me he had been branded a coward. It was impossible for him to find work, so to support them both she took a well-paid job at the Tivoli Theatre.

Will and Jessie made a point of visiting us in Victoria every so often after my father was back on the scene. I always thought them terribly sophisticated. During one of these 'noblesse oblige' visitations I travelled to Ballarat to join them all at a bistro, about as cultured it got in country Victoria. At the table, Jessie leaned in close and dropped a subtle hint that my few rough edges could do with polishing. Perhaps I might consider leaving my new life in Melbourne to live with her and Will in Sydney in a sort of Pygmalion situation. This came as quite a shock. No-one in the family had ever been invited to inspect the outside of their historic Milson Point shack, never mind step over the threshold.

Much to the horror of the family, off I went to live with them in their Sydney home. I drove to Sydney from Melbourne in my newly acquired second-hand, push-button, automatic Valiant. Arriving at their Mitchell Street house, I was met at the door by a kimono-clad Jessie bearing a violin tucked under her left arm, and a cold, fresh gin and cucumber for me in her outstretched right hand. Their home was on Blues Point in North Sydney, the first train stop after the Sydney Harbour Bridge. The small, slightly tilting, two up, two down, wooden two-storey house was the original home of Billy Blue (convict, settler and ferryman), for whom Blues Point was named. It was brimming to the point of overflowing with eccentric if dilapidated charm. There was a tiny, rickety balcony facing the full splendour of the Sydney Harbour Bridge off my small bedroom/library.

Auntie Jessie informed me that as a child, I used to make birds' nests in her blonde Afro hair, a tight, completely impenetrable fuzz. Once on a visit to Fiji, she was obliged to participate in a Kava ceremony in her honour. The locals, believing her to be a pale version of themselves, perhaps threw the word deity into the mix. Short, pale and with a nose not out of place on a toucan, she was in possession of an intellect most men of the era would consider a detriment. Beautifully spoken and university educated, Jessie was a joy to be around. My good old sponge-like thirst drank in every word I heard her utter.

Sometime after I'd moved in with them, Jessie felt we were now intimate enough to show me a sepia photo of her standing on a stage playing the violin. She was wearing an enormous picture hat, tilted at an 'oh so very' urbane angle, and a pair of high heeled shoes. Nothing else. The Tivoli musical-hall style theatres in Sydney and Melbourne were way ahead of their time, allowing nudity on stage as long as the girl didn't move. So, this was darling Jessie's Tivoli gig—sawing away nude on the violin in a subtle enough way for her to be considered becalmed.

What did Jessie see in me to prompt her to take the large step of inviting me to live with them? I have thought about this long and hard. I don't believe I was at all effeminate or owned any other affectation which would lead a person to consider me a budding homosexual. I most certainly was not, in my mind at least, giving off any hints – subtle or otherwise – as to my burgeoning taste for 'men of the opposite sex'. Certainly, I had not spent enough time with either Jessie or Will prior to their invitation to lodge at their home for them to discern any sort of conclusion regarding my leanings toward the arts.

There was obviously some faint hint of something causing a blip on their radar. Whatever it was, I am eternally grateful.

I've always considered my time in their slightly lunatic household as my formative years, my Auntie Mame years. I developed my taste for fine food in that home. Meals were always *ad hoc*, but invariably verged on five-star restaurant quality fare. Jessie was a fabulous cook and insisted on experimenting with every exotic recipe she could lay her hands on. Theatre attendance was a must. Dressed in all our splendour, she and I went to entertainments ranging from grand opening nights to experimental street stuff. In 1969, when '*Hair*' opened at the Metro Theatre in Kings Cross, Jessie and I decided flowing kaftans were the go for opening night. Sitting on her tiny lounge room floor for hours cutting and hand sewing together, we conjured up two black and white 'pop art' kaftans to wear. Thinking we were as smart as paint, we arrived at the theatre on the night to discover our seats were directly behind Graeme Kennedy. He appeared to be the only person in the theatre not wearing a kaftan. Bugger—we could have been such a hit.

I found a rather strange job in Sydney. The House of Curzon, or Curzon's as it was known, was a small, private department store located between Pitt and George Streets specialising in women's high fashion. A permanent runway located on their second floor allowed them to present continuous showings. One of my tasks was to hang two-metre lengths of white butcher's paper vertically in the Pitt St windows, then quickly sketch or paint willowy, big-eyed girls wearing likenesses of the fashion items on show upstairs. Huge crowds of onlookers would gather outside, clogging the footpath and yelling and screaming to be given the line paintings as soon as they dried. Crazy, but very effective in gathering an audience. The showings upstairs would then be packed with anxious females clutching their paint sketches bunched up on their knees waiting for 'their' garment to appear on the runway. We could have wallpapered the house in Mitchell Street with those paintings. The bloody things were everywhere.

Some might possibly think of me as ungrateful to decide to pack my small portmanteau and decamp to Kings Cross. This was never the case, not at all. Once I had hesitantly brought the matter up, I only received encouragement. I believe the whole point of my sojourn in the Mitchell Street house was the development and polishing of whatever personality and independence I possessed. To groom me to the degree where I felt confident enough to take flight. When the move was finally accomplished, I felt so much more in charge of my life than when I first tasted freedom in Melbourne. A bit of patient fine tuning had worked wonders.

Next stop was a small flat in Greenknowe Avenue in Kings Cross. There was a couple living above me, one of whom was a glamorous female TV personality and ex-model. Below me lived a not so glamorous, talented, hysterically funny, beloved, gap-toothed, male comedian. The not-infrequent arguments upstairs were often promptly followed by the clackety clacking of winkle picker stilettoes carrying their wearer to the refuge of the sanctorium below.

I'd saved a bit of money, so I decided I would do away with the small, bourgeois lounge cum dining area, and turn my front room into a garret-like studio. Selling my paintings on the streets of the Cross was the aim. I had no trouble producing art pieces; churning them out by the dozen. Selling them was another matter entirely. The despondent, bare-footed, long-haired, hippie-type me would sit opposite the El Alamein fountain next to my slow-selling wares, gradually painting my old $50 VW Beetle to look like a tiger – all broad orange and black stripes – with a $60 fine sable brush. What happened to the Valiant? I arrived home one day to find a collection company had repossessed it. As my father had co-signed, and he'd gone bankrupt, they'd swooped on it.

The Cross in the late '60s was entirely different from what it has now become. During the time of the Vietnam War, it was the place to be for Australian and US servicemen on R&R. Sure, it was full of vice, strip joints, bars and whores, but there was an innocence to it all. Or was the innocence mine? I certainly never felt unsafe on the streets. The street girls were not the drug-addled, scrawny types who haunted those streets in later years. They were fun, colourful, mini-skirted, beehive-hairdo-ed, camp-as-Xmas girls who were often as not, putting themselves through university.

Still in the firm belief I was batting for both teams, I dated Barbara, a bubbly redhead I'd met while working for Curzon's. This cute, funny, effervescent girl was such a live wire, and rode a motorcycle, her helmet painted to look like a tortoise. Watching this crazy gal hurtling along the streets of Sydney with a tortoise on her head and her long, wavy, flaming locks streaming out behind her was a sight I treasured. Babs and I often headed up the coast to Terrigal near Gosford on Friday evenings after work. Friends would hire a couple of onsite caravans for the weekend, and a few more pie-eyed, wanton days would be lost to memory.

That's the thing about that particular decade—they say if you can remember the sixties, you weren't there. Adore her as I did, things between us were moving in the brick veneer direction, not a vision I cared to entertain. A moonlight flit, the coward's way out, was planned and precisely executed. I packed the VW with Heinz tinned vegetable salad, a sleeping bag, a .22 rifle and headed off, over the Nullarbor Plain to Perth, some 4,500 kilometres away. A bit of distance was the order of the day. I understand why women didn't realise I was gay because I hadn't fully grasped it myself. There were still things, many things about which I had no clue.

On the way from Sydney to Perth, I stopped off in Melbourne to see some friends. While I was there, one of them told me that the Lido nightclub would soon be holding auditions for *Oh! Calcutta!* and suggested I try out for it if I wanted to make a little extra money. 'The only problem,' he said, 'is they are auditioning for girls and guys who will perform naked.' Me: 'Hey, who cares—I'm not ashamed of my bits 'n' bobs.'

The Lido, for those too young to remember, was an underground establishment. I don't mean in the furtive, semi-legal sense; it genuinely was underground. It was located at 184 Russell Street, on the corner of Little Bourke Street, about a block down from Her Majesty's Theatre. Looking in the front door, all you could see was an enormous chandelier, supposedly the largest in the Southern Hemisphere. Entering, you walked towards this chandelier and straight down the stairs passing beneath it. The décor was tiered table seating, with each level in a different shade of green, getting darker the farther you went back. Positively stunning. David McIlwraith, the owner, produced shows as well as bringing in international artists, including Lido dancers from Paris. It was unquestionably the most sophisticated showroom in Australia.

Come the day of the auditions for *Oh! Calcutta!* I turned up at the appointed time, and after filling out no end of forms, was led down to the stage area. Dozens of hopefuls of both sexes were at these auditions. McIlwraith said to us all: 'Right. Strip. This show has total nudity, sitting in on this audition is the current headliner here at Lido—the fabulous Miss Eartha Kitt. If you can't do it now, you can go.' Those of us who were into it buffed up and faced the front row. The bodies not measuring up were given the 'don't call us, we'll call you' treatment. I got a part. *Oh! Calcutta!* never opened. There was so much fuss regarding nudity, the censors of the day banned it before it began. McIlwraith was furious and made a statement to the press saying if he couldn't open this show, he would sell The Lido and leave Australia for good. Which, sadly, he did.

I carried on to Perth with a side trip to Daylesford where my parents had moved to. What a shock my lay preacher grandfather and my newly minted, born again, ecclesiastical father would have today. That sleepy little town, partially deserted, pillar of all things Christian, is now chock-a-block with LGBTIQ (Are they in the right order, did I miss any?) persons and is considered the gay country heart of the State of Victoria. I now live in Castlemaine, a mere stone's throw away.

CHAPTER 6

GO WEST YOUNG MAN

The poor old VW was capable of a top speed of around 60 kilometres per hour, so it was a long and hot trip over the desert. The unsealed part of the road over the Nullarbor was all rocks and ruts which threw my old bomb all over the place. Once I got closer to Perth, my $50 car didn't have the guts needed to get over the hills. The brakes didn't work and I held the gear stick in place with my knee. I caught the slipstream of a semi-trailer which hauled me over the Darling Ranges outside Perth and I eventually made it into the city.

Carried along by the evening rush hour traffic, I ended up on Stirling Highway beside the beautiful Swan River. Deciding to follow the river around for a bit, I turned left onto Hackett Drive, and stopped at Matilda Bay in Crawley to take in the deepening evening view of Perth city some six kilometres downriver. Spectacular, what a sight to behold after such a gruelling trip and certainly worth it. I opened and ate a can of salad from my diminishing pile and then hunkered down in the back seat, to get a good night's sleep. Around midnight I was roused by the first of many police visits whilst living in my VW. On that occasion, the explanation of having just arrived was accepted with a warning from the officer of the 'let's not catch you again' variety.

Perth, fourth on the list of the most isolated cities in the world, is quite remarkable for its size. It was then, and is much more so now. Perth people adore their city, and many revel in its remoteness. A sort of reverse chip on the shoulder, a case of what you can't disguise, emphasise. It didn't take long to feel part of the place, especially after meeting my someone special, and I was quite content to call it home.

Sleeping rough in the car or on the beach came to an end when the Police gave me a final warning. I think they were forever stopping me just to have a sticky beak at the inside of the crazy vehicle. I recalled a friendly colleague from my Sportsgirl days was from Perth. Could he be back here? Could I remember his name? It was a strange name. Propersomething, Proper … john, yes Glen Properjohn. Getting myself into a public phone box on Eric Street in Cottesloe, I pawed over the tatty phonebook. Luckily the Ps were still intact. G Properjohn. Dialled and waited.

'Glen? Glen is that you? It's Tom here. Tom Robb from Melbourne.'

'Oh my God, where are you? he gasped back.'

'Well, I'm in a phone box on the corner of Marine Parade and Eric Street, Cottesloe.'

'Really? Well turn around and look in the shop window behind you.'

And there was Glen, sitting behind his desk in his Beaut Sausages trendy knick-knack shop on Eric Street. Glen, who owned a freelance window dressing business on the side, very kindly invited me to live with him in his mother's home in South Perth and he also gave me a job. So, there I was, established in Perth. Glen was pretty well connected, with low friends in high places and high friends in low places, as would be seen some years later with his scandalous connection to the murdered Perth Madam, Shirley Finn. I soon met anyone who was anyone. Perth then was not the metropolis it is today. In 1969, the entire State of Western Australia, a state so enormous it could swallow most of Europe, had only recently reached a population of one million people.

It was the time of the Poseidon nickel bubble and Lang Hancock's iron ore mines; the economy was unquestionably booming. I went to more fantastic, outrageously lavish and expensive parties in Perth in those days than I ever witnessed in Sydney or Melbourne. The sky was the limit where cash flow was concerned. My undignified car became something of a mobile landmark over the following year. None of my new friends was ever too proud to ride in it. On the grand opening of *Boys in the Band*, I pulled up to the red carpet outside His Majesty's Theatre (the 'His' in the name never went away in Perth). Giant searchlights swept the sky and a barrage of TV crews eagerly awaited the limousine arrivals of the celebrities. Imagine me pulling up and the passenger-side door bursting open, and at least half a dozen glitteringly compelling 'A list' women and men tumbling out. They included the spectacularly luscious Maureen Maricic, who was soon to marry Australian rock icon, Johnny O'Keefe. The TV persons were not impressed; I could hear repeated hissed instructions to 'move it', 'get this piece of shit out of the way'.

A year on, after local Police advised me that an indigenous family was currently residing in my now largely unused VW, I decided to sell it. Fifty dollars changed hands, exactly what I'd paid for it. Who knew it would prove to be such a great investment? After a quick priming with petrol in the carburettor, the old girl noisily shot rust out of the exhaust, and in a cloud of smoke, took off down the street. They just don't make cars like that anymore.

Arriving home to Mrs Properjohn's one evening, I found there was a phone message asking me to call Rex Reid? How amazing. I'm so far away from Melbourne, and here is Rex living in Perth and working as Artistic Director of the West Australian Ballet Company. I'm still not sure exactly how Rex knew I was in Perth, or how to get hold of me, but we were travelling in the same very, very, small circles in little Perth. It turned out Ann Church was in town to paint three of her set designs for the WA Ballet Company's fast-approaching season at the Playhouse Theatre. Darling Ann. Love her as I did, there was no hiding the evidence of her more than passing love affair with the booze. Rex informed me Ann had been in Perth for two weeks and there was not one solitary brush stroke on a single flat. Apart from a sortie to Jacksons Art Supplies where she almost bankrupted the Company buying every sable haired brush in stock, the only accomplishments so far had been much artistic prancing about the studio. No end of poetic poses beside windows, soaking in and remarking on, the view of the park next door, but nothing in the way of splashes of paint on sets.

Rex asked whether I remembered any of Ann's works. I replied, 'Of course. Every brush stroke.'

'Good,' he said, 'how soon can you start?' Three ballets were to be staged, and forty-eight hours remained before opening. The flats were laid out on a deserted factory floor near the old Perth Markets. The first few hours were spent sketching the designs with chalk. The next move was sheer brilliance, even if I do say so myself. Window dressers. This town was full of those wonderfully artistic people. Off to David Jones, Boans, Ahearn's and Baird's department stores to plead my case to display managers.

The following morning, a team of eight boys ready, willing, and oh-so-obviously able to attack the sets, rolled up for work. During the long night I had cheekily set out the flats, in what could only be described as 'painting by numbers' and, arming my little group of volunteers with appropriate paint colours and brushes, I pointed them towards the blank canvasses saying, 'Go to it fellas'. I played the part of director and detailer and Ann, sitting on her canvas director's chair on a raised dais, gin, ice bucket and glass close at hand, more sheets to the wind than the entire Spanish Armada, superbly played the part of enthralled creator supreme. Two days later, as the first act of The Comedienne was under-way, I was putting the finishing touches to the giant red heart on the other side of a revolve. I jumped off, pot and brush in hand as it started to turn, my big heart glistening under the spotlights, wet but finished.

During the interval, I was at the crush bar getting a well-deserved stiff triple when Ann yelled from the low Playhouse dress circle steps behind me, 'We did it darling!', and promptly collapsed into my arms. Dear, sweet Ann died a couple of years later, in 1975. Hugs, my darling.

While working on the sets, we were constantly visited by people involved with the production, especially Rex and the leading dancers. I often caught Luis Moreno, the premier danseur of the company, spying on me. There was a 'will we, won't we' thrill to the witchery which I was hesitant to break. His stunningly handsome face and equally beautiful body were magnetic.

Rehearsals became an opportunity to see this Spanish fireball, star of the Perth ballet world in tights and leotard and I certainly took every chance to catch yet another glimpse. Luis appeared to be doing the same, his chiselled face with its head of tussled deep black, rehearsal dampened hair hovered here and there around my workspace. I loved hearing his deep, sensual, heavily accented voice as he and Rex discussed the sets' progress.

Love at first sight, is an overworked cliché. But for me, a twenty-two-year-old guy still coming to grips with his sexuality, the sensation in my gut, a palpable churning, was new and confusing. The torture, and it was indeed torture, thankfully didn't last long. I was way too shy to make a move, but Luis, accustomed to worship from near and afar, introduced himself at last. From that moment, it became apparent to all, sparks were flying. The scandalous night of the opening of The Boys in the Band and *that* car, saw my group and the ballet group ending up at the same venue for an after-show nosh up. It was also the night Luis invited me home to his tiny flat in Beatty Park. I quickly learned being an outlaw, an abomination did not exclude me from the giving and receiving of love. That the sexual act between men could be more than frantic, anxious gropings in bushes or public toilets. Or that the creation of a home and home life was not the unique privileged domain of the heterosexual—a joyous revelation.

This is how I met the love of my life. We moved in together a mere two weeks after that night, and parted amiably thirty five years later.

CHAPTER 7

FIND ME A HACKSAW

Luis was born in Spain under the heavily oppressive Roman Catholic regime of Generalissimo Francisco Franco. A nastier piece of dictatorial work than Franco would be hard to find. A mere 1.63m or 5'4" in the old money, he ran a brutal regime and treated Spain as his personal fiefdom.

The Spanish Civil War (1936 to 1939) was particularly hard on Luis's family. His father, Pepe, was an officer in the Republicans—the losing side. For several decades afterwards, the family was on tenterhooks, waiting for that tap on the shoulder, that knock at the door that would see him carted off, probably never to be seen or heard of again. This happened to a great many of his fellow officers and compatriots. The family devised a discreet but dangerous warning system. Luis's mother, Aurora, would receive a phone call in the dead of night and Pepe would vanish for however long it took. This left Aurora with the burden of running the family parquetry business while raising their three children until it was safe for Pepe to return home. Vibrational remnants of these anxious and exhausting times were still felt when I arrived in Spain in early 1970. A military father schooled in the old ways, a dictatorship which brooked no deviation from its super strict state laws as well as Catholic morals meant Luis's boyhood dream of becoming a dancer was always in triple jeopardy.

A dancer, bad enough, but a gay dancer promised it was simply not going to happen. Franco caused a massive artistic brain drain—he considered all artists to be 'parasites'. Many fled into exile or were executed. Sixteen was considered old for classical training, yet Luis secretly started taking dance lessons at Miss

Karen Taft's studio near his home in Chueca, central Madrid. Ironically, it's now the gay heartland, and the ground floor of his old apartment block is a gay sauna. Back then, the need for secrecy meant filling a bag with dance gear and later, clandestinely washing it. A great deal of skulking and lying was involved. Eventually, his older brother, Eduardo discovered what he was up to, and the ensuing massive uproar resulted in his ejection from the family home.

Luis was always considered a gifted dancer; his mind and body worked in perfect unison. Classical ballet was the aim, but in the Spain of the time, there was no classical ballet company, so he took himself off to France. Classes and auditions, auditions and classes. Luis's tenacity soon brought him to the notice of Roland Petit, dancer/choreographer and Artistic Director of the Marseilles Opera House Ballet. And so, it began.

During his time there, Luis was able to work with such inspiring guest artists as Margot Fontaine, Rudolph Nureyev, Rosella Hightower and Jean Babilee. A more fabulous entry to this wonderful world could not be imagined. Restless and longing to soak up more, more, and even more, Luis moved to Brussels and joined the innovative Company of Maurice Bejart. From Brussels, he then went to England and London Festival Ballet under the direction of the great British ballerina Dame Beryl Grey.

The onward and upward bug was soon biting again. Luis, as it turned out, possessed the same transient tendencies as I did. He found himself in Johannesburg South Africa, with the Performing Arts Council of the Transvaal (PACT) Ballet, where he was finally allowed to discover himself, and dance discovered him in return. While he was in South Africa, he was being partnered more and more often with a petite Australian dancer from Perth who was making a name for herself, Jenny Miller (later Petal Miller or Petal Brown and finally Petal Miller-Ashmole).

This partnership led to an invitation to join the new, professional full-time company of the West Australian Ballet under the then Directorship of its founder, Madame Kira Bousloff, as a guest dancer for the Festival of Perth. Later during this period, Luis introduced Kira to Rex Reid while he was visiting Perth giving Master Classes, which then led to Rex being appointed the first Artistic Director, other than Kira, later the same year. Luis fell unconditionally in love with Australia, and with me. He is still the dearest person in the world to me and we visit each other whenever possible. Now he is back in Madrid living in the family home he was ejected from at age 16. I am back in Victoria. You need my leg, darling Luis? Find me a hacksaw.

I met Peggy Snow a few days after meeting Luis for the first time. I was in my car, parked directly across narrow one-way King Street from the West Australian Ballet Company studio, which was actually Kira Bousloff's studio. After about ten minutes there was a rapping at the passenger side window. I leaned across to wind the stubborn old window down. A honey-haired, bespectacled head thrust through, attached to a middled aged chubby woman, decidedly in command.

'Are you Tom?' The face with the very British voice barked at me.

'Yes, I—'.

'Luis is running late and get your hair cut!' My hair was shoulder-length, how extraordinary, I wasn't sure whether this was a request from Luis or a spontaneous command from this rather brusque total stranger.

Peggy Snow came out from England by ship as a ten-pound Pom in the early '60s. Quite how she became friendly with Kira I don't recall, but friends they were. Best, fast friends. Kira's ballet school was quite large and extremely well-regarded. Peggy was her secretary and general dogsbody—she kept the books and manned the door collecting fees. A formidable woman, loved by few and feared by many, Peggy ruled the financial side of the school with an iron fist. Woe betide any mother who was late with her child's tuition fees or who turned up at a concert rehearsal without the prescribed costume in a satisfactorily completed state. On meeting Luis for the first time, Peggy took a shine to him, not something she often did to anyone, and became his self-appointed unofficial secretary, driver, aide and protector. There was more chance of sidling up to the Pope in those days than getting anywhere near Luis Moreno, who was by now Premier Danseur of the WA Ballet Company.

It was an open secret Peggy was more than enamoured with her fiery Spanish charge. Unhappily married with three children, one boy about the same age as Luis and a younger boy and girl, Peggy more or less lived a life of her own. Once we were properly introduced, I found this crusty older woman to have a wonderful attitude regarding what people thought, or didn't think, and she had a wit and irreverence which was irresistibly appealing. It wasn't long until we became friends. Wonderful friends. After Luis and I started living together and Peggy left her husband, we decided we would look for apartments in the same building. Eventually, satisfactory places were found, one apartment above the other, in Highgate, close to the city.

That's how our relationship began. Enamoured or not, Peggy was undoubtedly very good to and for Luis. She did everything for him, managing his professional, and more often than not his private life, beautifully. He got a well-ordered existence, she basked in his nearness, fame and sensuality. Peggy even became his personal dresser, a situation which led to many a blow-up in the Company. Not everybody was endeared to our Peggy; she could be uncommonly insensitive and rude.

I was also close to Kira Bousloff. Born in Monte Carlo to Russian parents who fled the mayhem, Kira spent much of her younger years in Paris and Monte Carlo, with most of her adult life lived in Australia. Although I don't think she ever set foot on Russian soil, she felt passionately Russian and proud of it. I once took her backstage to meet Rudolph Nureyev. Seconds after the introduction in his dressing room; these two Russian souls fell into each other's arms in an intense and profoundly moving embrace. I backed out of the room and quietly closed the door. Thirty minutes later, Kira appeared with a tear-streaked face, saying it felt like finding a long-lost son, it had shaken her to the core.

Kira came to Australia with Colonel De Basil's Ballets Russes de Monte Carlo in 1938. At the end of the tour Kira, along with then-husband Serge Bousloff and several other dancers, decided to stay on in Melbourne rather than go back to a Europe facing the perils of the impending WWII. In

1952, the couple went to live in Perth, where she started the West Australian Ballet Company. Kira always said Perth's uniqueness attracted her. From the moment she arrived by ship during the Ballets Russes tour, it felt like home. Kira was friends with a lot of mostly European older ex-ballet dancer/teacher-types, whose company I came to enjoy. One, in particular, Madame Nadine Wulffius, (White Russian, daughter of Countess Alekseyeva Yaroslavskeya) was as nuts about all things Egyptian as I was. We could chat for hours about what we did and didn't know about ancient Egypt. Madame Nadine seemed very, very old, even way back then in the mid '70s. I always wondered if her profound knowledge of ancient Egypt might well have been first hand.

Towards the end of 1970, Luis and I made up our minds to leave Australia and go to Madrid to start the dream of creating our own glamorous cabaret/nightclub show. Air travel was prohibitively expensive in those days. Besides, if we went by ship, we would each be given the standard ten cubic feet of space in the hold. A precious benefit enabling us to take the entire contents of the house, saving us the expense of re-purchasing everything in Spain.

The only available ship which suited us was the ageing P&O SS *Orsova*. Oh dear, what a hulk it turned out to be. Built in 1954, the *Orsova* carried 1,503 passengers and was commissioned especially for the England–Australia run. It mainly carried 'ten-pound Poms' and many thousands of economic refugees from Greece and Italy—on a trip which took four weeks through the Suez Canal. On the fifth of June 1967, at the beginning of the Egypt–Israel Six-Day War, Egypt had suddenly and unexpectedly closed the Canal, trapping fifteen cargo ships inside. These became known as the Yellow Fleet and were trapped there with Egyptian forces one side and Israeli forces the other until the re-opening eight years later. For us in 1970, this meant a detour around Africa, extending the sailing duration to six weeks. We duly booked the only affordable cabin, located down in the bowels, and set about having crates made to pack our meagre furniture and belongings. I painted all these crates bright yellow using leftover paint from some garish sets. We were still using some of the smaller ones as costume trunks thirty years later.

As departure day loomed, I was incredibly excited. This was my first time out of Australia and my first time on a ship. The only person to see us off was Peggy, predictably terribly upset and overwrought. She put on her best British brave face and clowned about a bit to take the edge off, but it was still very sad. Luis and I were wearing matching knee-length black fur coats and considered ourselves the height of ship-boarding fashion as we watched our trunks hauled up in a cargo net.

It was time to leave Australia and we stood at the deck railing watching Peggy watching us. Luis threw her a red carnation which she comically stuck between her teeth in a Carmen-like pose. As the Scottish Pipers played 'Now is the Hour', coloured paper streamers thrown by passengers to friends and family on the dock were now our only link to land. Fremantle Port has a North and South Mole, manmade embankments which allow a deep, clear channel to run several hundred metres out to sea. Peggy rushed to her little Fiat Bambino and drove out along the South Mole as far as she could, waving until the very last glimpse.

Peggy ended up travelling back and forth from Australia many times over the years, joining us in Spain, Italy, France and Japan. Sometimes there would be a knock at the door and there she was. The problem was that her time with us often stretched beyond reasonable. She left the two younger children, the girl was probably aged fifteen and the boy maybe thirteen by then, with Kira, who, delightful woman she was, would never have been awarded Mother of the Year. One peek inside Kira's fridge was enough for anyone to know a lettuce leaf and half a tomato would never feed two growing children.

When I broached the subject of going home, the tears and the clutching of pearls would eventually lead to me backing off. The matter would rest there until my tears of frustration out-gushed hers. That pattern continued for years; there was no way to get through to her that she had responsibilities at home. We were also obliged to pay for her living expenses, money we quite often couldn't spare, but that fact didn't appear to sink in either. Loving the woman as I did, her tenacity eventually had to be accepted. Later, after we bought a house back in Perth, we installed Peggy in residence while we travelled and for her to be the chief cook and bottle washer on our hectic, short bi-annual visits home.

Peggy was a marvellous cook and housekeeper, and she could hand bead costumes with the best of them. She turned out some excellent costume beading over the years. When I auctioned off the costumes thirty years later, a good many were from that original period and still as good as new. She remained living in our Perth house until her untimely death in 1985.

CHAPTER 8

ALL AT SEA

On our first night at sea, Luis and I entered our extremely tight cabin to unpack a little and change for dinner. The cabin was so damned small. On the right-hand side were two narrow bunks one above the other, on the left a miniature sink, and straight ahead a child-size wardrobe. At my head-height, running through the middle of this tiny cabin were two seven-inch-thick pipes wrapped in white painted canvas. We had to duck beneath them every time we moved. I swore I could smell bilge water.

Outside our cabin door on the right was the metal hull of the ship with – believe it or not – a hinged, steel-covered porthole. Why was there a porthole below the waterline? It gave me the horrors as it seeped seawater continually. There was no toilet in the cabin; communal facilities were located a way off down the passage and resembled something from a cheap, C-grade movie about a rotting and doomed cargo ship. Thick, white, cracked paint covered the floor and every surface. Paint had been applied so often it was like thick icing in some places, fractured and rust-stained in others. 'Gentlemen, please adjust your dress before leaving' was painted on a sign near the exit door. Unlike cruise ships, this was an ocean-going liner. The difference was vast, not only in the design and shape of the ship but also in the facilities available, the treatment of its passengers in the different classes, and the fact we were not cruising from exotic port to exotic port, but were actually en route to a specific destination.

When the dinner gong sounded, we made our way up the never-ending stairs between decks to the dining room. Passengers were allocated tables and seating which remained for the duration of the voyage. We initially shared our designated table with two geriatric gentlemen, utterly oblivious they were dining with two young gay men. On the first night our rather gorgeous waiters were definitely on the make and ignored our two wrinkled companions completely. After fifteen minutes or so of this entertaining flattering and fawning, an older, more sombre waiter appeared, and very politely informed us a table of passengers on the other side of the dining room had asked if would we care to join them? Yes, we would thank you.

Our saviours turned out to be a delightful lesbian named Toby who had acres of flaming red hair, and her friend and travelling partner, an equally fascinating and handsome young gay man called Pat. After introductions and the shuffling of seating arrangements, Toby announced to the waiter, with haughty authority, that we would be seated at their table for the rest of the voyage, and so we were. They had boarded the ship in Sydney and witnessed our fur-clad arrival on board in Fremantle. Toby had immediately commented to Pat, 'Well that's the end of any service in the dining room.' The ship's officers, deckhands and engine room crew were British. The Purser's department, cabin stewards, restaurant waiters, galley and laundry staff were a combination of British and Goanese. The Goanese guys were mostly gay, or sex-starved enough to give it a try. It's a pity we were not permitted to mix freely because they were friendly and charming and handsome.

The crossing from Fremantle to Durban, South Africa, was reckoned to be the roughest in thirty years, and the storm ropes were out the entire trip. Doors to the outside decks were often locked and huge waves would frequently crash right over Deck Three where the dining room was situated. I soon realised I was not a good sailor and spent many days on my bunk. These bunks were not like the solid, comfortable beds on cruise ships today. Instead, they were fairly slack old wire bases with a thin mattress on top. As the ship pitched and rolled, so did the wire base, only more so. A heave to the right would be followed by sinking into the mattress, a heave to the left, the mattress would rise in the middle, then it would start all over again. A groping, shaky stagger to the toilets would be met by the overwhelming stench of sour vomit slopping up and down the floor, increasing the intense, debilitating sickness. 'If this is travel and adventure in all its wonder then take me, God, I've seen enough already.' Fortunately, all things pass, including seasickness, and as Durban appeared on the horizon, I was fit and well and looking forward to planting my feet on foreign soil.

Luis and I disembarked with Toby and Pat, all of us looking forward to this twenty-four-hour stay in Durban. The exotic drama of Africa was immediately apparent. Row upon row of Zulu rickshaw pullers bedecked in beads, colourful feather headdresses, and clad only in grass and fur-trimmed loincloths met the ship. I was a little hesitant at first when it was suggested we ride with them into the city, uncomfortable to be drawn along by a human being acting as a beast of burden, however I was soon convinced these guys earned a very good living and were keeping a tradition alive.

Halfway through our journey, Toby, who was travelling in front of me, suddenly shot out of her rickshaw and landed with a thump in the dust. The rickshaw went up in the air and collapsed on the driver. A loose spoke from the left wheel had jammed into the side of the rickshaw, resulting in the catapulting of poor Toby. She jumped up completely unharmed and laughed until she cried. Or, as she put it, 'till tears ran down her thighs'. The rickshaw puller was also unharmed and very apologetic. I shifted over a bit, and lovely, good-natured Toby continued into the city with me.

I soaked up the new experience of being in a foreign city. The people were colourful and friendly, but the underlying racial problems and the policy of apartheid disturbed me a great deal. When mailing my postcards, I stood in the wrong queue to buy stamps. I went to the wrong counter, I used the wrong toilet. It was confusing and very disturbing. On the streets, completely contrasting quality of buses pulled up to service the separate queues at the different stops. Visiting the movies, I was shocked by a pre-movie ad featuring the image of a slovenly, overweight, headscarved 'Mammy' type black servant pouring dishwashing liquid down the sink. The accompanying voiceover asked, 'Are you tired of your maid wasting dishwashing liquid?' It was incredibly offensive. Unfortunately, the negative impact of the city still colours my memories.

A few days later, we entered the harbour of Cape Town. This entrance was breath-taking, with the city low on the horizon and the spectacular Table Mountain a looming backdrop in the hazy distance. Cape Town was a much smaller city. I wanted to go on the Table Mountain tour, but there wasn't time, so I satisfied myself with looking at its dominating magnificence. Cape Town has marvellous markets; the Indian section had tables and tables of exotic fabrics at lower than reasonable prices. Luis and I staggered around for the rest of the day juggling rolls of textiles. All in all, I'd had quite enough of the discrimination and confusion, and I was pleased to make my way back to the waiting ship.

Facilities on the *Orsova* were minimal. A makeshift cinema – consisting of a screen the size of a double bed sheet on a tripod with dining chairs set out in front – was erected in the dining room after second sitting each evening. The Second-Class pool was a tad over the size of a double sink and was towards the rear of the ship, or behind the 'aft' funnel. Obviously, the ship's designers had *never* travelled second-class, or they would have realised tiny, hot cinders from the funnel constantly landed on any diehard sun worshipper. It was like being bitten by ants every few minutes. Luis was eager to get his shears into those rolls of Cape Town fabric, so we did a deal with the Purser. We could use the dance floor for cutting out in exchange for Luis giving Modern Dance classes. I would keep time on a ship's drum. That's how we availed ourselves use of some of the first-class doings.

On board entertainment was a dance band, with the Entertainment Director contributing the odd song in a grating voice. News sheets of the ship's progress and the name of the passenger who had rightly guessed yesterday's advancement, plus a shortlist of the various activities to look forward to, were 'posted' under the cabin doors overnight. I've never been terribly keen on group activities, but one caught my eye: a hat competition. Right up my alley. I hadn't yet learned to make hats professionally but was definitely willing to give it a bash. Toby dragged me to the hold where she revealed she was travelling with a trunk jam-packed with feathers, trims and some scrumptious fabrics. What else would a qualified costume designer be taking all the way to London? The two of us sat and sewed all day; and we turned out a couple of sure-fire winners. Sadly, this was not to be. A rather boring yobbo type wearing his wife's bra on his head won the prize.

The rest of the voyage is a bit of a blur. Three days out of Cape Town, I started to feel very uncomfortable in my lower back. This sensation worsened over the course of the next couple of hours and by lunchtime of the third day, I was in complete and exquisite agony. The pain was unbearable, and Luis helped me to the ship's doctor. With no diagnosis forthcoming, I was placed in one of the ship's two hospital beds, and a drip was inserted into my arm. I imagined pain relief was being administered via the plastic tube because I immediately felt more comfortable. After a 24 hour period, the drip was removed, the pain returned instantly. So, there I was, undiagnosed and hospitalised for the remainder of the trip. Whatever they were pumping into me must have made me drowsy, because I don't remember those few weeks at all. I do remember calling for the nurse at one point, telling her I was seasick, she said it was impossible for two reasons. One, I hadn't eaten for a week and, two, we were tied up motionless at the dock in Tenerife, Canary Islands.

Luis and I had only paid for passage from Perth to Lisbon, where we intended to get a train to Madrid along with all our boxes and crates. We were tipped out at Porto de Lisboa with our large amount of baggage. I was assisted out of bed by Luis and the nurse but was so weak from being on a drip for so long, I simply couldn't stand up. Luis dressed me and a wheelchair was found to deliver me ashore. The wheelchair was quickly whisked from under me once we were on land and I was then propped up – half sitting, half leaning – against our belongings.

As the Captain and Ship's Doctor approached, I thought, 'How nice, they've come to wish me well.' No, they wanted to hand me the most staggeringly enormous account for treatment and have me sign a document stating if I died, it was not their problem. Charmed, I'm sure. We had very little ready money, and I had no intention of paying anyway. The Australian Ambassador was sent for, arriving directly from the golf course in a foul temper. Luckily, Luis spoke Portuguese. I understood nothing of the conversation that followed between this little group. As it turned out, the Ambassador wanted nothing to do with my situation, saying, 'that they can't be responsible for every Australian who has the misfortune to be ill on a ship in international waters.' Between him and the Port Authorities, who would also not take responsibility for a sick foreigner, it was decided we were to proceed immediately to the airport, and board the first flight to Madrid. The baggage would be sent on. Well, that was okay because somebody other than us footed the bill.

Shortly thereafter, we found ourselves in the air headed for Madrid. Luis had called his father from Lisbon airport, and an ambulance would be waiting for us on the tarmac. What an entrance. Of all the shows I produced for over forty years after that, nothing ever beat it.

The poor old *Orsova* truly was past her use-by date, and in 1974, she was retired, sold to Taiwan and scrapped. I've probably shaved with her repurposed remains.

CHAPTER 9

SPAIN AND MY STONY START

Although very weak from my shipboard illness, I was still incredibly excited to arrive in Spain. Hustled, along with Luis, into the waiting ambulance, we set off for the local emergency hospital, siren screaming. It was Spanish football final day, and the streets were packed. Even with the wailing siren, we were going nowhere because there was nowhere to go on the packed roads. The resourceful driver mounted the kerb and we proceeded, probably very carefully, on the footpath. Feeling great elation at finally being in Spain, I sat up a little to watch the commotion. Luis furiously kept shoving me back down saying, 'Lie down, for God's sake. You're supposed to be at death's door.' We pulled up at Emergency and two attendants wheeled me into a rather large room, with only one bed sitting smack in the middle.

Around the walls, patients were slumped, semi recumbent, on the floor. I was put onto the bed. Shortly after, a doctor arrived and after much prodding and poking, questions and answers, he entered into an interminably lengthy consultation with his colleagues. I was lifted off the bed and set against the wall with hoi polloi while the newest arrival took my place. The little cadre of medicos came to the conclusion I was suffering from kidney stones. Consensus was, the attack having passed, I could go home.

Home? We hadn't even seen it yet. Dressed and then helped outside, I laid down on the back seat of a taxi while Luis and his father squeezed into the front bench-style seat with the driver. Madrid's taxis then seemed a pretty dodgy lot—held together with hope, they had the cornering ability of fun park rides. On one particularly sharp turn, the door at my feet flew open and

I slowly but surely began to slide out. My cries for help were going completely unnoticed until I was able to make a feeble grab at an arm draped over the back of the front seat and they wrestled me back in. I came very close to making an exit from Spain just as theatrical as my entrance.

Luis's mother, Aurora, was a tiny little fireball. Only five feet tall, or maybe not quite, she had meticulously groomed greying hair and impeccable make-up on her still beautiful, scarcely lined face. Her unmistakable will of iron was plainly obvious, even though I couldn't understand a word. This little woman hunted for, and found, an entirely appropriate apartment on Calle Hilarion Eslava for us. The street was named for the nineteenth-century Spanish composer and defender of Spanish opera and Zarzuela (Spanish musical), Miguel Hilarión Eslava y Elizondo—a theatre person, how appropriate. One of those very old-fashioned but absolutely charming cage-style lifts took us to the third floor where there were two apartments, ours being on the right.

The apartment was 'U' shaped and huge, built around a large air shaft it shared with the only neighbour in a mirror-image setup. There was an enormous sitting room on the left that could easily fit eight beds, great for the dancers if we ever got that far. Along the passage were two bedrooms then after a left turn there were two more bedrooms and the dining room facing the street. Two bathrooms, laundry and kitchen were on the 'interior' or air-shaft side. Although fully furnished, there was still plenty of space for our belongings when they arrived. To my amazement, in our bedroom was a double bed. Remember, this is Generalissimo Franco's Catholic Spain, a Spain that brooked not the slightest hint of sexual deviance, the Spain where Luis's mother grew up, and had never left. Where did this amazing little woman get the guts to not only go against everything she was been brought up with, but also the stringent laws of her country and the very heterosexual mores of her macho husband, to whom she was married at an innocent sixteen. Indeed, a strong, strong woman. We were over the moon.

Obviously, I was the first and immediate occupant of that bed. Aurora (from now on Mama), cooked a vast plate of something delicious and ladled it down my throat. I slept the sleep of the dead until early next morning. After such a restful sleep, weak or not, I wanted to go exploring. Nothing, absolutely nothing, will ever be as thrilling as that first day on the streets of Madrid. The people *looked* Spanish, the buildings were old and elegant and completely unfamiliar, the thoroughly incomprehensible language, even the air itself felt distinctive. The Metro was clean, efficient and cheap—three pesetas no matter how far you went and trains came by every three minutes. Even the smell seemed alien. The impact of that first day was never ever repeated. Even though I visited, lived, and worked in twenty or so countries in the years after this, nothing was ever again so powerful. I loved it.

Of course, later there were things about the place that I didn't particularly enjoy. Not being able to communicate was incredibly frustrating and I did my best to learn Spanish as quickly as possible. Over time, the excessive, oppressive Catholicism was overwhelming. I witnessed religious processions which included self-harming penitents. Horrifying. Spitting on the streets bugged me. All, or mostly all the older women, wore wretched and gloomy black or dark hues, like the 'New Australian', immigrants back home. And I finally saw where the 'look' of European male immigrants came from as the men wore sports jackets, even while digging ditches. Despite being told homes were spotlessly immaculate, bathing seemed to be a problem, as body odour was high. I even saw men and women nonchalantly pissing in the streets.

The odd shopping trips with Luis or Mama were enormous fun. Every day, Mama would shower and change from her housecoat into something smart and fortunately, colourful. A fresh application of lippy, a quick check of her immaculate hair, a grip on the vinyl trolley, and off we went. The subterranean markets, spaced every few blocks, sold every foodstuff imaginable. The aromas of the spices in open sacking, the rabbits, chickens and other small animals and birds – plucked, skinned and hanging overhead – was a novel experience for me. The fruit and vegies looked fresh, plump and tempting, the dried legumes of every description puzzling. The 'Who's first, *usted Seño*ra?' approach to service, the yelling, bawling and hollering of the vendors added to the delightfully deafening din of the shoppers. I found it all entertaining and intensely real. No soulless supermarkets, soothing music or cold steel trolleys here. Every woman in Spain shopped daily for food. Of course, every home possessed a refrigerator, but the food intended to be cooked and consumed that day was purchased that day. Mama was a fabulous cook and invitations were of the 'open house' variety. The big family gatherings on Sunday were especially enjoyable—something I had never known before.

And so, we settled into Madrid and made the apartment liveable. There was plenty of space for a sewing room, storage and entertaining. It was time to try and turn our dream of creating and presenting our own showgirl shows into reality by getting our first show up and running to earn some much-needed pesetas. A showgirl show is a Moulin Rouge-style entertainment featuring feather and diamante clad dancers. We decided to make the costumes for the biggest numbers first and hopefully, we could get a few spots guesting in revues. Meanwhile, I had this wonderful city to continue exploring.

Our first show in Spain, was at the famous Teatro Apolo Barcelona, as guest ballet for a Colsada revue starring Tania Doris. The theatre was relatively small, hardly on the glamorous side, but it offered well paid work. It meant travelling from Madrid to Barcelona by train, the 'Talgo'. I was looking forward to seeing Barcelona. An avid reader, I already knew much about this historic city founded by the Romans in the Middle Ages. The Old Roman walls can still be seen around the Cathedral of the Holy Cross and Saint Eulalia, constructed between the thirteenth and fifteenth centuries.

A book I'd read described the possibility of following much of the wall system as it still stands today. Despite large portions of the wall being incorporated into newer buildings, it is certainly still visible. I walked and walked that fascinating area enjoying the unexpected sight of geese wandering around a little garden inside the Cathedral. I soon learned the geese are a symbol of the Patron Saint of Barcelona, Saint Eulalia, after whom the Cathedral was named. The number of geese kept at the cloister is always thirteen, representing her age when she was killed by the Romans.

During my wanderings, I often came across peculiar-looking buildings. These edifices – old, but not ancient – looked a bit dilapidated and uncared for, but were unmistakably designed by the same architect. Strange, twisted-metal balconies and free-form concrete masks. Nobody could tell me who the architect was. I dragged Luis along to see them. He agreed they were fascinating constructions but had no idea who the designer might be. Later we visited the unfinished 'Church of the Sagrada Família'. Begun by Francisco de Paula del Villar in 1882, Antoni Gaudí became involved and took over the project in 1883. By the time of his death in 1926, one solitary spire was completed. That's pretty much how we saw it in the early '70s. There was a wall around the site, so looking from the outside was as close as you could get; it was not yet the incredible tourist destination it has become today. That one 'dripping' tower was awesome, and I knew straight away, this was my architect. It was so obvious the buildings I'd seen previously, and this church, were designed by the same person. Now everyone is aware of Antoni Gaudi and his works, but back then, for some unfathomable reason, there was little or no interest. Maybe it was a Franco thing; he despised the Catalans, even going so far as to forbid the speaking and teaching of the language. Gaudi, heavily influenced by Egyptian, Indian, Persian, Mayan, Chinese and Japanese art, is now a demigod.

We settled into the Hotel Abrevadero (Horse Trough), a mere block from Teatro Apolo, at the end of the Carrer Nou de la Rambla, an infamous little street running from Las Ramblas to Avenido del Parallel through the heart of the equally infamous Barrio Chino. Chinatown. We spent many months in and around this district and not once saw a single person of Asian appearance. That exotic tangle of alleyways and streets was home to sneak thieves, pickpockets, pimps, petty criminals, artists, intellectuals, transvestites, homosexuals and prostitutes. I loved every cobblestone in it. This section of Barcelona was an area of great ambience and charm, for all its dark and foreboding reputation. As well as the Teatro Apolo, it was the location for many of Barcelona's famous theatres including the Teatro Condal and Teatro Victoria. The most famous of all, El Molino was home to Barcelona's acclaimed variety and outrageous drag show. Even in the times of Franco, this place managed to stay open, drawing huge nightly crowds, and was considered an institution and local icon. The comic drag stars performing there were well and truly past their prime – if they'd ever had one – but maintained such huge followings, all and every sin was lovingly forgiven.

Teatro Apolo was the home of the Chicas Alegras de Colsada, famous in Spain at that time, and Tania Doris was the latest in a string of 'stars' to grace Señor Colsada's stage. Tania was not a slight girl or the most graceful ever to parade around a 'pasarela', the catwalk that runs around the orchestra pit off the apron of a stage. Although quite attractive when standing stock still, I thought she was a most clumsy and awkward girl. Evidently, Señor Colsada obviously thought otherwise. He was a short, squat, ugly little man, and seeing the two of them out and about after the show at night was a sight to behold.

I must give it to Tania, (as I know Colsada was) she made quite a career for herself and is still going strong. The review finished the first half with a song dedicated to 'La Dama del Paraguas', a quite camp 1855 sculpture of a woman with an umbrella. It is a revered symbol of Barcelona as water sprays out of the top of the umbrella, making 'La Dama' stand in eternal rain. Tania sang her song dressed as 'La Dama', atop a tall replica plinth complete with rain, and when the curtain came down you could hear as far out as the lobby, the thud of Tania's bulk as she de-plinthed onto the stage. I always waited for it; it was part of my day. Those poor Colsada girls, they worked so hard. Two shows per day, six days per week. Some were getting on a bit and had worked in the Apolo for decades. Their dressing rooms were small versions of their homes: plants, photos, hot plates and even the odd child asleep in a box under their make-up desks.

Henri Bustos, possibly the most sought-after man in the feather costume trade in Madrid, made us a massive blue feather tail, a good two metres in diameter, to be worn by our lead girl Hanni, performing en pointe to 'Saint Louis Blues' in a fun number choreographed by Luis. I always climbed up to the flies to watch this favourite of mine. I vividly recall the occasion when management changed conductors without telling us and the new guy played our number at almost double-time without once looking up. Poor Hanni was burning holes through her pointe shoes trying desperately but unsuccessfully to keep up. I was heaving candy at the conductor in a futile effort to get him to look up. They bounced off the drums, the cymbals and the musicians, but not once did he raise his head.

CHAPTER 10

FEATHERS IN A CAP

Our run at the Teatro Apolo was soon over, and we were grateful. Money is money, but it was definitely not the most prestigious venue. We were back on the Talgo heading to Madrid and as no other work was waiting, the near future looked a little bleak. Venue owners knew many show owners were desperate, especially if you had a show rehearsed and a full complement of dancers. Dancers could afford to hang around for only so long without work. If you couldn't come up with work for them, another 'ballet' would snap them up. Ballet is a strange term in English for a cabaret show, but in Europe, a show such as ours is called a ballet. There were already a few established ballets in Spain, and we were 'the new kids on the block'. All's fair in love and war and tits' n' feathers.

As the fluent Spanish speaker, poor Luis spent many long hours in agents' waiting rooms, doing everything but sleeping across the doorway. There were a handful of beautiful venues in Madrid but some, like the 'Lido', owned permanent shows and the others could afford to be super choosy. Why take a chance on a new group when shows that have previously performed successfully at a venue are only too willing to do a return engagement? Then there was the clever ploy of: 'Sure we can give you a chance. You put on a show for us for free, and if we like it, we'll sign you.' That's a big, expensive chance because the dancers must be paid from somebody's pocket – ours, obviously – and, at the very least, the venue gets a free show. We did this several times. We were very sure we would be picked up at the beautiful El Pavillon inside the grounds of the fabulous Retiro Park in the heart of Madrid. Our show went well, but there was no follow-up phone call. Then, a week or so later, just as the dancers were preparing to look for other work, an agent called and said the management of Pasapoga, having seen the show, would like to make an offer.

Amazing news, wonderful news. Opened in 1942, Pasapoga was then the most prestigious venue in Madrid—smack in the heart of the city at *37 Gran Via*, the main avenue and best address in town. This marble, red plush and gold leaf decorated nightclub attracted the cream of Madrid society. Expensive and dignified, the club extended over two floors, the top floor being a mezzanine overlooking the stage. During the 50s, it was a favourite hangout of the high-ranking Nazis that Franco sheltered after WWII. Show business luminaries throughout the world performed there at their height, including Frank Sinatra and Xavier Cougat.

We were thrilled by this miraculous offer. A successful show at the prestigious Pasapoga was an entrée to every major venue in Europe. This extract from Wikipedia:

> *Its horseshoe-shaped floor plan, in the style of traditional theatres, and its exuberant decoration, with columns and wall paintings imitating old frescoes, hosted concerts by artists such as Antonio Manchin, Frank Sinatra or Rosa Morena. Scenes from Pasapoga appear in the 1952 film 'The Eyes Leave Traces'.*

Opening night drew near and we were all ready to go when Pasapoga management informed us they wanted to include a singer in the show. Now, this is a colossal problem. Firstly, we must find one in a hurry, secondly, there was to be no increase in payment. Our agent came to the rescue with the name of a British singer called Genevieve, who was in town looking for work. Princess Genevieve actually—she was married to an obscure Italian Prince from some long ago, dubious Principality. The Prince was a tiny, weedy, very gay, little man, who followed his Princess everywhere, like a Chihuahua. We arranged an interview and met this *chanteuse* at our home. A quick rehearsal was organised with the maestro, at the appointed time and on asking for her music, he was met with a totally blank stare.

'What music?' she said. 'I thought you would supply the music.' This situation was rapidly going from bad to worse. Music was produced by the maestro and on her cue, a thin, almost inaudible squeak turned out to be her singing voice. This hole was getting deeper by the minute. Genevieve apologised explaining she was recovering from a sore throat but would be just fine by tomorrow's opening and not to worry. Famous last words of 'it'll be right on the night' echoed in my head. The maestro stayed up all night copying music for her, paid out of our pockets as we intended to deduct the cost from Genevieve's wage. When I questioned the very (let's be kind) buxom Genevieve about her costumes, she said, 'Oh, don't worry about that, I have heaps of glam turbans and stuff, I'm mad for costume auctions and have loads of Elizabeth Taylor's old dresses.' Liz had a weight problem, sure—perhaps Genevieve had sewn them all together.

On the evening of the show, she appeared hours before curtain up and immediately started applying her make-up. The dancers arrived, and except for the excitement of this being the beginning of something new, all was calm and professional. Genevieve's dressing room door remained closed. I occasionally gave a soft knock to ask whether everything was okay. An assured voice always answered, 'Fine.' The five-minute call went up, I knocked on Genevieve's door and barged straight in. There she was, sitting in her underwear, still applying make-up three hours later. It's true, her eye make-up would have been the envy of the most discerning drag queen, but come on, girl, it's five minutes. Get dressed. She pointed to what looked like an un-spooled bolt of midnight blue velvet fabric draped beside her on the floor, explaining it was her dress.

'Would you help me?' Sure.

'Let's go.' She held one end while I did several laps around her with the other and jammed a turban on her head. What a disaster she looked. Pushing her to the stage door, I gave her one last shove as her music started. I took off for the mezzanine to watch. Oh, my stars. The voice was not one iota better than the day before, and on top of this, she'd lost a shoe. I was horrified. She performed that one night only, and nothing was surer than a polite, or not so polite, request to not come back.

As it turned out, the management had deliberately given us a quiet night to open and were kind enough to tell us the show was precisely what they needed. Shows at the time were elegantly posey and we were more active, more 'dance-y'. They did inform us the following night would be packed with Madrid's finest and they expected to see a new singer of some quality. There would be no sleep until Harry, a dancer friend from South Africa, came up with a telephone number for a South African singer who arrived the day before. This was Deni Lorren. I should qualify that. This was the fantastic, amazing, unbelievable Deni Lorren. Deni was contacted and more than pleased to find work so quickly. She arrived on time for band rehearsal the following day with a suitcase full of music and a small trunk of beautiful gowns. Giving the maestro a nod, she let fly with one of the most unbelievable and powerful voices I have ever heard—in quality, a cross between Bassey and Streisand. In looks, she was a tall, blonde 'Jessica Rabbit' sex siren. Oh, Deni, my darling, I loved you then, and I love you still. Wherever you are.

On one occasion we were having people around for some bash at the apartment and of course, Deni was invited. Most of our guests were already in attendance when Deni arrived dressed in an orange, crocheted, unlined micro-dress over flesh-coloured underwear. Now this is a woman with curves and, admittedly, she looked spectacular, but her attire wasn't exactly early '70s urban Madrid daywear. 'Sorry I'm late', she said, 'but whenever I take a cab in this city, they seem to go the longest way round. I don't mind 'cos I never get charged.' The evening was hitting its straps when a great hubbub could be heard through the open dining room window. Looking out of the bedroom window I saw a tremendous crowd of men gathered on the pavement below, all looking up, calling and whistling. There was Deni's generous, scantily clad arse sticking out of the dining room window as she perched on the sill. Oh, Deni. What a woman. We lost track of Deni over the years. I do know she went on to do some recording with the Argentinian composer Waldo de los Rios, who was enjoying considerable world acclaim at the time, and remembered for his ability to transform European classical music into pop music. Sadly, the very talented Waldo suffered acute depression and committed suicide in Madrid a few years later, in 1977.

The Pasapoga survived until relatively recently and was at one time a popular gay haunt. The magnificent façade has been kept as a historical site. Thank you, Pasapoga for a wonderful start to our very long careers.

Our early years in Spain were spent trying desperately to get a permanent show up and running as quickly as possible. Pasapoga was a grateful first step, but now we needed continuity. The next move was to design more costumes, and either make or have them made. Madrid was blessed with some of the finest costume and hat makers in Europe but unfortunately, the costume person we chose to use did not belong to such impressive company. As a consequence, we took the decision to get in some sewing ladies and make everything at home. Our apartment was enormous, so space wasn't a problem. The problem was money. We'd made a gargantuan hole in our meagre savings, so I decided to call a few friends and look for work. Luis was the sewing expert and needed to be on hand, while I was the 'as yet untried' producer, designer, hatmaker, with more time to spare.

CHAPTER 11

READY FOR MY CLOSE-UP

Madrid in the early '70s was chock-a-block with American, English and South African dancers. The Americans – the guys anyway – were mostly draft-dodgers from the Vietnam War, but the rest were in search of work, and there was plenty to be found in Madrid. Live theatre was everywhere, and you could be in the country for just three months to qualify for residency. There must have been ten or more full-time productions running. In addition to this, there was cinema. This was a time when most of the American moviemakers set themselves up in Spain. Why? I don't know, but they were all there. The decade had opened with Hollywood facing a financial slump, so maybe that was it. Many big studios were set up on the outskirts of Madrid.

I became friendly with a South African girl, Sandra Labroque, who was a resident casting person for Metro-Goldwyn-Mayer (MGM). I'd met Sandra at the house of our friends, the South African dancers David and Harry, and when I gave her a call, she was wonderful. 'Sure, I have work for you. Come out to the studios tomorrow,' she said. I was there like a shot. Sandra pulled a few strings, and I was hired the same day as a resident extra. Those of us fortunate enough to be resident extras were required to attend the studios every day. MGM sent a minibus around Madrid picking us up from our homes. Luxury. We would sit in the cafeteria all day playing canasta, waiting to be called.

Sometimes we would work on two or three films a day, getting shunted from wardrobe to make-up to set. Most times I didn't have a clue what these movies were about or even what they were called. Did I care? I was making ten US dollars per hour, up to ten hours per day, six days per week. We are talking more than five hundred dollars per week. When I'd left Australia, I was being paid sixty dollars per week as resident designer with the WA Ballet Company. Such an amount of money went a long way in Spain in those days. You could buy a 'plato combinado', a set three-course meal, including wine and coffee, for fifty cents.

I had lots of fun on those movie sets and did a lot of stuff which was just bloody awful and must certainly have ended up on the cutting room floor. One of the most memorable films for me was *Travels With My Aunt.* George Cukor was directing and what a thrill it was to be on set every day watching him work and soaking it all in. His most unforgettable films include *The Women*, *The Philadelphia Story*, *Holiday*, *My Fair Lady* as well as *A Star is Born* (featuring Judy Garland in one of the grandest screen performances of all time). We started filming *Travels With My Aunt* with a super, big female lead, but after a falling out with George, she was replaced by Maggie Smith. Mum's the word regarding exactly who the original lead was, but let me say, she was delightful. I wouldn't dream of saying she knew my name, but this darling lady greeted everyone on the set equally and ate with us in the old bus that served as a canteen. No huge retinue following her about, no gofers chasing after her; and she fed lines off-camera to the other actors—something very few actors do. She knew her business. I remember well a time she suggested a particular light be moved back six inches. She knew from the heat she wouldn't be lit properly.

Ms Smith on the other hand, was very cold, and very much on her dignity. There was a huge cortège of people around her, plus her husband and other hangers-on. She would never be on the set if her stand-in could do the job, for example, back-of-head shots. I knew nothing of her in those days, and maybe I was influenced by the stark difference between the two actors. I am now a huge fan and will see absolutely anything she is in. I received the most delightful note from her after praising her remarkable performance in *The Lady in the Van.*

I was allocated an elevated role in this particular movie, with a half dozen words to deliver to a seated Ms Smith and her co-star Louis Gosset, Jr. For this distinctive performance, I was paid twenty dollars per hour and given a screen credit. Yes! Plus, my pay packet said *Thomas Robb, Disc Jockey (it actually said Dic Yoky in* Spanish) as that's the role I was playing, instead of *Thomas Robb, Extra.* Ah, the heady feeling of stardom.

George Cukor and I became friendly on the set. He was having an affair with a young Australian guy at the time and gave him a job. I don't know his official title but when George yelled out for *'Mas fumar'* (more smoke—the set was supposed to be a Parisian night club), this young man would trot around the set with a smouldering piece of emery paper. In my role as the nightclub disc jockey, I was to visit the stars' table with an arm full of LPs, shove my head between theirs and say, 'Is there anything you would like to hear?' before being waived away and sauntering back to my DJ desk to continue sorting, bopping and glancing around the room. Positively award-winning stuff. My costume for this scene was a super tight pair of broadly striped dark grey and white jeans, a pale grey shirt and a black sleeveless pullover tucked in. My crotch was right 'in shot' and at the same height as the heads of the two stars. Ms Smith used to do her trade-mark rapid eye and head movements and take a peek.

After the first day's shooting, George approached me and said, 'Tom, who asked you to pad your crotch? We watched the dailies last night and all I could see was this great bulge between the actors' heads. The distortion of the stripes over the bulge really played hell with the camera, and we've wasted a day's filming.' I hadn't stuffed my crotch. It was all me. I've never been ashamed of my equipment, but nobody ever said it was all too big. Well, that's a white lie, Luis complained, on many occasions, about my bulging scrotum. It was the 70s, and tightest of tight trousers were 'in'. The type you lay on the bed with a coat hanger in the zip to get them done up. I rather thought it was fine and normal and if anything, a bit of an advantage. George harrumphed saying, 'Well, get off to wardrobe and tell them I said to give you plain black trousers.' When I next stood between the two stars, I distinctly heard affirmative murmurings from what has become a very well-known voice.

This little episode was the catalyst for much suffering of my poor package sometime later. After some nagging by Luis, I submitted to the surgeon's knife only to have the whole affair turn out rather badly. As a result of that butchery episode, I spent an agonising period with the offending orbs infected. The resultant blackening and swelling made the size of the originals insignificant, forcing me to wear extraordinarily large, baggy tracksuit pants and to adopt the ambling gait of a sailor who hasn't seen dry land in decades. At one time, I was seriously considering a wheelbarrow as a tote for my watermelon-sized scrotum. Further surgery through my abdomen saved the day; I now pass for completely normal in the region. Anyway, it didn't matter, I believe the whole scene was cut in the end. I don't know because I haven't seen the movie to this day.

It was the greatest honour and privilege to watch George work. He just knew. That's all there was to it. He just knew. There was a crowded disco dance floor scene in the nightclub, and I recall clearly to this day George shouting, 'Take the girl at the back in the red dress out, she's self-conscious.' Imagine being able to pick out a self-conscious person in a crowd scene. In another scene, two high-class prostitutes were to walk down the vast curved staircase into the club. George felt the actors were not walking properly, went to the top and said, 'Like this,' and came vamping down looking exactly like a high-class hooker. He was an old man wearing mufti, but all you saw coming down those stairs was a hot, expensive lady of the night.

Travels With My Aunt did well with the Oscars that year. Maggie Smith was nominated for Best Actress; Anthony Powell won Best Costume Design; John Box, Gil Parrondo, Robert W Laing were nominated for Best Art Direction/ Set Decoration; Douglas Slocombe, Nominee: Best Cinematography; Me … no mention.

Sir Robert Helpmann and George Cukor were great friends, and probably knew each other through Katharine Hepburn as they were both dear chums of hers. Hepburn lived with Spencer Tracy in a bungalow in George's back yard. While we were filming *Travels*, Bobby came over from England to visit.

I'd known Bobby for quite a while by then and this pleased George, we could perhaps knock out a bit of fun. He'd often asked me what on earth was there to do in Madrid, something which might bear a touch of the camp about it. During Franco's time any man who even hinted at gayness would disappear from the streets, appearing some weeks later with his head shaved and having survived on nothing but a diet of castor oil. Those poor guys were wrecks afterwards, more than a few were known to have died. Hard to believe Spain was one of the first countries in the world to approve gay marriage, in 2005.

The furtive life was still the case during this time in Spain, although some of the private parties I attended in Madrid were nothing short of scandalous. Two friends lived in downtown Callao in a very old building. The apartment was on the top floor and was one of those peculiarly European places where the low ceilings followed the up and down of the roofline and dormer windows—tilt your head left to take a slash, to the right while washing your hands, that sort of thing. Absolutely full of charm if you didn't mind paying out for chiropractic fees now and then. These guys loved getting into drag and would hold some of the best parties I have ever been to. Drag was de rigueur; nobody would be admitted without a nice frock and much of it was a total bad taste send up. They were having one of these famous events that coming weekend, so I asked George how he felt about it. It was a rush to see who could get to the wardrobe department quicker, him or Bobby.

In the early '70s, Spain still maintained the 'sereno' system. All apartment buildings (and Madrid is all apartments) must be locked by an external metal grilled door by nine pm. You carried a key to exit your apartment block, but if you forgot it, or someone else had it, you had to put your hands through the bars from inside and clap to get out. The key didn't work from outside; you just stood in front of the door and your clapping would – if you were lucky and he wasn't getting pissed on cheap *tinto* somewhere – bring the sereno, or neighbourhood guard. He carried keys to all the buildings within a block or so, and you must tip him to let you out or in. The night of the party in central Madrid, there was probably a dozen or so of us already there. Everyone had imbibed a few bevies when all hell broke loose downstairs. The taxi bearing Bobby and George arrived and deposited them at the front door. Rather than a circumspect, barely audible clapping to summon the sereno, these two Ugly Stepsister look-alikes had fairly burst into a full flamenco routine. Heads were stuck out of every window in the street. So much for discretion. The next sound we expected to hear were police sirens as they came to take us all away.

CHAPTER 12

THE DETONATORS

My time at MGM was fun, and I wish I could remember all the movies I worked on. I can recall the *Sinbad* series with John Phillip Law, the tall, gorgeous Blind Angel from *Barbarella*, because we were all painted green from head to toe. 'A harmless vegetable dye,' we were assured. Harmless it might have been but come off it wouldn't. Long sleeves and high collars were very much the go for days after. The scene was in a cave where a multi-armed Indian-type goddess came to life and caused havoc.

Film crew, extras, bit players and stars are alike when it comes to filching the best prop items on sets when a film is 'wrapped'. That particular call is eagerly awaited if you've been eyeing off a nice little décor accoutrement during filming. It's every man for himself. First in best dressed, was the rule. A bronze miniature of the demonic goddess was on a table outside the set entrance, all eyes were on it, waiting to hear, 'That's a wrap!'

During *Travels*, Augusta's (Maggie Smith) nephew Henry's (Alec McGowen) London kitchen set led onto the Paris nightclub set, and I often walked through it to get into place. If they were shooting from my side, the wall would be removed, and I could walk straight to my position. If I had to walk through the kitchen set, I would brush through a beautifully beaded hanging doorway curtain. High quality, big glass beads in several shades of blue and plenty of them. One good, hearty tug and that fab curtain later entered the costume repertoire for our own show—appearing in any number of guises over time, including years later, ending up draped from hips to arms on the topless models in one of our finales. A friend dived onto the divine little goddess statue in Sinbad. It quickly disappeared into the folds of his costume, then into his dance bag, and took pride of place over the mantle at his home. Unfortunately, we got called back for some retakes; all hell broke loose when the statue couldn't be found.

While I was working for MGM, Luis and I were offered work in Rocio Jurado's first TV special, 'Rocio y los Detonadores' (Rocio and the Detonators). Rocio was already a big star in Spain, but I don't think anyone realised just how big a star she was to become. From humble beginnings – mother a housewife and father a cobbler – Rocio took on the role of breadwinner. After her father died, she worked at shoe making, fruit picking and various other menial jobs. Rocio was nicknamed the 'Awards Girl' because she won every singing contest she ever entered and kept on collecting awards for the rest of her life: Gold Medal of Fine Arts, from Don Juan Carlos I, King of Spain (1995) and Adoptive Daughter of the Province of Seville (2007) were just two of the many.

This TV special was typical '70s Spanish TV nonsense, centering around two groups—the goodies and the baddies. The baddies were a group of females, our girl dancers, who were trying to take over the world. Baddies taking over the world, how original. They chose a very practical uniform, knee-high, black lace-up boots, black PVC hotpants, bright yellow and black PVC jackets and black hair braids of the type predominantly seen on females young and old, (and some males), arriving home from a holiday in Bali. Wasn't a good look then and still isn't. Obviously, discretion was not a priority. Difficult to explain the plot now because I never got a handle on it then. Suffice to say the baddies were continually being foiled by the goodies, the boy dancers. The guy's outfits were black PVC trousers, with belted tight-fitting black PVC jackets. No braids.

Rocio apparently possessed some range in her voice which was going to allow the baddies to set off worldwide nuclear explosions at a time of their choosing. This set the scene for a gay romp around southern Spain with the baddies setting up poor Rocio as the Detonator, hence the title, constantly being thwarted by the goodies. The continual change of location gave Rocio a fantastic opportunity to have a massively varied wardrobe. Southern Spain has rich climatic variations, from the snowy mountains of the Sierra Nevada to sun-drenched beaches, all within an hour's drive of one another. Rocio possessed a body which was a designer's dream. Slim, but with curves exactly where Spanish men wanted them, relatively tall for a Spanish woman, with a beautiful, expressive face—it was easy to understand her stardom.

When filming began on 'Rocio y los Detonadores' in Granada, I was in the middle of some movie or other and simply couldn't get away. Obviously, I was filling a vital void in a crowd scene of a major spectacular which no other extra could possibly have handled, so Luis took off with our troupe to Granada, and I was to join them as soon as I could. Shortly before Luis left, Deni Lorren asked me to design a dress for her. A heavily beaded bra in black oil slick bugle beads with a multi-layered diaphanous dress in dark blues and aquas hanging from it was sketched and approved. Luis made the dress before travelling south for filming, leaving me to bead the bra. After an incredible length of time and a huge quantity of beads, it was simply gigantic. I delivered it with dress attached, and Deni tried it on. Horror of horrors, none of my fine handiwork showed at all. Those immense cups barely covered her nipples and the beautiful, expensive, beadwork pointed to the floor. It still looked magnificent.

All good things must come to an end, and soon it would be goodbye to my very lucrative little movie stint. Money was still not flowing into our bank account in proportion to expenditure—it never did seem to reach deluge status. Every penny we earned was spent on living and costumes. As soon as I was ready to join Luis and the crew, I made my way to Granada by the cheapest transport possible, hopping from one town to another on local trains. There was little for me to do on this TV special other than to manage and run interference for the twelve dancers. Hours and hours which felt like days and days of hanging around waiting for setups, lighting, sound checks and the interminable takes to be completed; but such is the way of film work, no matter your involvement. In Granada, the filming was inside the grounds of the fabulous and historically famous Alhambra Palace. How they got permission to film in there I don't know. The Alhambra was and is a top-of-the-list tourist site and a Spanish National Treasure. What a joy and honour for a wide-eyed Australian boy to be there, never mind experiencing the added gift of filming.

There were scenes to be shot at the entrance gates, the battlements overlooking Granada, the Court of the Lions' fountains and several other much-photographed tourist sites. Crowd control was always difficult with countless busloads of tourists from all over the world continually arriving. Of course, the tourists snapped away at the filming as well—only too happy to be getting an unexpected double whammy on this leg of their sixty-cities-in-three-days package tour. The ascent to the Alhambra is a terraced, winding driveway, and on the drop side are shrubs about a metre high. Sitting at our crew camp one day, with not much to do, I stripped off my shirt and began taking a bit of sun on the hood of one of the crew vans. Very slowly and dimly Luis's voice penetrated my sun-soaked, semi-conscious bliss, and I looked up to see him waving and shouting from the terrace above. As I couldn't quite see or hear him properly, I got down from my perch and backed up to get a better view.

Still unable to see him, I backed into the bushes just a bit more and whoosh, I was falling through nothingness towards the terrace below. Those damn bushes were not growing from a bed at the edge of the roadway but, horizontally out of the perpendicular edge. Out, quick right angle, and up. In my blind, frantic groping, I managed to get a grip on the horizontal part of the bushes which grew outward before it went up. After hauling myself up, I emerged dishevelled, in front of the entire film production peering open-mouthed over the top of the bushes of the terrace above. Never did find out why I was being called.

On another occasion, we were filming at the enormous Arabic keyhole-shaped gateway into the palace. Seemingly, those villainous hot panted baddies spotted an opportunity to grab Rocio back from the saviour-like clutches of the goodies. Exact details of the attack escape me, however there was the necessity for a fittingly sombre, black, horse-drawn hearse, complete with black ostrich plumes waving on each corner, to be drawn up by the side of the gate. The machine gun-toting baddies were doing their best to dance in heels on cobblestones and trying to include the heavy machine guns into the choreography without braining themselves or each other. They were real, functional machine guns rather than some light-weight props and an accident waiting to happen.

The next location was the coast. I have an idea that it was Castell de Ferro or somewhere nearby because I do remember castle ruins. We were put up in a very comfortable cliffside hotel overlooking the beach, the sun continued to shine, and it was all very southern-Spain-tourist-brochure weather. Filming was to take place nearby in a typical, white-washed village, with geraniums hanging from every windowsill. Whitewashed walls, terracotta tiles, sharply winding cobbled streets, obligatory be-shawled, wrinkled, black-clad grannies on wickerwork chairs crocheting and gossiping outside every doorway. Should this have been mocked up by the set department as colloquial, it would have been rejected as overkill.

This scene was a complicated setup. The baddies were once again going to wrest Rocio from the goodies. Same plot different location. A winding section of the village was selected as perfect for the scene, the occupants of the houses were evacuated to their neighbour's or relative's homes or the local tapas bar, and duly compensated for the use of their street. Giant foam making machines were brought in, and the street was filled completely with soap suds. Right up to the roofline. Not an uncommon scene in these sleepy villages, I'm sure. Rocio and the goodies were to be in front of these suds – why the foam was there was never explained – a wind machine was to blow the suds away, revealing six enormous vertical cardboard cartons in staggered formation along the street. Nothing unusual here except … those dastardly baddies were to break free from inside the cartons in complete surprise. A simple little scene.

What could possibly go wrong? Everything. The suds wouldn't stay put. The slightest breeze revealed the tops of the cartons too soon, the baddies were slowly expiring in their PVC costumes inside airless cartons on a hot day. There were problems making the cartons break open where and when needed. They became soggy and collapsed onto the heads of their occupants. The baddies' make-up ran down their faces when they finally tore themselves free. On and on, and on it went. Just another day on location.

After getting the scene in the can, I decided to walk along the beach the few kilometres to the hotel. Not far along I was approached by a particularly belligerent, shotgun-wielding local and told, in no uncertain manner, to get off the beach. It's private. As an Australian, I didn't realise a beachfront could be privately owned. There was a rather charming, rustic restaurant at the hotel, and we took all our meals there. Here it was brought home to me that star status and good breeding are not necessarily mutual. Sitting at the table next to Rocio and Tola, I was shocked to see Rocio intermittently spitting, or throwing onto the floor, food not to her taste or liking. At the end of each course, she grabbed a fist full of white tablecloth and cleaned her mouth and hands with it. I couldn't look at her in quite the same light from then on.

Only one other location sticks in my mind. The Sierra Nevada is a short twenty-one-kilometre jaunt from Granada, and more strikingly different weather you cannot imagine. From the warm-to-hot, boxy streets of old Granada to the windy, freezing snowfields of the Sierra Nevada is a mere one-hour drive. Twenty-one kilometres in an hour might seem a long, sluggish drive, but while you are en route, it seems to go straight up. Of course, the twenty-one kilometres is as the crow flies; the actual journey is a combination of twists and turns, hairpin bends, sheer mountains on one side and equally sheer, jaw-dropping drops on the other. The driver of our company bus was, in my opinion, a homicidal maniac bent on taking us to his maker with him. On several occasions, I was physically restrained from jumping from the bus in abject terror. Still, we made it, and it was so very beautiful but so very cold. None of us was prepared for such a plummet in temperature but luckily, the costume department produced a pleasant surprise. Instead of the flesh-exposing costumes worn previously, the goodies and the baddies were given lovely, warm, padded ski suits in appropriate goodie and baddie colours. Enough were left over for the entire crew, so there were no complaints.

'Rocio y los Detonadores' was a tremendous hit at the time and was repeatedly aired right up until 2009. The director, Fernando García Tola, was at his peak. As ever, Luis did a magnificent job of the choreography—especially when you consider the surfaces the dancers had to cope with. Everything from ankle-twisting cobblestones to sand and snow.

Seventeen years later at the magnificent Gran Palace Showroom, an hour outside of Barcelona in Lloret de Mar, we were a few years into a five-year show residency. One of the special guest artists was Rocio Jurado. A global superstar by then, Rocio had come through the years looking a little heavier but very, very, good indeed. Backstage, when Luis came up and tapped her on the shoulder, there was instant recognition and squeals with hugs all round. In 2006, at time of her death from cancer aged 61, Rocio was the greatest and richest singing star in the Spanish-speaking world. A delightful lady and a massive, hugely respected talent.

CHAPTER 13

WILD DOG ISLANDS

By 1971, our first contract outside of Spain – though technically still on Spanish soil – was two months at the 'Number 1 Club' in Las Palmas, Canary Islands. The islands were named from the Latin for dog, *canis*, after the native wild dogs once found on the islands. Canariae Insulae means 'Island of Dogs'—nothing to do with canaries. An active volcano near Las Palmas called Cumbre Vieja is due to erupt any time. Scientists predict when, not if, this volcano erupts, a massive, already unstable piece of rock, twice the size of the Isle of Man, may break away and create a wave some hundred metres high which will devastate the west coast of Africa and the east coast of North America, causing global chaos. As I write this, Las Palma's Chumbre Vieje has been spewing lava for six weeks, glad we got our visit over with when we did.

We'd worked hard on the costumes for this run of our International Fantasy Show, and almost every peseta we made went into them. Luis is an excellent costume maker and made costumes for all our shows over thirty years. He worked so hard, making costumes through the nights and mornings, rehearsing our show in the afternoons and giving classes in the evenings in exchange for the use of the Miss Karen Taft's studio for rehearsals. I was getting a handle on the job of producer. The budget, sourcing and costing, music royalty payments and the endless paperwork. I'm hopeless on a sewing machine but, more than capable with handwork such as beading.

The MGM gig had made us a bit of money to help keep us going. Mama was a marvellous seamstress and spent many long days and nights in that room in our Madrid apartment sewing, sewing, sewing. We also employed a lady named Leonora on a part-time basis. A hairdresser by trade, she ran a little salon near the 'Rastro', Madrid's famous Sunday market/flea market. El Rastro means 'the trail'—most likely derived from the tanneries which used to be in the area and the trails of blood left behind the dead cattle being dragged along. Look hard enough at El Rastro, and you'll find anything from birds and animals to antique lace, rare books, curios, and anything stolen in Madrid the night before. Equally popular with locals and tourists, author Hans Magnus Enzensberger once wrote, 'El Rastro is the final border between Europe and Africa.' Though my Spanish wasn't very good then, I laughed so much with Leonora. She must have been mid-forties, quite tall for a Spanish woman, a little on the hefty side, wore monstrously high stilettos, the shortest tightest skirts seen in Spain so far, bleached blonde hair teased within an inch of its life and piled high. I'm sure, being a good Catholic woman, she thought the higher the hair, the closer to God.

The feathered tails created by Henri Bustos were the only things, apart from shoes, made outside our own little sweatshop. 'Tails' in the parlance of our style of shows are the outrageously enormous feathered concoctions worn on the shoulders of dancers. When Lido in Paris started the fashion of the wearing of these feather arrangements they were indeed 'tails', stuck into the back of a bikini bottom. Once g-strings came into fashion (ours were the first touring shows to wear them in Europe and it was thought very daring) tails were too heavy to be supported so made their inevitable way up the back to rest on the shoulders. Younger dancers now refer to them as backpacks.

I made every hat in every show. This was born of necessity. Dancers from the Lido told me of Angelita, who made their hats, and how to find her. Angelita, also lived near the Rastro and worked from home. Her tiny apartment was completely covered in feathers, sequins, fabric and diamantes. They were in every nook and cranny. Rolls of braids, bias bindings and edgings spilt out of every drawer. Finished hats were in the passage and bedroom. Her poor patient husband – on retiring at night – removed hats from their bed for years. I had never seen such beautiful hats as this amazing lady, and her little band of helpers turned out. Although the confections Angelita made were definitely outstanding theatrical creations, there were two problems. One, she was expensive. Well, no, that's not right. The money she was asking was more than fair for such beautiful work; it's just we simply couldn't afford it. The other was these monstrous feathered edifices were a nightmare to pack. We needed a cane skip for each one, and the amount of baggage we were carting around was already huge. Angelita had made our first hats and I very gingerly pulled one of these constructions apart and learned the tricks behind the towering height, balance and weight. From then on, I made every hat in every production, what's more, they pulled apart for packing taking up far less space, reducing baggage and transport costs. It was the same story with the feathered tails. I showed Angelita what I'd done; she was amazed and wanted to know every detail. I was delighted to show her in exchange for a few hatter's tips.

Airfares were out of the question in those days. Way too expensive and we were ten or twelve people plus costume trunks, so we booked passage on the little ship doing the Algeciras–Morocco–Canary Islands run. Truck to the station, train from Madrid to Algeciras, truck and taxis to the port, ship to Las Palmas. Simple. No, nothing was ever so simple when you were trying to organise anything in Madrid. Firstly, the truck taking the trunks to Charmatin Station never showed. This led to me, Luis, Aurora and Leonora, rushing up and down the main streets of Arguelles flagging down taxis. A sight I'll never forget is Leonora hitching her already minuscule skirt up over her ample thighs and legging it down the street after a passing taxi, high heels in her hand.

One trunk per taxi, in the boot, end-first with the bulk of the trunk sticking out precariously was the order of the day. Ten trunks, ten taxis and off to tangle with the notorious Madrid traffic in a headlong dash for the train. It took time to corral the taxis at the busy station, unload the trunks, pay the fares and manhandle the heavy baggage by ourselves to the train platform. We were young and strong and desperate. Just as we got the last trunk stacked next to the baggage wagon, the train, ever so slowly, pulled away. Twelve horrified dancers' faces were leaning out of windows and doors as the train slowly chugged its way along the platform with us waving, running, screaming, and sobbing in frustration. Instructions were somehow relayed we would catch the dancers up in Algeciras and they, having each been given their tickets, were to board the ship no matter what. What a horrible, sinking feeling it was to watch the train and those faces getting smaller and smaller.

That departing train was the only direct way to get to Algeciras before the ship left. There were later trains, but nothing would get us there on time. Nothing for it but to take tiny local commuter trains from town to town, getting off and on with the trunks and hoping, simply hoping, there would be no linking delays and we would make it on time. Those little country trains for local commutes carried no baggage wagon. We squeezed the trunks through the narrow doors and stacked them up on top of seats, hugely annoying the other passengers and paying fares for each seat we took up.

The connections often meant there were mere seconds to change trains, or hours to take turns either playing guard or walking around these picturesque little villages in search of whatever food we could get. Bobadilla is one of those tiny little white-painted villages in the middle of nowhere. I recall taking a photo of Luis asleep on the piled-up trunks as we waited for the next leg of our frustratingly slow journey. At last, we made Algeciras, unable to find a truck or even enough taxis, we heaped the trunks and personal luggage onto a station porter's pushcart and, with minutes to spare, pushed, tugged and shoved the bloody heavy conveyance all the way to the port. Oh, the glamour of owning a theatrical touring company.

At the docks, we were met by excited squeals from the dancers hanging over the ship's rails. It looked as though all was well in the end but, in Spain under Franco in 1971, nothing but nothing was ever going to go smoothly. It was deemed by whoever deems these things, we were to be considered late embarking, and although we could get on board, the trunks, now on the dock at the bottom of the gangway, couldn't. Ohhhh, the frustration.

A heated exchange now took place in Spanish between Luis and a very butch female purser. I was not fluent at this stage but was certainly getting enough to know what was going on. I turned to the dancers who were asking for an update saying in English, 'Fucking Spanish. Nothing goes as it should except when you don't want it to.' Then the storm broke. Well, a storm inside the ship, between the purser and me. 'ANTI-SPANISH!' she screamed, 'ANTI-SPANISH! GET OFF THE SHIP! GET HIM OFF THE SHIP NOW!' Me and my tongue. Will I never learn to hold it? Of course, this bull dyke is an officer on a ship dealing mainly with tourists. Of course, she speaks English. Luis verbally battled and cajoled away with what seemed like the entire officer contingent. Eventually, for a reasonable donation to the homeless sailors' mission, we were allowed – Luis, me, the dancers and our baggage – to head for the Canary Islands.

The ship stopped briefly at Morocco less than an hour later. After dinner, we went straight to the cabin we were sharing with the two male dancers. It was immediately apparent our cabin had been ransacked; the contents of our suitcases were dumped on the floor. After careful inspection, the only discernible item missing was my passport. This seemed too, too convenient. The only thing taken was the passport of the person guilty of an anti-Spanish utterance. I reported the theft to an extremely uninterested officer and crashed. Enough drama for one day, believe me.

Las Palmas was in sight, getting through Customs and Passport Control was going to be a problem for me. Turned out when we arrived it wasn't; there weren't any. Docking at a large tin shed, the gangway was heaved against the side of the ship and that, amazingly, was that. The first day, I wrote to the Department of Foreign Affairs in Canberra, there being no Australian or British representation on the island, explaining what had happened. Within the month, I received a plain envelope containing a blank Australian passport with a letter inside saying to fill the passport out, get a photograph taken, stick it in, and visit an Australian or British Embassy or Consulate, as soon as I was near one, to get it stamped. What an extraordinary thing. Can you in your wildest imagination see such a thing happening today?

Las Palmas was unquestionably idyllic. Sun, palm trees, beaches, lovely apartments and the sweetest venue owners with a truly classy little nightclub, 'Club Number 1'. Two thirty-minute shows were required, and every effort was made to make us feel welcome and comfortable. The performances were broken into ten-minute segments with different sight acts, or attractions, inserted into the breaks. These acts were changed every few weeks, and we met some delightful people. The MC was a Cuban girl who sang before and after our show. Stunningly beautiful she was a delightful person. We became very friendly, and it was tragic to listen to her tales of the tribulations she went through to get out of Cuba. Her girlfriend/lover, also Cuban, was a journalist with a local newspaper. Needless to say, we got some excellent reviews. Never hurts. I'm sure they made wonderful things happen in their lives. I certainly hope so.

The island is dumbbell-shaped, and the club was situated on the thin strip of land between the Port and Playa de las Canteras, the main beach. This strip of land is only three or four streets wide, so access to absolutely everywhere was super convenient. Our apartments, provided by the club, were only a block away, and they were very comfortable. One apartment per floor, two people in each. There was an air shaft running through the bathrooms connecting all six floors, and we would use this as an internal communication system. I can still hear the call, 'FLEET'S IN, GIRLS,' followed by the sound of stilettos clacking down the stairs outside. Oh, those girls. What a lovely, lively bunch of sweethearts they were.

The first gay bar I ever visited was a notorious tiny bar located quite near to us, unbelievable in the days of Franco. You could be arrested and disappear from the streets for sticking your pinkie out as you walked. I guess Canary Islands, although Spanish territory, was considered far enough removed to be allowed the odd concession. We were taken there after work one evening and treated to one of the funniest drag shows I've ever seen. This bar was minute and tucked away up a side street off the wharves. You'd never find it on your own. The clientele was as much fun to watch as the show. Observing beefy, bruiser, sailor types brawling over the few eligible queens was like living through a few chapters from a Jean Genet novel.

Our two months on this magical little island were up before we knew it. Next stop, Pova de Varzim, Portugal. This time we were packed and ready to depart, luxury upon luxury, by air.

CHAPTER 14

OUR FIRST CASINOS

We flew to Lisbon via Madeira. The take-off from Madeira is frightening as the runway ends at the top of a cliff. I concluded you're going to be airborne one way or another. Once we'd landed in Portgual we caught a train to Povoa de Varzim and arrived in the early evening, for a month-long contract at the Casino da Povoa on the beach. The train station was a dilapidated, shed-like affair with no platform at all, just steps down from the train then a good jump to an unpaved road. Such an elegant arrival for showgirls. Povoa de Varzim, thirty-five kilometres north of Oporto, had been Portugal's most popular and well-known northern beach resort for decades. As with many of Portugal's cities, it emerged from the Roman conquest in the second century BC, and although in the '70s there was a population of some fifty thousand, it still maintained a very rural, fishing-town ambience.

Despite arriving on schedule, we were met, not by a top brass welcoming committee but a big, frumpy, peasant-ish, middle-aged, gipsy-looking woman. With hand signals and streams of loud, rapid, Portuguese, she conveyed to Luis, who managed the language quite well, that she would assist us to the casino. The trunks and personal luggage were unloaded onto the dirt road by railway staff, and we looked around for a truck or other suitable conveyance. There was nothing to see, except a rather bent, weedy, little old man and a horse-drawn cart with no horse. The woman yelled at him, cuffing him about the ears. It became obvious he was her husband. The poor little fellow started loading our luggage and it was clear he was struggling. His beefy wife picked up the heaviest trunks, those usually needing two people to lift, and heaved them single-handedly onto the cart. Once they were stacked and ready, she backed this bent and twisted little man onto the shaft of the cart and with much heaving and pulling, he set off down the road, leaving us all open-mouthed in astonishment. It was apparent this was not his first foray into this particular form of labour, every twist and turn of his poor, deformed body married perfectly with the shaft and T-bar of the wagon. I've never forgotten it.

When the casino came into view it was a very welcome sight. A stylish 1930's building with a two-storey central section and two single-storey curved wings, each side fronted a wide, long, sandy beach—truly magnificent. Later in 1977, it was listed with the Portuguese Institute of National Monuments. When we arrived, the welcoming party appeared, and amid apologies for not being able to meet the train, and noticeable embarrassment at the mode of transport provided, we were escorted into the casino, shown our large dressing rooms and given a quick tour. A gorgeous stage fronted an equally lovely showroom with much gold leaf and fancy plasterwork. After stowing the trunks, we were led down and across the street to our guesthouse accommodation, a Pension. Private guesthouses specialising in artists' accommodation are the normal way of things for touring artists in Europe, the equivalent of British theatre digs. Anna, the woman who opened the door, greeted us warmly and took us up to the dining room where casino artists, already in residence, were tucking into their evening meal. 'See this,' she said as she pointed proudly at a monstrous platter of thinly sliced, garlic steaks and an equally large side platter of tomato salad. 'This is the type of food I serve every night.' True to her word, that's exactly what we got every night for a month: garlicky steak and tomato salad. Anna, dear, this would be delicious once a week but, please, a bit of variety.

In the 1970s, in order for the Portuguese population to obtain a passport—males had to do two years of military service and females two years of domestic service. This system was shockingly abused. The well-heeled could circumvent it with a few quick jottings on a cheque, but the poor and middle classes must perform this hard labour with no complaint, and for pitiful pay. Anna had the services of one of these unfortunate girls, and she treated her abysmally. I'd often see the girl about town, both arms laden with food shopping and a hessian bag of potatoes on her head. She cleaned, polished, carried and served like some slave in a mediaeval tale, and her name was, wait for it: Cinders. Povoa seemed poverty-stricken. It was coming into spring, still quite cold but sunny. The Pension was opposite the casino, off the beach. From my window I could see black-draped shapes gathering immense mounds of seaweed, then loading them onto horse-drawn carts. They would climb up to sit precariously in amongst their harvest before driving bumpily off down the cobbled streets. Toothless, shoeless and bent double, these poor women toiled away endlessly.

Portugal is so beautiful, and we were kept busy doing touristy things. One afternoon we were given a long tour of the casino's wine cellar where hundreds, and hundreds of webby, dust-covered bottles of Port were stored. 'Take whatever one you want' they said. We didn't need to be told twice. There was little to do in Povoa once the small shopping area had been thoroughly gone over. The surrounding terrain was virtually as flat as a pancake all the way to Oporto so Luis and I decided to rent bicycles and go discovering. Most of the roads were cobblestones, so it was a bit bone-shaking, but we got out and about seeing quite a lot of old Roman ruins in the nearby countryside. These included a long and unbroken aqueduct still supplying water.

A place we definitely wanted to see was the town of Barcelos where the famous unofficial symbol of Portugal, the good-luck rooster, came from. Everyone has seen at least one of these colourful china or plaster roosters with their high, red cockscombs and oversized tails. At thirty kilometres away it was too far to ride there, but buses ran regularly. In Portugal, the rooster is a symbol of faith, good luck and justice based on the legend of 'the Old Cock of Barcelos'. The legend tells of a pilgrim from Barcelos travelling through Spain who was accused of stealing silver from a wealthy landowner and sentenced to death by hanging. Time and time again the pilgrim pleaded his innocence. On the occasion of his last appearance before a judge, who was about to get stuck into a roasted cockerel, he swore that if he was innocent, the rooster would stand up and crow. The pilgrim was led away but, just before he swung, the rooster did indeed stand up and crow. The astonished judge then hurried to the gallows to free the innocent man. Years later, the pilgrim returned to Barcelos to carve a statue of the cockerel. The legend and symbol were born. Impressed, we bought a whole family of these plaster roosters ranging from half a metre to a wee one. Sadly, none have survived.

Performances were running smoothly, and management was happy but we needed to change a dancer. The brother of Jillian, a delightfully bubbly British girl, died in a nasty car accident. The poor girl was suffering badly and it was decided she should take leave and go home. Ingrid, a German dancer from an agency, was to replace her, and on the evening of Ingrid's arrival, I was a bit stunned. No spring chicken this fräulein. The agency photos I'd seen showed a far younger person. Ingrid was a great show dancer, certainly clear enough from rehearsals but I was more than a little concerned about how she would scrub up.

On the night of Ingrid's debut, I learned a few of the old professional showgirls' little tricks. Firstly, she covered her entire face in a red base, dried it with a little fan then applied her regular foundation over it. I'm still not sure why this does what it does, but it took ten years off instantly. Next, the eyes were attacked. She skilfully applied the required browns, creams and beiges – 'no colours please, I don't like all the blues and greens' – and finished off with a double pair of thick black lashes. She looked bloody marvellous. Now for the boobs. Ingrid's knockers had seen better days, and rather resembled two empty hot water bottles. Off with her largely unsuccessful day bra and on with the opening number show bra. She lifted up each bosom in turn, and rolled it carefully around her gloves, poking wayward fingers in. The result was voluptuous, slightly over-filled cups any page-three girl would be more than happy to own. She looked gorgeous. Oh, Ingrid, I do sincerely apologise for any of my misgivings.

Christine, another British dancer, had a phobic fear of birds. A very dexterous magician preceded our finale. Like many of his profession, he worked with white doves, producing no end of those little creatures from scarves, hats, audience members pockets and nooks and crannies all around the stage. These birds flitted away and sat amongst the showroom light fittings until the end of his act. On his cue, they would fly back to him to be taken offstage. Just the thought of these creatures out there in close proximity freaked Christine out, but trouper that she was, she soldiered on.

That was until a night when one little escapee birdie decided it would ignore its master's orders and stay perched on a light fitting near the ceiling to watch the finale. Christine spotted this bird immediately she entered the stage, and like a shot, it took off, flying straight for her. A showgirl in full flight heading for the exit and the street beyond, shedding her enormous feathered hat and various items of costume as she high-tailed it towards the main street is not the prettiest sight. Cutting her off at the corner, I managed to calm her down and return her to the dressing room with my jacket over her shoulders, but she was never the same girl afterwards.

After quite a few similarly interesting interludes, the Povoa de Varzim contract quickly reached its month's duration. Yet another unexpected country, province, city entered into my diary. Walking on history, that's how I viewed my travels made thus far. Western history that is. Australia possesses a people whose history goes back some 60,000 undocumented years. Being western we wrongly view the world through our history, and the making of the modern world as the only important perspective.

CHAPTER 15

UNLOVELY LONDON

I always found London damp, grey, miserable and dirty. I know very well that is not true, but it's how it has always appeared to me. Maybe the misery and bone-chilling cold of Ballarat in Victoria, Australia has forever tainted my view of damp places. I often visited London to conduct auditions. Mostly, I'd try to get in and out in one day. In the beginning, I stayed in rented rooms in Victoria, near Buckingham Palace. These rooms were run by a funny old Cockney duck called Mrs Beaver, a sweet, pleasant, and mundane little woman. The first time must have been the mid-'70s, and it was a good deal colder than I anticipated. Evidently, I looked pitiful because Mrs Beaver offered me her departed husband's warm clothing. I've no particular aversion to wearing the raiment's of the gathered, but these proffered pieces were a little odd, to say the least.

It appeared Mrs Beaver's spouse happened to be a WWII German submarine captain. She told me just quietly they were not the most beloved family on the street when he was alive. All water under the bridge to me but, yes, fine, I'd be grateful for some warm clothing. What did this strange little lady hunt out for me? His old German uniform greatcoat and leather gloves. I must admit, I did wear them, if only to the nearest Army and Navy Store for my own supply where an elderly assistant looked longingly at my attire.

London is a marvellous place to be a tourist but see the sights and get out are my feelings. On my list of things to see was the Peter Pan statue next to the Serpentine in Kensington Gardens. The 1905 version of J.M. Barrie's Peter Pan in Kensington Gardens was illustrated by Sir Arthur Rackham, a distant antecedent. The Palace of course, Houses of Parliament and Covent Garden got a look-in but little else. On subsequent visits for auditions, I much preferred to get in early morning, do the audition at Pineapple Dance Studios and head out by plane to Paris for the night. Much nicer.

After one visit to London and Mrs Beaver, I was to meet Luis in Paris for a couple of days off. After arriving at our favourite little hotel near the Eiffel Tower, alongside the Maison de la Radio, I realised I left a stash of some thousands of dollars taped behind the mirror in my room at Mrs Beaver's. I liked and trusted the old gal—but not enough to call and reveal my hiding place. So before leaving Paris, I called and made a one-night booking asking for 'my favourite room'. Two minutes after arriving, I retrieved my stash, paid for the night and was on my way to Madrid.

On another occasion, which was Christmas and the time of the IRA bombings in London, I much admired the decorations which were laser beams in various colours bouncing their way up and down Oxford Street and Regent Street. I was on my way to Australia. Airline strikes were in full swing, at Christmas time, what else is new? I'd already changed my ticket twice and was walking into the Qantas office in Bond Street to do it a third time. Prepared for the cold, I wore my luscious, warm black fur coat. The one I had worn so noticeably on the ship. I approached the counter and was asked to be seated. In the middle of the room was one of those old '30s-type round, tufted, diamond-buttoned upholstered sofas with a high, central, conical backrest.

Sitting with his back to me, I could see another man, with obviously exquisite taste, in much the same coat. Well, I'm certainly not going to sit next to him, am I? So, I sat as far away as possible on the opposite side. Shortly afterwards, a woman called out, 'Sir Robert?' and this person got up. It was Bobby Helpmann. I grabbed the edge of his coat as he went past, saying, 'Obviously fake.' He looked down that imperious nose as only he could and opened his mouth, snide retort ready to be spat out, before realising it was me. Bobby laughed; we agreed to wait for each other and went off for a bit of coffee and gossip. He was having the same problems as I was getting home, and we were booked on the same plane out the next day. That aircraft didn't get to take off either and, after waiting around the airport all day, we were finally bussed to a nearby hotel. Bobby took Barry Humphries up on his offer of a couple of freebies for his *Edna Everage, Housewife Superstar* opening in the West End that evening. People were still not comfortable attending theatres because of the bombings, so there were plenty of seats at all venues. Be assured, Barry certainly wouldn't be offering free seats otherwise.

The eventual flight home was a nightmare. It took more than two days to get to Australia, as we were diverted here and there several times. The toilets were full to overflowing, and one night was spent at the Bombay airport, on the tarmac. During the night, we were taken from the plane in groups of twenty or so to walk around the tarmac and stretch our legs. There was a crew change in Bombay, and if it hadn't been for a rather stupid steward dumping Bobby's fur coat on the floor after holding it up disdainfully and saying, 'What's this doing in the flight attendant's locker?', I would have been bored to sobs. Bobby's delightfully scathing rage sure as hell beat any in-flight movie.

In the late '70s, I was forced to spend a few days in London. I took myself off to the Albury Theatre in the West End to see the Cameron Mackintosh revival of *Oliver*. Having not booked a seat, I was relegated to the side to wait for a cancellation or a no-show. The performance was about to begin when I was informed, I would not be seeing it that evening. I was about to leave when a rather plump man stopped me at the doorway. After telling me he was involved with the production and about to go to his box to see the show, he enquired whether I would care to join him. Well, I'm no newbie to the theatre. I could tell right away there was going to a cost somewhere along the line. Nonetheless, I nodded enthusiastically and followed him upstairs. The performance was magnificent, starring Roy Hudd as Fagin. The odd wandering hand up my thigh didn't interfere with my appreciation, but after the show was a different matter entirely.

It was suggested, having eaten the steak, as Judge Judy would say, I was now expected to pay for it. It turned out we would be taking a tube ride on the Bakerloo line. I thought, surely an opportunity will present itself to slip away discreetly. We reached his station, and immediately outside, he stopped at a phone box to call his apartment—possibly checking whether the coast was clear. I took those convenient few seconds to clutch my pearls, make a mad dash down to the station and jump on the first arriving train. Poor man, I bet he cursed the bloody Australians to hell.

After a couple of years of staying at Mrs Beaver's, I started looking for more comfortable accommodation. In the late 1970s, I'd worked in Cairo with a comedy trio called 'Joe, Jack and Johnny'. I knew Jack (his real name is Jazz) owned a lovely home in Brixton with plenty of spare room, so I stayed there. Many years later, in 1990, at the time of the Margaret Thatcher's Poll Tax riots, I was staying at Jazz's, preparing to hold auditions over two days. One Friday night, I decided I might as well go and kick up my heels at Heaven, the London 'Superclub' in the arches beneath Charing Cross railway station, off Trafalgar Square. Billed as The Most Famous Gay Club in the World, this humongous nightclub was the London equivalent of New York's Studio 54. It regularly featured artists such as Madonna, The Pet Shop Boys, Kylie Minogue, Eurythmics, Grace Jones, Amanda Lear, Eartha Kitt, Cyndi Lauper and Cher.

Jazz's home was a couple of kilometres past Brixton Station. That night I turned out to be the only passenger on the bus going to the station and I sat near the female driver who commented on my accent. We got within a block or two of the station when a colossal crowd could be seen on the road ahead. Seconds later, a hammer hit the front window and cracked it with such a resounding bang it frightened the crap out of both of us. She swore like a sailor and spun the bus into the nearest side street. 'Shit. This is my first night by myself,' she told me, 'I've just finished training.' We drove around for quite a while, but it was soon apparent she was as lost as I was. After passing over the same bridge several times, I told her so. She admitted she was 'a bit disoriented' and asked me where I was going. I told her 'Heaven', she said apart from reading in the papers about its reputation as a drug dive, she knew nothing of it and never been but would take me there. How bloody marvellous, arriving at this notoriously prominent nightclub in a chauffeur-driven double-decker bus.

It didn't end there. After letting me out, she closed the bus and came in with me. The bus was left double-parked in the middle of the street directly outside the club. What a great old night, me in my trendiest glad rags and her in her bus driver's uniform. After dancing together for the longest time, we were separated. When I finally staggered out of the club in the wee hours, the bus was gone. Whether she took it, or it got taken away by the bus company, I'll never know. At the very least, I'm pretty sure the darling girl would have lost her job.

CHAPTER 16

NEXT STOP, THE WORLD

Luis and I gave up the Madrid apartment. We were hardly ever there and had become busy making costume repairs between contracts, with everything stuffed into our spacious hotel room at the Hotel Aguilar in central Madrid. Between one and five o'clock in the afternoon was siesta time, when most businesses in Spain were closed. One day we heard a loud racket coming from the room next door. Curious, we popped into the corridor and knocked on the door. Apparently, we gave the occupants a fright—they thought we were management come to complain about the noise. Two attractive young American women were in the room, Pam and Janice. Pam had been flamenco-ing in her new, custom-made shoes. She told us she was studying flamenco in California. Janice, was a fashion model from New York.

As it happened, we were looking for a couple of dancers for our upcoming contract of six weeks in Italy, and asked Pam if she'd be interested in auditioning for the spot. She was at the end of her holiday and ready to go home, so she declined. We then asked Janice whether she could dance. She'd had some modest modern dance experience, including a stint in an amateur chorus line, and was willing to audition—which she did and passed with flying colours. Though not a professional dancer, Janice was quite at home on a stage.

Both Luis and I got on incredibly well with this vibrant young woman. So well in fact, she moved from her cheaper pension and took up residency in Pam's old room next door to us. We ate together at the modest dining places nearby, became close friends in a very short time, and remain so to this day, nearly fifty years on. Not knowing anyone else in Madrid and travelling on a tight budget, Janice spent much of her spare time outside rehearsals with us in our room. I taught her the art of good beading, and she helped bead costumes as needed.

Janice was a tad taller than our other dancers, thin as a reed, thin but shapely, the perfect figure to drape almost anything on. We had not, up until that point, presented what are usually called models. These girls are typically taller than the main dancers, and wear somewhat more elaborate costumes with much higher and more extravagant hats, so their choreography is not as robust as the other dancers. For visual balance, pairs of them usually occupy opposite sides of a stage. Janice was perfect for this. We only needed to find another one to make the pair. Through a London agency, we hired a tall dancer, Josephine, to fill the other model slot and paid her fare by train from London to Madrid. We didn't have deep enough pockets for airfares in those days.

Meeting her at Atocha station in Madrid, I enquired how her trip was. 'Dreadful,' she said in a very upper-class accent. 'The gentleman in the carriage with me had budgerigars in his pocket, and they got out.' Josephine was a strange bird herself. Not a great beauty, a bit on the Windsor no chin side, but with milky white skin and perfect breasts. She moved well and looked great on stage. Strangest eating habits, though. I could never sit opposite her at a restaurant. She would cut her food into minuscule pieces, stab a morsel with her fork, hold it vertically at eye level studying it from every angle while furtively glancing around as though the entire room might be watching. The tiny scrap would then be popped into her mouth and chewed the regulation three hundred times, all the while scanning the room with fleeting peeks before swallowing. Meals were rather lengthy affairs with Josephine.

Our first Italian contract was near year's end in 1972, performing at the Grand Casino Municipale in San Remo, a city on the Mediterranean coast. Followed by the Casino de Campione d'Italia, on the shore of Lake Lugano. Founded in Roman times, The population of San Remo was fifty-seven thousand and was one of the Italian Riviera's most popular and best-known destinations. One of our lead girls for the tour was Gladys Maria Sanchez de la Cruz. 'Call me Lala.' She was allegedly the last person allowed out of Cuba in 1972. She quite intentionally started an affair with some sort of high-up official Communist cadre who arranged her departure. At the airport in Havana, they gave her no documentation, made her strip, dressed her in what can only be described as sacking and shoved her on a flight to Madrid. We wanted to give her something, and the only thing she wanted was a watch, as they took her father's watch from her. Spain had issued her with a flimsy paper interim refugee document, but her lack of a proper passport was a nightmare for the poor girl. Every time we crossed a border, she would disappear from the train, turning up, often days later, ready to perform none the worse for wear.

Christine, she of the bird phobia, was still in the troupe. Her mother visited, sharing a room with Christine and Janice in San Remo. Mother was 60 and drove an electric milk delivery float for a living. She was on leave because she'd managed to plug it into the wrong recharging socket, burning it down to a charred frame. Opening night, I seated her at a nice little table to watch the show, during which I saw her steadily crumpling to one side. Rushing out, I caught her just before she hit the floor. I carried her to the dressing room area, laid her on a cane trunk in the passage and covered her with some costumes and feather fans. I rushed back to my duties but, before going, asked if I could get her anything. She said no but, 'Make sure nobody sees my tits or toes.' When her mother recovered, I asked Christine what she'd meant. 'Oh, her boobs have dropped quite a lot,' she said, 'and she has hammertoes. Doesn't like anyone to see them.'

Novice Janice's debut was a great success. She possessed the most stunning face. Although not required to be a brilliant dancer, she moved beautifully, and was arrow straight. She would glide around the stage using and showing her costumes to their best advantage, and she had a wonderful flirty way with the audience that is essential in showgirl world and simply can't be taught. You either have it, or you don't. Janice most certainly had it. Although she wouldn't appreciate me saying this, Janice was more drag queen than showgirl. Drag queen is the ultimate compliment in showgirl glamour. I have heard some of the most beautiful leading ladies state, 'I'm a drag queen trapped in a woman's body.'

Campione, on the shores of Lake Lugano, is not officially part of Switzerland. It's both an enclave and exclave of Italy, enclave being a portion of a State being surrounded by the territory of another State, exclave being a portion of a State geographically separated by the territory of another State. Over centuries, it was passed back and forth by different Bishops and Popes as gifts, and little thank you's for the support of various Holy Wars. After the unification of Italy in 1862, this tiny 1.6 square kilometre parcel of Lombardy land – less than a kilometre from the Italian border as the crow flies, but 14 kilometres by road – survived as Italian soil. In 1933 it was officially named Campione d'Italia. During World War II, the US Office of Strategic Services or OSS (the precursor to the CIA) maintained a unit in Campione using it for operations into Italy, to which the Swiss turned a blind eye, as the Swiss are known to do.

Once again, we arrived in the early evening. The casino arranged rooms for us at an artist's guest house or pensione, the Hotel Ideal Garni, literally metres from Mussolini's white and grey striped stone arch marking the border. The owners of this pensione were retired Swiss pastry chefs. I cannot possibly tell you how wonderful the food was. Breakfast was fresh home-baked bread rolls, almost hollow, and still warm, ready to receive a liberal dob of butter and fresh strawberry jam. Evening meals were the fare of top-class restaurants with unspeakably delicious deserts. We arrived a few days before Christmas as the Christmas–New Year entertainment, and Christmas lunch was a menu I still dream about. It included a traditional Swiss Christmas log instead of pudding, complete with little coloured marzipan animals and birds scampering over it. Oh, the kilos to be worked off after that gastronomic sojourn.

The casino was a short walk away. Everything, including Switzerland, was a short walk away. Although the original building was replaced in 2007, the old casino was then a magnificent, striped stone '30s structure on the water's edge with a big stage and comfortable amenities. Across Lake Lugano by ferry was the city of Lugano. All shopping was done there. Lugano is beautiful, especially at Christmas time with the streets decorated, the toy shops and the snow. It was magical. Shirley Bassey was living there at the time. There was always the thrilling possibility of catching a glimpse of that megastar. I did see some very glamorous women hiding behind oversized sunglasses, but I don't think any of them was her. However, she just might be saying, 'Do you know, I saw Tom Robb once on the street in Lugano.'

Luis was never big on taking long walks, but Janice and I shared many walking adventures during the year we travelled together. Our stated theory was: if we can see it, we can walk there. One morning, we climbed toward a village we could see on the hilltop in front of the pensione. We took opposite sides of a shallow ravine, searching for a proper trail when, as Janice crossed to my side, she stepped on what looked like solid ground but plunged feet first a dozen metres or so down a steep incline, landing in a small pool of icy water at the bottom with one leg bent under her and the other splayed out. She wasn't moving. I was terrified. To this day, I don't know how I got down to her or how I did it so quickly. I honestly thought she would have at least multiple fractures, but she blinked at me a few times and rose like Lazarus, saying she was just fine.

As long as she kept moving, Janice's leg seemed okay, but as soon as we got home and she sat down, her knee began to swell. I was all for getting her to a doctor, but she would have none of it. Luis, of course, went nuts over our lack of responsibility. The very idea we were to be one model shy was unthinkable. Luis parked her under his infrared lamp for the rest of the day. By the time we left for the casino, the swelling had subsided, but her knee was a nasty shade of puce with hints of plum. New Year's Eve was our biggest night of the tour, and Janice insisted she could perform. She put as much makeup on her knee as her face that night, swallowed a handful of aspirin and got on with the show, gritting her teeth in what looked like a broad smile but was, in fact, she said, a grimace. The audience never knew. Nevertheless, Luis treated us both to a tirade of abuse in every language he speaks, which is quite a few.

After a successful month in the casinos of Italy, we were offered a six-month tour of Japan. At first, we were very much in two minds about whether to accept or not, we had so many questions. Luis had been there years before, dancing with Luisillo and his memories were all good. Still, we were not a cultural show, and wondered what sort of reception we might expect. Would the dancers be agreeable? I was a product of WWII, and with all the prejudices drilled into me since birth, Japan was still very much the enemy and had never been on my to do list. Hard to contemplate that line of thinking now, but that's how it was, even twenty or so years after such a dreadful, deadly conflict. The subject was brought up with the dancers. Some were enthusiastic; others declined and were replaced through agencies. 'Japan, how exotic' was the main conversation theme. There was a hiatus of eight weeks between our return to Madrid and our departure for Tokyo. I was hoping we could swing a bit of work in between so we could hang on to the dancers. Again, ensconced at the Aguilar, Luis dived into creating new numbers, and I swung into producer mode. Finding replacement dancers for those who did not want to go to Japan, arranging work visas, sourcing the new music needed, materials for new costumes, having new shoes made, making new hats, the list goes on.

Luckily, we were asked to fill in for a month at Club Ciros in Barcelona before we left for Japan. Club Ciros was a small venue, so we didn't need our full complement of dancers. Those staying on worked while the new ones rehearsed during the day. Before and after us were other artists or acts and one in particular that stuck in my mind was an exquisitely beautiful, tall, black girl, who did a most fascinating and outlandish tassel twirling routine. This agile and intensely sexy woman jiggled and wiggled her way around the stage, shedding items of clothing and ending up in a beaded g-string, two diamantéd and be-tasselled pasties stuck on her nipples and a rather large tassel on each hip. Then the fun started. The tempo picked up, and off she would go, ninety miles an hour, working the tassels and the audience into a frenzy. How she never strained something, I'll never know. First, the left pastie would be set twirling clockwise, then the right one anti-clockwise, then one hip followed by the other. All in perfect control, like a Maori poi twirler. She would stop and start individual tassels and reverse them in any order. I always watched in total awe and amazement. She brought the house down. This fantastically mesmerising act should surely have been performed by an artist with an equally fantastic and exotic name, or so you would imagine, but no. The name this alluring creature decided to bestow on herself was Fay Gray.

It came time to leave and catch the night train to Paris, from where we would fly to Tokyo via Moscow. We reached the station in time, the couchette train was boarded, and after a simple supper of bread, sausage, cheese and wine, off to sleep and the exciting prospect of waking up in Paris.

CHAPTER 17

IS THAT THE SHOW?

After the overnight trip of thirteen hours duration, we arrived at Paris's Gare de Lyon station the next morning. I've always loved train travel and have never had a problem sleeping. It's a shame most of these services no longer run, having been replaced by the TGV fast trains. There is something romantic about a leisurely meal in an elegant dining car and arriving back to your compartment to find the bed made up by the conductor.

For our one-night stopover, I'd reserved rooms for us all at a modest hotel located centrally near the Lido. Excited to be in Paris, I spent a couple of hours doing a quick tourist tour with Luis. Early the following morning, it was off to the airport heading for Moscow on Air France, where we would change planes for our last leg to Tokyo on Aeroflot. It's impossible to go on without a word or two about Moscow airport and Aeroflot. Sheremetyevo Airport was the most dour, bleak airport I had ever experienced. It featured dreary, typically severe communist-style décor and sour, sullen staff. There was only the one shop selling a dismal array of cheap souvenirs, the most authentic being sets of *matryoshka* dolls, or Russian nesting dolls, in various sizes and qualities.

What I particularly wanted were some Russian roubles. I bought a set of dolls and handed over my US dollars, hoping to get roubles in change, but I got US dollars back. I did ask for my change in roubles but got a curt reply in a very thick accent. 'You give dollar, you get dollar.' So much for that. I eventually got my roubles from a kind Russian gentleman seated near me on the plane. Luis thought he'd heard our flight called shortly after my doll purchase, and we took off at a trot to round up the rest of the dancers. Suddenly from nowhere, we were surrounded by angry, rifle-toting men in uniform shouting at us. Someone translated quickly, telling us it was illegal to run in the airport. Oh, dear. Visions of forced labour in a Siberian Gulag passed before my eyes. We were, however, allowed to proceed at a sedate pace, without further hindrance.

The dancers corralled, we set off with the rest of the passengers to board. I'd never seen a jet without engines on the wings, this one had three clustered around the tail. I've since learned it was a YAK42. As soon as we boarded this strange aircraft, Luis said, 'I think we're a bit early. The cleaners haven't got off yet,' referring to the women clad in almost floor-length red woollen coats and some type of matching hat. 'Luis, please, they're the hostesses.' The flight itself started out – and ended up – dicey. We soon discovered this was not an airline strictly adhering to International Air Safety regulations. Some seats were upright, and wouldn't go back, some were in the back position, and wouldn't come upright, some had hopelessly inoperable seat belts, and others no seatbelts at all. It was not the most comforting start to a four and a half thousand-mile flight over frozen wasteland. The evening meal was announced, we were served a passible chicken something or other.

After dinner, I needed a drink so pressed my buzzer. Well, I would have pressed my buzzer if there was one, but neither Luis nor I could locate it. So, I left my seat, and approached the curtains through which I'd seen the cleaners/hosties disappearing. My polite knock on the bulkhead produced a resentful, red-hatted head thrust through the curtains and a 'Vat you vant?' spat at me. I told this charming creature I needed a glass of juice or water or some form of palatable, thirst-quenching beverage if she really didn't mind. The curtain was snapped closed, followed by what sounded like the lid of a manhole being unscrewed, some noisy splashes, a bit of rustling, and a glass of something resembling orange juice was thrust out at me.

After a restless night, breakfast was brought around, consisting of strawberry jam with what appeared to be the leftover chicken from the night before. Tea was served from an enormous, battered teapot, which looked as though it had seen service over an Australian outback campfire, and the fasten seat belts (yeah, right) sign lit up. We were about to descend into Haneda Airport, Tokyo. That was the first and gratefully last time I have ever experienced a descent that felt like loping down giant stairs. We seemed to drop in an alarmingly stomach-heaving way, level out, drop again, and level out, repeatedly, until touchdown.

Haneda Airport is right in Tokyo, by the Bay. There to meet us was our Japanese agent, co-owner of Akaska Kyodo Booking Agency, Joey Uematsu. We'd never met prior to this and happily, our passage through passport formalities was uncomplicated. Customs was not so easy. They decided they wanted a thorough inspection of the costumes, so we agreed Luis, the dancers and Joey's assistant would go ahead. I would stay behind with Joey to wait on Customs clearance. Joey turned out to be a delightful person. He shared his agency with his sister and her daughter Atsuko with offices in Akasaka. We called the sister Mamasan. Atsuko, I remember all too well, was an absolute pain in the arse. Years later, when I was with different agents, she reared her ugly head with a rather nasty piece of extortion, more about that later.

Customs, for the first and last time in our experience of Japan, were being super thorough. The whole business was taking way longer than expected or was indeed reasonable. It wasn't until around nine p.m. that the trunks were released. We made a train of trolleys and wheeled them to the car park. Joey had a large, white van at the ready. Between us, we manhandled everything inside, and I ran around to the passenger side to get in. Joey also ran around to the passenger side. I immediately thought, 'Oh, they must drive on the other side here,' but no. Joey doesn't drive. I'm in Japan for the first time in my life, in the airport car park of one of the biggest cities in the world and found myself asking, 'You want me to drive?' No point sitting here belabouring the point. Get behind the wheel and hope above hope Joey at least knows where we are going. This being my first experience of a Japanese freeway, I was positively terrified. The drive to the venue would take at least an hour and a half, and Joey kept an eye out for the turnoff. Once onto the turnoff, Joey had arranged for people with torches to wave me towards the next few turns and eventually to the club, which seemed to be pretty much in the middle of absolutely nowhere.

Luis was waiting outside and started grabbing frantically at the trunks, saying there were only thirty minutes left until showtime. Thirty minutes? You must be joking. Even at its very quickest, the show takes at least an hour to unpack. There were cloth drycleaner-style suit bags for each dancer. They were made with long metal zips and lots of pockets for bras, g-strings, jewellery, shoes and smaller items like fishnet stockings, so they were not a big deal. Just hand out the bags to each person and let them get on with it. Their make-up was done, so were ready to go. The costumes, likewise, were just a matter of unpacking, sorting into names and hanging on racks.

What took forever were the feathered tails and the hats, which needed assembling and, most of all, the wigs. Back then the girls wore big beehive wigs which were, in fact, hollow wire cage-like affairs with a human hair fringe six inches or so long, wrapped and sewn around and around, so what you ended up with was a Busby-like thing. This hair was divided into sections, dampened, and rolled in hair rollers twenty or so per wig. When the rollers were taken out, each curl of hair was brushed into a rolled curl and pinned to the curl below. A long process with so many wigs to do. These wigs were the bane of the dancer's lives as they needed to be set each night after the show. I admit I used to feel sorry for the girls and often ended up doing them myself. Unrolling, brushing and setting, however, was always done by me. You can imagine I was simply not going to get a couple of hundred rollers out of wigs and have them brushed and pinned in thirty minutes. So, I tore the front section of rollers out leaving the hair in unbrushed, tight rolls and the back section still in rollers. I told the girls, 'No matter what the choreography is, don't turn around. Whatever you do, don't turn around.'

A placement, entrance and exit rehearsal had been held earlier in the afternoon, while I was still at the airport. The layout should have been firmly planted in the dancer's heads. Dressing rooms were on the first floor opposite the stage. How to get to the stage? Easy, you go across a catwalk supported by steel wires over the audience's heads. What could possibly be more difficult than trying to go quietly back and forth across this ridiculous, narrow walkway? Luckily, there was sufficient space stage-side for quick changes. To keep a circular, uncongested path of movement to and from the stage, all entrances were down the onstage stairs, and exits via the small stage level stage-right door. Except for the finale, where the reverse would happen. A five-foot-eight girl in heels wearing a three-foot-high hat was not going to fit through a typical Japanese door only five-foot six inches high. The solution was for the finale girls to await their entrance squatting in an inelegant line, entering the stage hat first, and straightening up ladylike immediately clear of the doorway. Not particularly dignified but certainly manageable. Right, everybody rehearsed and briefed, opening-night nerves under control. We're all professionals, queue music. Let's do this.

How I wish we had video equipment back then, and someone had filmed that show. It really is the only way anyone could believe the absolute disaster that unfolded. It's a miracle our opening night in Japan wasn't also our closing night. The entrances were made from the top of a wide staircase with lights on the left and right handrails. Halfway down the stairs, a dancer feeling a little off-balance reached out for the railing to steady herself and shorted the lights. The entire club was blacked out. Not a single light anywhere. There's some stumbling, the line is slightly broken, nothing too serious, and as the girl lets go of handrail, the lights are back up. Next line of girls starts down, same thing, unsteady, grab the railing, blackout. The dancers on stage are completely disoriented, and the line on the stairs is a mess. Now, the lights are back up and the girls – thoroughly confused and all instructions forgotten – go into the choreographed turns. 'No turns, girls, please.' Hair rollers start pinging around the room like a blast of birdshot. Drinks were knocked over and patrons were peppered by dozens of these plastic missiles. There was utter disarray on and off stage.

The opening mercifully over, the girls made the most graceful exit possible under the circumstances as the dancers for the next routine started making their way down the stairs. This was of a space/futuristic flavour. A small spaceship prop on wheels is waiting stage centre as Luis and Jannick descend the stairs costumed in brief but obviously cosmic-appropriate silver and black.

They were followed by two elegantly metal-clad celestial topless beings whose job was to take up the silver chain reins of the spaceship and drag it, Luis and Jannick slowly and smoothly around the stage while an intimate adagio duo takes place. It should have been superb, sophisticated, sensual and artistic, except Jannick, tangled and stuck tight by her costume on one of the overhead catwalk support wires, was helplessly looking down at the scene on the stage below. Luis was left alone to be seductive all by himself.

This show was taking one hell of a duck dive, and the subsequent routines fared no better. Directly before the finale was one of the most successful numbers Luis ever staged. It consisted of three butterflies, one deep pink, one blue and one green. The dancers clutched enormous wings of crystal nylon fabric attached to several metres of spring steel held high and wide. Beautiful, feathered masks covered their faces, and looped jewels draped their bodies. Luis worked out an intricate, and very cleverly managed routine with the pink butterfly who, once lifted, rarely touched the ground, and appeared to be flying. It was beautiful. She was carried on his back and spun and twirled over his head while the other butterflies fluttered, gently waving their wings, making a glamorous and colourful backdrop to this exquisite routine.

Oh, you know exactly where this is going. Almost immediately, Luis trod on a piece of the pink butterfly's long wing and slipped. In a supreme effort to recover gracefully and professionally, he managed to drag the butterfly onto the floor on top of him, where she became completely immobilised. The metal wing extensions on her arms effectively prevented her from getting up, so there she stayed with Luis pinned underneath. The two topless butterflies frantically hovered and flapped around the prostrate couple attempting to shield them from the gaze of the audience while they struggled to right themselves. By the time the music ended, the dishevelled pair rose to beat a retreat up the stairs with what little dignity remained. Except Luis completely forgot to use the stairs. In his flustered rush to leave, he took off through the door stage-right where the entire ensemble was squatting in a tight line, waiting to make their entrance through the tiny door. The resulting collision knocked everyone backwards like dominoes, each into the lap of the one behind, the force knocking their huge hats forwards to hang by elastic on their chests.

I watched it in ultra-slow motion, what a ghastly, sinking feeling. Apart from the other two male dancers who had back-pedalled and entered via the stairs, there was not another soul on stage for the entire finale.

The show over, the dazed audience gave sporadic, fitful and polite applause while the tangle of dancers tried to U-turn down the passage and make their way out. I will never, ever in my life, forget the look on Joey's face as he came backstage afterwards. He simply said, 'Is that the show?' In that moment, visions of the Burma railway loomed. Is that all he's going to say—not lose it and utter words such as lawsuit or breach of contract?' Joey did none of this. He was certainly not new to the business. He and his sister owned a very successful show called Tokyo by Night which toured Australia some years before. Besides, as I was to learn, that is not the Japanese way.

Joey let us pack slowly in silence and prepare to go to the hotel booked for us in the nearby town. Nothing was said to the dancers. We were all equally aware of the debacle which just took place and similarly aware of the series of events leading to it which were out of our control. After all, this was our one-night-only, out-of-town tryout, and we were all desperate to make the best possible impression. Luis and I were utterly beside ourselves with shame and anxiety. Accusations and recriminations were not going to help one bit.

CHAPTER 18

REPRIEVED

The following morning, I was up early determined to see what I could of Japan before surely being packed off home. The town was relatively small, and we were in a hotel on a little main street. I walked and gawked, loving the look of the oiled wooden buildings, and the greens of the densely forested, not-too-distant mountains behind the blocks of low grey tiled roofs. I went into a bakery and bought what I thought was a bun oozing chocolate. My first bite told me it was most decidedly not chocolate and although not nasty, I spat it out in shock. It was sweetened red adzuki bean paste, something I came to enjoy immensely. I strolled towards the back of the town, and up a track through a tunnel of green overhanging branches, over a little stream, and up rough, time-worn wooden steps to a picture-postcard sight I can still bring to mind. There in front of me was a small bright red-painted wooden gateway formed by two uprights, and two overhead crosspieces. Two small mossy stone dog or fox-like animals with faded little red bibs around their necks sat on equally mossy stone plinths each side of the arch. I was to learn these gates were torii, traditional Japanese gates found at the entrances of Shinto shrines, where they symbolically mark the transition from the irreverent to the sacred and are said to be a resting place for birds so they might sing to the gods. Beyond was another arch, and another until I lost sight of them around a bend. I went on through these archways along the path which twisted in and around the trees, and the hilly, rocky landscape until I came to, what looked like, a small, dark wooden altar of some sort. It was about two metres high and one metre wide and deep, two more of the dogs guarded it. There seemed to be nothing on the little platform inside except some dusty leaves and a few coins which looked quite old. I fell in love with Japan at that moment. Emotion flooded over me until I broke down in sobs at the thought of having to leave this place which suddenly seemed to be home.

Joey arrived after breakfast and, although not pleased, was not angry. He humbly blamed himself for rushing us into an opening night we could not adequately prepare for. He said the obvious quality of the show shone through the series of disasters the night before. While we would be going on to Tokyo, we would not perform that night as planned. He requested management give us the whole of the following day to settle in. Not a mention regarding the management of the previous night's venue. It was never brought up again. Joey was a true gent, and although things didn't work out in the end between our companies, we always held him in high regard. His niece Atsuko was a different kettle of fish entirely.

During the afternoon we were taken to our Tokyo hotel, the Fukudaya, a Japanese-style hotel located a walkable distance from Shibuya Station. Shibuya grew up around a castle owned by the Shibuya family and became a town in 1909. By 1947, it grew so large it was incorporated as Shibuya Ward, a part of greater Tokyo. It was still a small suburb with only one department store at the train station when we arrived. Over the years since, I've watched this upmarket, quiet, residential suburb become a Tokyo nightlife hub, and a fashion centre with enormous multi-storied shopping centres.

Shibuya Station is also the site of the life-size bronze statue of Hachikō, the legendary Akita dog who, from 1924 to 1925, greeted his master each evening at the train station. After his master died suddenly at work, this faithful little dog continued to meet the train for the next ten years in the hope of seeing him. Passengers who recognised the dog started to feed it, and soon this little animal became a national symbol of loyalty. The breed grew hugely in popularity. Each year on the eighth of April, a solemn ceremony of remembrance in recognition of Hachikō's devotion is held at Shibuya Station.

Hundreds of dog lovers often turn out to honour his memory and loyalty. Although his remains were stuffed and mounted and kept at the National Science Museum of Japan in Ueno, his monument is in nearby Aoyama cemetery. This moving story has proved the catalyst for plays, books and at least one film.

The Fukudaya was my first encounter with a traditional Japanese-style hotel, guestroom floors covered in tatami mats, no furniture other than the suitably low tables for floor dwellers. Futons were folded and stored behind sliding doors of shallow cupboards during the day and laid out on the tatami floor at night as bedding. I was a little concerned to be asked to take my shoes off and leave them in the shoe rack in the lobby. 'What if someone takes them?' I said to Luis, who calmly reassured me people don't steal in Japan. Still disinclined, I took off my only pair of shoes, our personal luggage was arriving later with the trunks, and left them in the rack along with dozens of others. After showers and generally getting ready, we went downstairs to hail a taxi. Luis found his shoes and slipped into them. I hunted and hunted but couldn't find mine. Wouldn't you know it? The only thief in Japan had pissed off with my shoes. Footwear my size was not to be found in Japan, so some foreigner with submarine-size feet must have been overjoyed and seized the moment.

I went to my first business meeting in my socks. First our disastrous opening show, now this. Joey would be starting to wonder. At this meeting, we met Joey's sister Mamasan and her daughter Atsuko. Mamasan didn't speak English so said little, but Atsuko spoke English fluently and commandeered the conversation immediately. Clearly, she wore the pants, and Joey deferred to her in all things. I felt the little warning sign on the back of my neck which has correctly saved me from trusting people in the past. I was already wary, questioning and mistrustful of this woman. Luis felt nothing and called me foolish.

Once back at the hotel, we went out looking for something to eat, me still in socks. I was soon awestruck by a beautiful image which seemed so Japanese. In front of us was an old, bewhiskered man in a short, knee-length blue and white montsuki or long haori. A type of traditional wrap-around coat, with a pair of long johns underneath, and traditional tabi and geta, the woven cotton split-toe socks and wooden platform sandal-type shoes with the thong between the toes. I whispered to Luis how much I loved what he was wearing. The old chap stopped immediately and removing his outer coat, handed it to me with, 'Doso, doso, please, please,' and in halting English conveyed he wished me to have it. Luis, who'd been to Japan before, urged me to take it for fear of offending, which I did with many loud thank you's. This little man waved and took off down the street, thoroughly comfortable in nothing but his long underwear.

Our true opening night loomed, and we were thrilled with the venue, the famous Tokyo Latin Quarter in Akasaka. We would be privileged to work in this world-class venue many times, and years later, ours was the last show to appear there before the club closed for good in the late '70s. The finest venues of America, Britain and Europe influenced this exclusive nightclub. Here's a Wikipedia quote about it:

> *Opened in the early 1960s, the New Latin Quarter was arguably the finest nightclub in Tokyo and set the standard for entertainment in the East, drawing on influences from American and British/European pop, rock, R&B, jazz and blues. The clientele consisted of the rich and famous; businessmen; spy organisations such as the CIA and KGB, and even the Japanese Mob the Yakuza! The artists who performed there are now legendary icons, including Nat King Cole, Sammy Davis Jr, Pat Boone, Louis Armstrong, The Platters, Ella Fitzgerald, Tony Bennett, Andy Williams and Connie Francis to rock and pop royalty The Supremes, Ray Charles, James Brown, Cliff Richard & The Shadows, BB King, Donna Summer, Dolly Parton, The Drifters, Paul Anka, Dionne Warwick, Engelbert Humperdinck, Tom Jones, Barry Manilow and many more.*

Apart from such notables as Tom Jones and Andy Williams, one huge international star we were fortunate enough to work with at Latin Quarter in later years was the fabulous Mary Wilson, the co-founder of The Supremes. We worked with Mary and the Supremes way back in the mid-'70s and found them friendly and welcoming. We were to open the show, and do our usual thirty minutes, then The Supremes would be welcomed to an already warmed audience and do their full hour or more. A great highlight for Luis and me was to see, up close and personal, the Bob Mackie costumes they wore, each in its own trunk with shelves filled with spare beaded patches to replace areas where sweaty hands might often touch during performances.

I worked up the courage to ask if we might inspect these fabulous gowns, Mary was only too pleased to show us all their gowns and went into great detail regarding Bob Mackie's fussy fittings and the entire process. Mary told me they were worth around seven thousand dollars US each. Today that's a lot of money, back then it was a fortune. We became very friendly with the girls. Mary in particular, was charming and easy to talk to. We would go hunting for places to eat together as they were as starved for home-cooked meals as we were. I recall a cook-up in our hotel (where cooking wasn't allowed) and someone making a delicious curry with a cooker and pot out on the window ledge to stop the aroma drifting through the rooms. The Supremes had a male backing band with them. Trying to wake our girls the morning after the cook-up to go to the visa office, I spied a few extra pairs of black feet sticking out from under the futons.

Mary was very kind to me over the years. When I was preparing the opening of a very classy restaurant I designed for a friend in Fremantle in the '90s, I noticed The Supremes were in Melbourne. I called Mary, and she flew everybody over to open the restaurant for me at cost, airfares and hotel. Even after all those years of performing the same songs, Mary still took them through an extensive two-hour rehearsal and sound check. The show was awesome, and Luis and I sat up with them all night, drinking and rehashing the past. What a great lady.

The Latin Quarter hostesses were the most famous in Japan. These women dressed in the highest, most sophisticated manner of the day, and it cost a small fortune to have them seated at your side. Very much like the renowned Geisha, the hostesses enchanted with pleasant conversation, flattered and served their clientele, and were a mark of a man's social standing. Many of Japan's biggest business deals were closed at these expensive watering holes in those days, so the hostesses were privy to massive secrets and were utterly trusted. These powerful ladies watched the show with a discerning eye every night, and if they thought you were not up to standard, they could have you cancelled at any time. We made sure we went out of our way to be courteous and pleasant and were rewarded over the years with many little gifts and loud ovations but, above all, return engagements.

The Latin Quarter bandstand and stage was semicircular, not big, but big enough, with a door each side to the dressing room directly behind. The dressing room was quite large but there were several drawbacks. The doors to the stage were very low, shades of our first-night disaster, and running smack through the middle of the dressing room was an enormous square air-conditioning duct at my eye level. Rushing from one side of the dressing room to the other during a show one night, I collided full tilt with this duct and completely knocked myself out. In a fit of anger, I wrote on it with thick black marker: PAD THIS FUCKING DUCT. When we returned the next time, padding had indeed been added, and on the night Latin Quarter closed for good, I pulled the padding off to find my crude message still underneath.

CHAPTER 19

FALLING IN LOVE

From Tokyo, we went on a bit of a whirlwind tour, and quite frankly I can't remember all the cities: Niigata, Nagoya, Shimizu, Shizuoka, Himeji, Fukuoka … maybe more. Nagoya, Japan's third-largest city with its famous castle and gold dolphins, was especially memorable. Although the original castle was destroyed during WWII it was carefully and meticulously restored. During the days, we explored the streets of the many places we were visiting and had great fun checking out the local cuisine. There were little plastic models of the menu offerings in the windows of all the restaurants.

These perfect replicas fascinated me, we browsed until we spotted appealing looking items, and not speaking more than a few words of Japanese: 'please, thank you, good day, good night, chopsticks etc.', we'd go into an establishment, motion a waiter to follow us outside and point at the models of our selections. This system worked very well, resulting in many delicious culinary adventures. Another adventure of sorts was the commonplace occurrence of minor earth tremors. When we first arrived in Japan, they were unnerving, but given Japan's fame as an earthquake-prone part of the planet we should have been on guard. Amazingly, even the most trepidatious of us soon became quite blasé about them although, some of the more severe quakes in later years were a different story.

We performed TV shows in Osaka and were taken sightseeing to Kyoto, which completely overwhelmed me. Kyoto is probably number one on every visitor's list, foreign or Japanese. There are over two thousand historic temples, shrines and pavilions to visit. The most popular must surely be the

Kiyomizu-dera Temple, the Ginkaku-ji Temple, and the Sanjūsangen-dō Temple. The Kiyomizu-dera is a magnificent temple mounted on thick wooden supporting pillars. The massive supports, and the complex woven-like structure of the wooden Temple itself has no glue, nails or screws in the assembly. Mind boggling hand-crafted joints hold the entire structure together. It has lasted since the year 794.

The Ginkaku-ji Temple, or Golden Pavilion, sits beside a huge lake, gloriously mirrored in its flat glass-like surface. It was originally a fourteenth century construction but was razed to the ground in 1950 when a young monk attempted to set fire to himself on the slope behind the temple. The present-day building was reconstructed in 1955 and there is considerable conjecture as to whether the original gold leaf was as thick or covered as much of the structure as is seen now. Visual excesses were very much a part of the Muromachi period and gold was said to suppress negative feelings and purify pollution of the spirit. Today the entire building glows from top to bottom in its lavish gold epidermis.

The thirteenth century Sanjūsangen-dō Temple was also destroyed by fire during its long life. Buildings in Japan were chiefly made of wood and paper so when they fell, they didn't kill anybody and were easy to put back up. Fire is a major concern and I imagine there is not an original wooden building of any great age which has not gone through several reconstructions, partial or full. Between fire and earthquakes, houses in Japan were expected to only last three years. They were built to fall down.

Sanjūsangen-dō was extremely interesting to me because of its history of archery, long before my fascination in this activity was as great as it is today. The 118m-long west veranda was used for archery practice, and it is still used for that today, 400 years later. Tōshiya, the Festival of the Great Target attracts upwards of 2,000 participants annually as they vie for the coveted prize. Archers shoot at targets ranging from fifty to one hundred centimetres wide, from a sixty-metre distance. The Japanese prize archery for its lessons in patience and self-control.

I've been back several times since, and it's always like the first visit. After Osaka we travelled north to work in Himeji and visited what is considered to be the finest surviving castle in Japan. Almost untouched by the raids of WWII, this hilltop wonder consists of eighty-three buildings and was registered in 1993 as one of the first UNESCO World Heritage Sites in Japan. From our hotel we could see this fairytale vision in the distance. It was cherry blossom time and in the town of Himeji, the streets were decorated with branches of pink blossom tied to the lamp posts. The vision of soft pink clouds running down both sides of the streets was utterly shattered on close inspection, the blossoms were all plastic. Beautiful but somehow so wrong.

From there, we went to Teine Yama or Mount Teine on the island of Hokkaido, which was the site of the first Asian Winter Olympics in 1972. Hotel Teine Olympia, a resort on the side of the mountain, is twenty or so kilometres from Sapporo, a forty-minute drive before heading straight up. It was coming into summer, and we were to perform outside on a stage built specifically for us. This resort, located near the base of the former toboggan run, was owned by a big game fanatic, and there were quite a few animals scattered about in large holding areas. A German lion tamer was also performing in a ring not far from our stage. Families with children largely attended our shows, so the models weren't topless. Our dressing room was a little shed that the chairlift to the ski slopes passed over frequently. Behind that was forest.

Our shows became incredibly well attended, I guess that's why we were there. Day visitors thronged to the resort. We were so popular we were requested to stay back after the shows to sign autographs and this became a thirty-minute affair twice daily. The things I signed! I had my own little segment in the show to pad it out a bit, and to entertain the children. A large piece of white paper was set on an easel. Using a black felt marker, I completed unconnected sections of lightly pre-sketched animals. An MC would ask the children to guess what the animal was before I finished the drawing. This lovable man was quite a character, my lack of Japanese and his equal lack of English turned into some very funny banter. I recall drawing parts of a fox, and when completed he asked me what it was, I told him it was a fox, a word he was unfamiliar with so, I said it was an animal that chases chickens. The resulting translation for the audience was that I had drawn a Chinese chicken. I was inveigled, during these autograph sessions, to draw on people's assorted garments. T shirts were popular, trousers, shorts, dresses, and on one occasion, a bra. I usually made do with a quick kangaroo.

Directly behind the resort, the mountain was densely covered in vegetation. Not so many large trees but half a kilometre or so up were impenetrable forests of hugely tall and thick bamboo. I loved roaming up through those yellow and green forest paths, the constant falling leaves making progress hushed on a calm day. However, with a middling breeze, the air is alive as the slender top few metres sway, giving squeaky, swishing embraces to their neighbours on either side. Stronger winds cause more violent movement of the thousands of culms resulting in a clamour of creaks and cracks as embraces turn to slaps. There's a whole world of goings-on in the uppermost reaches of a bamboo forest. I'd go as far as I could until it seemed I must be at the top, and then quite suddenly, through a clearing, there would be nothing in front but a sudden drop away, and the Sea of Japan.

Standing so high, surrounded by the whispering grandeur of the forest, the land falling away to the sea over a thousand metres below, I imagined I could easily be on top of the world. And I was, on top of my world. The world of a young poor Ballarat boy whose humble beginnings held no hint, no forecast of the heights to come. I had only to lean left or right to touch some of the greatest riches on earth. The richness of nature, its awe-inspiring immensity makes man and his struggle for dominion over it puny and insignificant. I was so very in the moment. Such special occasions reminded me to be ever grateful and appreciative—I hope I have been.

On one occasion we were taken to the city of Sapporo to participate in a parade at the end of the Autumn Festival. We weren't aware of the chill still in the air, so got into our skimpy costumes and were driven on flatbed trucks through the streets lined with waving people who looked a damn sight warmer than we were. While in Sapporo there was time to explore the climate-controlled underground city which made shopping possible in the harsh winters of the far north. Now, vast underground shopping malls are everywhere but it was new to us back then. In the evening we performed a couple of routines on an outdoor stage to a massive audience. Following us was the incredible talents of a lady long admired: the unbelievable Peggy Lee. Backstage she looked amazing, if a tad tight in the facial skin department, but that voice. What a woman.

In Teine Yama there were often guest artists and one weekend, a team of Ainu were featured performing traditional songs and dances. The Ainu are the indigenous people of Japan's northern island of Hokkaido—long suffering, as indigenous peoples so often are. Their traditional clothing is exquisite with fantastic geometric designs in reds, blues, white and black. Their culture centres around the native sun bears. There are many songs and dances to do with these animals, which they consider deeply spiritual. In June 2008, according to Wikipedia:

> *The Japanese Diet (parliament) passed a resolution recognising the Ainu people as 'an indigenous people with a distinct language, religion and culture', acknowledging that they, the lawmakers, 'solemnly accept the historical fact that the Ainu people were discriminated against and forced into poverty with the advancement of modernisation, despite being legally equal, Japanese people.'*

Evenings proved to be very dull in Teine Yama, and three months was way more than enough. Fortunately, three months is also long enough to make a few friends and we got to do and see a lot more than your average tourist. The owner of the Hotel was quite tall for a Japanese man, and extremely fit-looking, probably 45 to 50 years old and not a hair on his shiny, tanned head. He took a liking to me. I cannot remember his name, I'll call him Teinesan.

Teinesan entertained us at night, put on mini banquets and tried to liven up our evenings. On one of these occasions, he saw me getting stuck into some deliciously sweet and juicy watermelon. For some reason this made him laugh, he asked if I liked watermelon. I told him I did, and the next morning woke to find the hallway outside our rooms lined with watermelons. Quite the collector, there were beautiful pieces of art all over the resort. Magnificent sculptures and paintings were everywhere. One series I particularly enjoyed spending time with was a collection of scenes made entirely of butterfly wings. These pieces shimmered and glowed and constantly changed in the light between day and night. Teinesan noticed my fascination with them. I'd been in Japan long enough to know you keep your mouth closed when admiring something or you might be handed it with much bowing and many dosos, and I was afraid these pieces would all end up outside my door, so I stopped spending so much time examining them.

There were many beautiful books in the public lounge, and I was becoming impressed with Japanese art. The economy of brush strokes producing such deeply meaningful works amazed me. Unlike most Asian art, there is nothing garish about Japanese art. To my mind, it was pure and classy. I bought myself some white cotton fabric and an embroidery hoop deciding I would try my hand at this style. I'd never embroidered anything before, so I made up my own stitches, and had a great deal of fun, spending many hours creating just two pieces. One was of women in kimono crossing a bridge in a rainstorm, the other of a traditional bride in a garden. Teinesan would watch me stitching away, I imagine he thought it a bit un-masculine, but he always made kind remarks regarding my efforts. When completed, he asked whether he might hang them in his sumptuous private rooms for the duration of our stay. I was thrilled, he was either being very polite, or thought them worthwhile. The resort was a ski resort in winter and a golfing resort in spring and summer. Weekends were full of golfing fanatics practising their swings all over the hotel. The Japanese love their golf.

Teinesan told me during one weekend, a very special friend was staying with him who admired my stitched pieces (calling them embroidery I thought was a bit grand) and would I care to meet this gentleman? Sure, why not? So, I met this rather dignified man who was politeness personified. He told me he was particularly impressed with my appreciation and handling of the Japanese art style, and he would like to buy the wedding scene. I'd been in Japan long enough to understand the custom of *presento doso*. I immediately told him I thought my amateur effort was unworthy of sale, but I'd be delighted if he would consider it a gift. Much bowing and quite a few arigatos later, I was back in my room, astonished my efforts were so much admired.

A few weeks after the experience with that refined gentleman, I received a large package, beautifully wrapped in a purple tie-dyed silk scarf knotted together at the opposing corners to make a little sling. There was a very fancy white card in Japanese, which when translated, was an exquisite thank you note from His Imperial Highness Crown Prince Akihito, who subsequently became Emperor in 1989. Inside the box was a full-size wedding hat complete with the two doves I wove into the wedding design. This, it turns out, was Teinesan's special friend, and it was he to whom I'd given the stitched piece. I was flabbergasted. I carefully took out the boat-shaped hat and touched it with great deference and awe. The birds were made from tiny pieces of different white and silver fabrics and stuffed with something crinkly. On my next visit to Sapporo, I sent this precious gift, along with the note, back to Australia for safekeeping. Sadly, it never arrived. I gave the other stitched piece to my doctor and friend Mark Choong on my recovery from cancer in 2006. Mark was a whiz in his diagnostic skills, his care throughout my treatment, and subsequent recovery was personal and touching.

Our first, but most definitely not last, tour of Japan ended back in Tokyo where we featured at the renowned and prestigious Club Golden Gessekai, again in Akasaka. While we were there, Luis received an invitation from The West Australian Ballet Company to return for a three-year engagement as Artistic Director, an offer too good to refuse. So, this would be our last tour for a while. I was more than happy to put my career on hold while Luis completed this important last step in his classical ballet life. As our departure date neared, Atsuko came to ask a favour. A fellow agent in Hong Kong had an act cancel on him at the last minute, and he was desperate for a replacement, just for a month. She implored us to help. We asked the dancers, but most declined, being more than ready to return to Europe, as contracted. Three dancers were happy to sign on, so Luis crafted a new little show for the five of us using our existing costumes, and off we went home, via a month in Hong Kong.

CHAPTER 20

THE MELTING POT

Landing at Hong Kong's Kai Tak in 1973 proved to be a heart-stoppingly thrilling descent. We passed through what appeared to be endless people's lounge rooms on our approach to the runway protruding out into the water. I simply knew this was going to be the most sensational and enticing city. Taking my very first hot, humid breath, from the doorway of the aircraft, it was the combined fragrances of jet fumes, street food and tropical rot. In no way was I disappointed. Not for one single moment. That descent was enough to get anyone's blood racing. When Kai Tak Airport was built in 1954, the scarcity of land in Hong Kong necessitated the construction of the infamous solitary Runway 13 on reclaimed land jutting into Victoria Harbour on the west side of Kowloon Bay. The approach to Kai Tak was notoriously tricky, with rugged mountains nearby to the north and the numerous high-rise buildings which grew up close around the airport.

Landings were dramatic to experience, and technically demanding for pilots. Kai Tak was popularly ranked as the sixth most dangerous airport in the world. The low-altitude manoeuvre over the crowded harbour required to line up with the runway was spectacular. I can promise you, over the years, I grew so familiar with some of those apartments at the end of the wings I could spot a décor change. When crosswinds from the northeast were strong and gusty during typhoon season, the big crabbing angles during final approaches was quite thrilling and often frightening. From its opening in 1954 to its closure in 1998, there were ten major crashes at Kai Tak resulting in 198 deaths and countless injuries.

During our first visit, Customs and Formalities were passed through without problems. We were met in the Arrivals Hall by our agent, a rather rotund Mr Tam Bing Wah, most aptly described as a non-PC characterisation of a Chinese gentleman. With his pot belly, jet black thinning hair and small, sparse, drooping moustache, he looked as though he'd stepped straight out of a Limehouse Opium Den from one of Sax Rohmer's Fu Manchu novels. Mr Tam, it turned out, was one of two top agents in Hong Kong, the other being the more upmarket Benny Tong. White stretch limos were provided to whisk us away to downtown Kowloon. We found out soon enough, we were heading for the scandalous, infamous, and more than slightly seedy, Chungking Mansions at the harbour end of Nathan Road in Tsim Sha Tsui.

As ill-famed as this building was, I thought it was nothing less than fantastically exotic. The entrance to this already dilapidated building, although it was barely thirteen years old, was teeming with hoi polloi, people from every walk of life, Indians in colourful grubby turbans, gellabiyaed Arabs, cheongsam clad women, wrinkled, shirtless old Chinese men, a sprinkling of Western tourists, and people with pushcarts, people bent double carrying heavy sacks of who knew what, others laden with ivory tusks. And what seemed like the entire world of hippy diaspora. Up to the thirteenth of seventeen floors, in a small lift with a whiff of unwashed exoticness, to one of the dozens of el cheapo guesthouses and hotels filling the building. With one thousand nine hundred and eighty rooms in total, Chunking Mansions has the highest number of guest houses/hotels of any building in Hong Kong.

Our guesthouse in the Mansions, was run by a Chinese couple who specialised in hosting theatre people, and the rooms turned out to be spacious and clean, if also a bit hot and stuffy. The owners cooked Chinese-style meals and there was certainly no complaint from me. I'm not adverse to a bit of perturbation. (Word de jour, perturbation. I love it). Chungking Mansions rightly deserved its seedy reputation. Three dark, dirty and airless shopping arcades occupied (and still do) the ground floor, and it is no stretch to say, if you can't buy it there, it doesn't exist. Restaurants, coffee shops, bars, and tea houses, both legal and illegal, could be found on any of the above floors. On our first visit, an illegal, late night/early morning coffee-shop-cum-bar on the fifth floor was operated by an ageing English transvestite who carried a live boa constrictor wound around her body and had a taste for underage boys. The snake appeared to be both a pet and a prop in her erotic/exotic nightclub routine. A strange place to frequent, you might think. Well, yes, but we finished work very late, at one or two a.m. It was challenging to find somewhere to eat at such a late hour.

The lifts, only two on each side of the building, were a nightmare. Estimates put over four thousand people residing in Chunking Mansions at any given time, and four lifts just didn't cut it. Apart from human cargo, these lifts often transported bundles, crates and mysterious packages. Somewhere in the building, someone had a thriving trade in illegal ivory, and I was often accompanied on my ride up by a dozen or more whole elephant tusks. Illicit mah-jong dens were plentiful as well because the rattling, shuffling and slamming down of the tiles in play often kept me awake.

The age of the building, its subsequent dodgy additions, and ancient, and unauthorised amateur electrical wiring made the place a vast fire trap. Blocked stairwells and locked emergency exits didn't add to the safety, there were numerous deaths of locals and tourists over the years. Chungking Mansions owned such a reputation, it has seen service as an authentic location in films, books and TV dramas. It was also known to be a centre for drugs and dealers as well as a refuge for petty criminals, scammers, and undocumented immigrants. Apart from, and including all this, I loved it. I thought it was absolutely sensational and stimulating. I was young then. I would most probably have second, third and fourth, thoughts about the place today. I'm assured it's still there and still the same.

Hong Kong contracts were notoriously arduous, with most agents demanding three shows nightly in three different venues. Admittedly the shows were only thirty-minutes long, but we carried only two shows with us, which meant the last show was to be packed up each night, and taken back to the hotel or kept by the agents' assistant. That show then became the first show the following evening, and the middle show stayed put. A proper pain in the arse because one show of ten changes per artist was unpacked and repacked twice nightly. This was the deal with Mr Tam, there was nothing for it but to comply, and get on with it. The first visit, we worked at Miramar Hotels' Ondine Room, Kowloon side, Pearl City Restaurant, under the Pearl City Mansion complex in Wanchai, and lastly, the Highball Club at Ocean Terminal cruise ship dock in Kowloon beside the old Kowloon Railway Station. A bit of a trot each night, but there were plenty of assistants from the agency, and it was fairly smooth going.

One appreciative audience member, Hong Kong businessman Phil B, took a great liking to us and invited us to a private party at his home on the Peak on one of our rare nights off. Another occasion, he picked us up in a chauffeur-driven, air-conditioned Jaguar. I'd never been in an air-conditioned car in my life. He took us for lunch at the grand old colonial establishment on the other side of Hong Kong Island, the Repulse Bay Hotel—that epitome of British colonial elegance with its striped awning colonnades, and usually a jazz band on weekends. The origins of the name Repulse Bay are vague, and many stories and myths abound. The one I choose to believe, only because it has so much romance, is that the bay was a notorious and ill-famed pirates' nest which interrupted foreign trade and was repulsed in 1841 by the British fleet. Absolutely no evidence exists of the truth of this story, but it has a certain swashbuckling charm. In 1920, the Repulse Bay Hotel was built and a bus route established to bring swimmers out from Central district. I believe that bus route is one of Hong Kong's oldest.

Shortly before our arrival in Hong Kong the first time, the ocean liner *Queen Elizabeth* had caught fire and sank in Victoria Harbour. The 83,000-ton liner was the largest ship in the world at its launch in 1938, and after its retirement, it had been purchased by Hong Kong tycoon CY. Tung, who intended to convert it into a floating university. Because the fire seemed to have started simultaneously in several places along its length, it was treated as a case of arson but never proven. Hundreds of people living and working on the ship were either evacuated or jumped for their lives. Fighting the fire continued for twenty-four hours, but nothing could save the doomed Queen. It was still there and we saw the rusty hulk exactly as TIME magazine reported.

'Next day, with her upper decks, collapsed and her massive steel hull buckled like so much soggy cardboard, the ship, still burning, keeled over. The Queen had died.'

After our first month-long Hong Kong stint in 1973 with agent Tam Bing Wah, all subsequent Hong Kong contracts were with Benny Tong's agency. After we won 'Show of the Year' in Tokyo, we were treated with a lot more deference. We made it into the annual book produced by Japan's theatre world that featured stories, interviews, and images of touring shows. A kind of showbiz bible used by agents from all over Asia to choose the shows they wanted to book for the coming year. This meant we would perform just two shows per night instead of three, and we could leave a show in each venue. Bliss. As well as the marvellous gift of only two shows nightly, we were given a bit of a boost in our accommodation standard as well. No more Chungking Mansions for us, three-star hotels in Mong Kok or Wanchai were now the order of the day. Oh, how the other half lives.

We once spent several days locked in our hotel in Mong Kok during a typhoon. For the duration of the typhoon, the sound of breaking glass and falling neon signs was all that could be heard over the howling wind and rain. When we were finally allowed to go outside, there was glass and twisted metal everywhere. I'd heard of a taxi which didn't get to shelter soon enough and was picked up and thrown into the harbour, killing all on board. An ocean liner broke its moorings. It was blown back and forth across the harbour demolishing parts of both the Hong Kong and the Kowloon Star Ferry terminals before it was pushed into safer waters and secured by some very brave tugboat operators.

In 1975, there was a half-day stopover in Hong Kong en route from Taiwan to Bangkok for a month's contract at the Galaxy Theatre Restaurant. An afternoon's shopping in Hong Kong was heaven after the rigours of Taiwan, and the dancers were given strict instructions to meet at the old Kai Tak Airport a good two hours before our flight. Luis and I did quite a bit of show shopping and had half a taxi full of replacement beads, sequins, fabrics, et cetera. The cab pulled up, we gathered our loot and ran for the terminal. Only when I looked for my passport did I discover I'd left my, what do I call it, manbag, purse, handbag, whatever, we all carried those little bags on a leather strap back then—in the taxi. Not only the bag, which was a Pierre Cardin, and my passport, but two thousand dollars of profit from a month's hard slog in Taiwan. Well, obviously I wouldn't be flying.

I got everyone else ready to board then took myself off to the Australian Embassy. Passports in those days were much more easily replaced. A kinder, gentler world perhaps. It was no big deal, and a new passport was in my hands in a couple of hours. Problem now was getting to Bangkok. I went to the airport, trying all the different airline counters. Nothing—I didn't care if there was a bit of country-hopping just as long as I got there. Nope, nothing. I was dejectedly walking away to try to give Luis a call in Bangkok when a girl from one of the counters called after me.

There was a non-scheduled Lufthansa flight leaving in thirty minutes. Strictly speaking, it was not taking passengers. This was a new aircraft being delivered, and after consulting with Lufthansa, this kind person secured me a seat. Not only a seat, but gratis. There was only one other person on board, the Boeing rep who was conducting the handover. Not even any cabin crew. The only condition to my travelling was, 'as Australia was at war with Vietnam and we would be passing over enemy territory', I was to be seated next to this Boeing official and have the window blinds drawn during that part of the flight. I could do that. So off we went. What a strange feeling to be travelling on this enormous, empty, wide-bodied aircraft.

Hong Kong stayed on our regular itinerary for many years, and watching it grow was fascinating, the land reclamation projects, the ever-increasing growth of buildings climbing the Peak, and the destruction of grand old edifices to be replaced by towering monstrosities. We worked in so many places I've entirely forgotten most. Still, the regulars like Pearl City and Ocean Terminal were always a pleasure and we were always welcomed with open arms. Sad to see the old Kowloon Railway Station gone. At least they kept the poor lonely clock tower. We used to jump on the train there to go exploring in the New Territories. One particular joy of mine was to get up early on a Sunday, catch the bus behind the Hong Kong Hilton near the Peak Tram Terminus, and go to Repulse Bay for a swim. Lunch was always at the old Repulse Bay Hotel on the pillared veranda with the awnings pulled down just enough to take the heat off, and the ceiling fans turning lazily overhead. Musician friends had a regular jazz gig there, and it was relaxing and pleasant to get nicely tipsy on the hotel's speciality cocktails and hitch a ride back with the musos. I'm sure that magnificent colonial hotel is sorely missed.

The tiger beetle crossing the Nullarbor to Perth, 1969.

Leading lady Hanni. The first show, Madrid, 1971.

Some cast on the outdoor stage, Cairo late '70s.

TOP The Circus opening with leading lady Jayne.
BOTTOM The Circus tribute.

TOP Leading lady Therese with Luis in The White Fox finale.
BOTTOM The White Fox finale

TOP Leading ladies Faye and Melissa in the Broadway tribute.
BOTTOM The Broadway tribute.

The author and Luis (right), Spain, 1989

TOP The Bond tribute.
BOTTOM Everyone loves a marching girl.

CHAPTER 21

TAKING A BREAK

One night while performing at the Miramar in Hong Kong, I received a phone call from the front desk. It was Clair, a West Australian ballet dancer and old friend who had also danced in our Barcelona Apollo Theatre show. An extraordinary-looking Eurasian woman, she was in the lobby with a friend and would like to see us. I secured her some house seats and said we would meet up after the show. The last I knew of her she'd gone to London, and was working with the Benny Hill show. That evening after the performance, Luis and I caught up with Clair in the lobby and met her partner, none other than the fabulous Benny Hill himself. Off we went somewhere for supper, and it was delightful to see Clair and to meet Benny.

Benny was absolute charm itself and he loved the gorilla routine in our show. Being the gentleman he was, he asked if he might buy the number from us. Buy it! My dear man, anyone else would just steal it. Please – by all means – use it with our blessing. Like most comedians, Benny's performance persona was totally unlike his real-life self. A more charming, modest, quiet man would be hard to find. Clair and Benny stayed together until his death in April 1992. What a fabulous, long-lasting union.

Every day in Hong Kong I made sure I went out to see, and explore as much as I could fit in. I love walking, it truly is the only way to know a place. I often tried to get into the old Kowloon Walled City, but never ever had any luck. Kindly, or perhaps diplomatic, people always turned me away. It was a massively overpopulated 2.6-hectare enclave of warren-like lanes and alleys. Buildings, both authorised and unauthorised, were stacked on top of each other like children's play blocks. Electrical wires and cabling ran in spider-web fashion along, above, and through every opening. Sanitation was a nightmare and fire always a constant threat. Small family factories churned out everything from plastic flowers to electrical appliances. Although the majority of its residents were not involved in crime and lived relatively peacefully with each other, the entire place was controlled by the Triads.

The Walled City was the base for every criminal activity in Hong Kong. Prostitution, drugs of every description, gambling and every other vice could be bought and sold there. It was a haven for thieves, murderers and every law-breaker in the colony. Even the police were afraid to enter. It was said that some thirty-three thousand people lived there at its peak. The Hong Kong government had tried unsuccessfully to have the place demolished since 1944. They were successful in 1993. A couple of gates and remnants of buildings were preserved as a reminder of the life and history there.

We quickly made many friends in Hong Kong, as always people wanted to get to know the dancers. Of course, it's the ravishing girls they wanted at their parties and clubs, but they had to take the guys as a package deal. There were still a lot of British police there in the '70s, especially amongst the Officers. A particular high-ranking officer became a good friend of mine, which led to me laying my hands on some lovely antiques. There were police watch stations along the Sham Chun River, and at night these were equipped with floodlights to spot crossing refugees. The colony received frequent complaints from village heads on the other side of the river about the lights disturbing their livestock. It was nonsense, of course. Everybody knew if they complained often enough, and loudly enough, a visit from the Hong Kong authorities would be accompanied by the odd small payoff. My friend, the high-ranking flatfoot would visit these villages, and I would don a police shirt and hat and go with him in a Black Maria. Highly illegal, I imagine, but not even worth thinking about when you consider the crime and corruption of that period. It was the time of the Cultural Revolution in China, and the village heads knew where every little treasure was hidden. Under haystacks, under barn floors, you name it, they knew. They also knew the going price. So, after a bit of light haggling, a nice screen or chest would be hastily retrieved from its hiding spot and deposited in the back of the police van. I still have a couple of treasures from those sorties. Shipping them home was easy, and there was no tax in those days for anything considered art.

Benny Tong came to see us off on the hydrofoil as we headed for our first show visit to Macau. Being a bit of a history buff, I was very excited to be visiting this both famous and infamous Portuguese colony. Built in the late ’60s, the three-storey Lisboa Casino was relatively new. The twelve-storey circular hotel section was added in 1970. Already a landmark, the distinctive yellow and white building topped by a gold crown could be seen from almost anywhere in Macau and was the more famous of the two casinos there at the time. The management spent a small fortune bringing the best artists in, and it was possibly the easiest contract we ever had. Four shows per week. Two on Friday and two on Saturday, with maybe a show added on Sunday. The rest of the week, we were free to roam around discovering this tiny, yet fascinating history-drenched place, with its narrow meandering streets and the ruins of the old St Paul’s Cathedral. On the wharf, bare-chested coolies could be seen loading and unloading traditional style junks. Macau was fabulously stuck in a time warp.

The hotel also brought in the world-famous Crazy Horse Show from Paris. As anyone who has seen these amazing ladies will know, they perform entirely nude—except for the odd hat, wig, belt or a bit of jewellery. The dancers are chosen from the most beautiful women in the world. The girls lived in the hotel with us and were delighted to have a bit of like-minded company. Their work schedule was tough, with three shows per day, and they were not permitted free range of the city for fear they would be molested. The poor girls always had security with them at all times. Their show was identical to the one I'd seen in Paris, complete with a huge tank and dolphin. A more beautiful and sophisticated show would be hard to find.

I think we performed in Macau three times over the years. The last time, I was present for the first opening of the border with China (Guangdong Province) since the 1950s. The ceremony was incredibly moving, watching family members and friends who hadn't seen each other in nearly thirty years greeting one another. After the 1974 overthrow of the ruling dictatorship in Portugal, the new Portuguese government determined it would relinquish all its overseas possessions. After well over four centuries of Portuguese rule, the Chinese government assumed formal sovereignty of Macau at the end of 1999. I believe there are many, many, more casinos in Macau now, and the dear old Lisboa has a monstrous new sister built next to it. I'm rather pleased I can remember it as it was, I have no desire to go back.

Now it was time to head for home. Not Madrid, but back to Perth where Luis had accepted the post of Artistic Director with the West Australian Ballet Company. While Luis was working for WA Ballet, I hawked my 'jack of all trades' abilities around the theatres. Around 1974, I was dressing the set for *The Importance of Being Ernest* at the Hole in the Wall Theatre. It was actually a hole in a wall, the tiniest theatre I've seen, the foyer was massive in comparison. We were getting towards opening night and I was frantically trying to get it all together, working on the set while dress rehearsal was underway. Miss Eartha Kitt was appearing at a concert in Perth at the time, a friend of one of the actors who'd invited her to come to a dress rehearsal. So, there she was, large as life, stopping the rehearsal every five minutes with suggestions or criticisms. It was so irritating, and I'll never understand why someone didn't say something, especially the director.

Most of my evening was spent up a ladder trying to get two humongous, heavy, and unwieldy red velvet curtains hanging correctly. They were almost dragging me off the ladder, and that rasping, interfering voice was making my blood boil. Someone or something tugged on my trousers, and there was the feline face of Miss Kitt, looking up at me, telling me the left side was hanging low. I politely reminded her if she cast her mind back to the last time she saw me, the left was hanging low then as well.

Soon Luis's stint as Artistic Director of WA Ballet was over. It was time to get our shows out of mothballs and take them on the road. When discussing our next tours we decided, if at all possible, we would prefer to work exclusively with Australian dancers. After all, we'd named our company Australian International Entertainment (A.I.E.) and there were several reasons why. Australians are so grateful to find work outside Australia, so well behaved, and exceptionally well trained. It was easier to manage a single nationality where visa applications were concerned, and to deal with one mentality and language. Touring can be very stressful for management. You are travelling with some very young people at times and must take the responsibility for them seriously. I think we accomplished that throughout our travels. When I browse Facebook now, for example, and see the strong friendships that were formed between the dancers twenty and thirty years ago still flourishing and with such strong bonds, I am pleased and proud.

An agent in Singapore offered us a couple of weeks if we could get there. From Singapore, it was not a big deal to go on to other Asian destinations, with each agent paying one-way. Hop, hop, hop, from country to country. I think we were nine or ten people at the time, and back then it was a lot of money to find for airfares. I had the brilliant idea that a shipping company might take us for free if we worked our passage.

In those days it was common to take a ship to Singapore then fly to London. I've an idea it was called ship/jet. Few vessels were operating from Australia but one making a fortnightly trip was the Russian ship *Turkmenia*. Dear old *Turkmenia,* 'the Turkey', as we fondly called it, was a bit rough and ready and carried around three hundred passengers. It was a small ship but much nicer, more intimate and friendly than these four-thousand-passenger monsters around today. The theatre gods must have been having a good day because I managed to get us on the 'Turkey', departing in ten days. The shipping company gave us a great deal, only one show required during the trip and of course, we had the run of the ship.

The Fremantle–Singapore crossing took seven days and was a delightful, reasonably smooth trip, especially through the Java Straits, past Krakatoa. This by the way, is west of Java, not east as per the famous 1968 film. The water was as flat and glassy as an oil slick, it was possible to look down into the crystal-clear water and see the marine life below. It was a small ship and from the lowest deck we were quite close to the water. Flying fish regularly flopped at our feet.

Crossing the Equator, we did the obligatory ceremony with the Captain dressed as Neptune, flanked by the dancers draped in bits of flimsy 'seaweed' beside him. I was accused of have 'multiple wives and not sharing with the crew' and was 'operated on' by the ship's doctor. Sausages, a chicken, and various other bits of offal were removed from beneath the sheet draped across me. I was liberally covered in flour and cocoa and mercilessly flung into the pool by the crew. Singapore ended up being a couple of weeks rehearsal at the Savoy Hotel then on to Hong Kong, Japan, Taiwan, Hong Kong again then back for a couple of weeks in Singapore. We spent approximately ten months circling Asia before heading back on the dear old 'Turkey' to Perth.

CHAPTER 22

THE SHOW WAS EVERYTHING

The Japan market was booming, and it became the main leg of our Asian tours. Regular twelve-month tours, covering Singapore, Japan, Hong Kong, Macau, Taiwan, Malaysia, and Thailand seemed to be reliable, and reliability was certainly needed. Considering we'd purchased a house in Perth big enough to store costumes and produce more, returning to Europe's uncertain market felt more like a step backwards. The Japanese agents were strong, and Japan's economy was booming, allowing venues to book us for the full six months permitted on a performance visa. Six months gave them plenty of time to recoup the cost of the airfares. Mostly, the Japanese agent would handle the entire Asian tour, arranging the selling on of the shows to other local agents. These agents were all very well established, there was never a problem with bookings. Of course, we had fabulous shows for them to sell, our costumes were always considered the ultimate in glamour, and our elegant, beautiful, well-trained professional dancers added prestige of the highest order.

The show, the show was everything, the show was all-consuming, the show was our lives. 'Tits 'n Feathers'—that's what we, in the business, called our type of show. There is Classical Ballet, Modern Dance, Burlesque, Cabaret, Contemporary etcetera, etcetera. Ask anyone who has performed in a our style of show, and they'll call it 'Tits and Feathers'. You could further explain our category by describing them as 'Casino shows, or, cabaret, Lido and Moulin Rouge types of show'. Maybe 'Showgirls' does it, but, since the release of the movie of the same name in 1995, that word has connotations, not of the positive sort. The film gives a totally unrealistic and untrue view. The dancers portrayed in it are beautiful but untalented. They are bitchy, untrained and little better than hookers. So, the word Showgirl, in our world is now more than a tad tainted. I guess Cabaret and Show Dancers are the acceptable go-to now.

The making of a show starts with a contract offer and acceptance. The shows for casinos generally called for twenty to twenty-five people on stage. All venues have their own requirements. These preconditions often go right down to the minutes and seconds on stage with set change, and costume change provisos. An average venue would request minor costume, and scenery changes every 90 seconds, and major changes every three minutes. Don't for one minute think you can get away with pretty dancers in cutsie costumes wiggling their arses off on stage for ten minutes and call that a number. Venues must be shown all costumes and set designs for approval long before revving up the sewing machines. These negotiations can be exhausting, much depends on the size of the venue, its staging capabilities (set change capabilities, stages going up and down, sometimes full stages with sets off stage ready to mechanically slide in and replace the currently used stage), the location of dressing rooms etcetera. Once designs are settled on, a venue will often whip up full working miniatures, and fly them to us with the stage engineer. These miniatures are gone through thoroughly, and every working detail perfected and timed before signing off by both parties. You'd better know your onions; any mistake can be outrageously costly and guess who foots the bill?

Then, it's time for an on-site inspection. Dressing rooms, stages, dancer's accommodation, food menus are gone through, or kitchens if we were lucky enough to get them. There is the backstage entrance given the once over, security checked, availability of transport if the venue is out of town. Stage entrances to be measured, backstage stairs, and distance to dressing rooms considered for costume change times, on-site medical availability and a thousand other little things. Only after all of this level of investigation and checking could I say: 'Boot up the sewing machines'. This was where the fun began. Find our production sewers, source fabrics, feathers, beads, sequins, diamantes. Feather quality, and feather dyeing is paramount.

Our source was Dita Feathers in Crown Street Darlinghurst, possibly the best feather company in the world. Ridiculously expensive, a single pheasant feather 1.5m long could cost $100. A few hundred feathers on stage and you can work it out for yourself. There are thousands of ostrich feathers and hundreds of metres of thick ostrich boa at $120 per metre to be ordered. The quality of the dyeing is super important. Cheap dyes poorly applied leave colour stains on costumes, and sweaty skin. Dita's dyes were frequently $1,000 per kilo. Nothing would make the colours of their meticulously dyed plumes come off on costumes or dancers. We always used wigs as no female dancer in our shows ever showed her hair. It is impossible to ask a girl to keep her hair in a long style and the same colour for two years. So, human hair wigs in the colour and shade of each girl's hair must be purchased. These long pieces run to $500 and upwards. The wigs are attached to the diamante crowns. And so it goes, on and on and on.

Dancers need to be found. Australia wide auditions were held, only the tallest, most well trained, stunning looking, fit and perfectly proportioned dancers were chosen. Reputation was considered, a dancers employment history was gone through thoroughly, one bad apple could screw up an entire cast. Our dancers had up to ten years of ballet training under their belts and were the cream of the crop, at the top of their game. Dancers are possibly the pinnacle of super professional athletes. An enormous physical and mental effort is required to perform two rigorous shows per night, seven nights per week. Australian dancers are known and treasured throughout the world for their beauty, physical prowess, dedication, and discipline.

Music must be selected, either from existing recordings or written for us, orchestras and studios to be paid for recording sessions. Quite often the bigger venues owned their own orchestra which played over the top of the soundtrack. Music was written for these musicians, and rehearsals taken. Should a venue require the dancers to be singing over the music, particularly during finales, then studio time was paid for the recording. Music was a costly part of our business, after all, the folk holding the rights must have their cut, and do so from each performance.

Each dancer must send a tracing of their feet to have their shoes made. Usually, the standard shoe supply per dancer was, one pair of flesh high heels, one pair of thigh-high black high heel boots, and one pair of white high heel ankle boots. Then there were the specialty shoes. For a show of twenty girls, that's a minimum of sixty pairs of handmade bespoke shoes plus the male dancer's needs. Are you still counting costs? Getting towards rehearsal time, there were visas applications, flights to arrange, accommodation, and rehearsal rooms to secure, tons of baggage to organise. The ever-dreaded fittings to be gone through, hat fittings are especially difficult. Dancing wearing a towering 1.5 metre hat is no small feat. Hats are always made with balance in mind, but there is still a considerable amount of skill involved on the part of the wearer—try balancing a lamp on your head while you do the vacuuming.

The routines themselves are the fun part. Much discussion between Luis and me about designs, practicability and cost often saw sparks flying. Nothing like two artistic gay guys, each wanting their own way, to set the cat among the pigeons. These opposing views were essential as each of us saw different difficulties which might result in the finished product. There were ideas in Luis's mind about the colour, and general shape of a costume. As he would explain his thoughts, I would sketch then paint the design. He always remarked on my ability to reach inside his head and extract his vision. A marvellous thing really, it made us a perfect team. Rarely did we make any mistakes costume wise, we couldn't afford those miscalculations. Luis totally understood the need for freedom of movement, and give in a costume, I knew equally as well the limitations of giant headgear. Between us we put out some very fine works. As for the sets and props, I pretty much had my way, and Luis was always grateful. One less thing for him to worry about.

For many years we used what was simply called the White Finale. This number was probably the most expensive we ever produced. The dancers wore nine-inch crowns topped with silver fox fur and white coque (rooster tail) feathers.

White elbow-length gloves, a diamanté necklace, white diamantéd G string and bra, with a floor-length full circle of white sunray pleated crystal nylon hanging from their hips, and the same from the backs of their shoulders to the floor. These pleated pieces were each trimmed with five metres of white ostrich boa. The topless models wore much the same but vastly exaggerated. Twelve-inch crowns, twice the width, and height in fur, and feathers, double the amount of pleated fabric, plus great bunches of silver fox tails hanging from in front of the shoulders. Of course, no bra, but we never allowed girls to be naked from the waist to the neck, so intricately beaded underwires called halters were worn under the bust. The guys wore a type of open bolero jacket, and full trousers of white fabric with a wide-open weave and tight at the ankle. Silver cowboy boots on their feet. An utterly stunning parade of glamour.

Then there was the ever popular Pink number which could be used as an opening or finale. Such inventive names, the White finale, the Pink opening. Obviously, a lot of thought and discussion went into those particular labels. The Pink number consisted of the crowns being utilised once again. At US$2,000 each plus wigs, we needed to get our money's worth. However, this time, they were topped by a hundred or so ostrich feathers. They were ombré dyed pale pink through hot pink to purple and set in bunches, one at each side and one in the middle, making this headgear around 1.4m wide and 1m high. Each girl carried two ombré dyed pink feather fans, each blade three feathers long, two metres wide when open. Hugely expensive, and enormously tricky to control. Purple and hot pink bras with pink diamanté epaulettes on the shoulders, pink guipure lace full circle skirts open at the front and hooked on to small purple bikinis, and a 50cm train edged with 4 metres of hot pink ostrich boa. These skirts were lined with specialised hot pink *bata de cola,* a stiff fabric used in flamenco skirts to keep the frills standing. The guipure lace flowers were hand sequined with light pink at the waist ending in purple at the end of the train. Accessorised again, with purple elbow-length gloves and a diamanté necklace.

To describe each performance number we produced would take another book. Suffice to say, over the years there were openings, finales and middle numbers in the theme styles of James Bond (including motorcycles on stage),

Flash Gordon, Tropical, a blue opening, a brown and yellow finale, circus, Broadway musicals, Inca, marching girls, and many others. The Inca number, with the beautifully trained lead lady Therese, needs a special mention. When it was first performed on the vast Sheraton Walker Hill Casino stage in Seoul, it was the biggest, most expensive stage set ever on an Asian stage. The set was a dark foreboding jungle, a massive stone temple with a monstrous god head set in the middle, and two ridiculously fat 6m long snakes, one on each side. These snakes rose and swayed accompanied by appropriate light and sound effects of lightning and thunder, knocking the temple down sending impressive styrene stone building blocks tumbling. The godhead's mouth was three metres wide, and out of it, at a specific, very crucial time, spewed eleven tons of constantly recycled water. This deluge raced down stone steps past fleeing dancers making its way to the astonished and slightly alarmed audience. The tsunami-like wave was caught by a clear Perspex screen, and the relieved theatregoers brought the house down with appreciative applause for each performance.

There you see and begin to comprehend the work involved. What you don't see are the myriad things that didn't go to plan. Always, absolutely always, dozens of problems cropped up. Each one required its own unique solution, even if much the same difficulty had arisen previously. That's when the seasoned producer and director tackles them head-on, and results unfold without impacting the smooth running of an immaculately produced show. I've seen other production of this size which are completely top heavy in management. Directors and their assistants, choreographer and assistant, pay masters, tour managers, and on and on. We were just two people; we couldn't afford to bring in outsiders. Three new shows on the road at the same time needed to make $15 million in one year just to cover costs.

You may begin to wonder why we would put ourselves through this again and again. True, the work was tough, and all consuming, with little time left for a home life or any time for each other. But we lived and breathed our work, almost to the point of obsession.

CHAPTER 23

MOVING ON UP

The tours of Japan continued, my high opinion of the country and its people, unchanging during my years there. A six-month stint in Japan was always something to look forward to, whether it be in a club in downtown Roppongi or, in a remote mountain hot springs spa/onsen hotel. Altogether, I can count more than thirty cities and towns where we performed, from the southern end of Kyushu to the northern coast of Hokkaido, and I'm sure I missed a few. Kagoshima was a fascinating place. Sakurajima volcano insisted on erupting almost daily around four pm, covering the city in a fine grey, ash-like, dirty snow called black rain. An umbrella was essential because the ash had a certain acidic sting on the skin. The first day it erupted, I recall our darling dancer Anthea bolting out of a hairdressing salon with hairdressers in hot pursuit, her hair still in their foils. Typical, surely, Anthea and fire! Dear Anthea's name will inevitably pop up quite often, and Anthea moments, although sometimes frustrating and unfathomable were always, nonetheless, consistently amusing and memorable. My darling Anthea lost her long fight with cancer in 2021. She managed to come to my 70th birthday here in Castlemaine and I will always be grateful for that.

Six months' work in the one place, or even two lots of three months was preferable. Tours only lasting two weeks in various Tokyo nightclubs or a week here, and a week there in different cities were exhausting. Once we even did a couple of weeks of one night stands out of Tokyo, often going as far as

Yokahama, five nights in a row to a series of Ichi Ban, Number One, clubs. That was decidedly tough. We would be picked up early afternoon from our hotel in Akasaka by mini-bus, drive the forty kilometres which can take a couple of hours in heavy traffic, unpack the costumes, rehearse, eat, wander around a while, perform two shows, pack up again and drive back. Repeating that process day after day is not fun in anybody's language. Still, watching one dancer, Suzy, apply makeup without a mirror in the seat next to the driver as we bumped along was very entertaining. Amazingly, she managed an immaculate makeup job and never once poked herself in the eye with a brush or sponge applicator, though the eyelash glue could be a bit hit and miss.

Over the years from 1972 to the mid-1990s, we changed our Japanese agents three times. First, we were with Joe Uamatsu's Akasaka Kyodo Booking and his dreadful niece Atsuko, but that was only one six-month run. Afterwards, we were with Mr Hamada's B.B. Kikaku Agency and his crew of assistants, a delightful man who was forever taking the entire show out to eat, and always acted in a proud father-like way towards us all. Ultimately, we settled with Sankyo Promotions. Mr Kato, or Kato San, and his team were equally good to us. The changeover came about because of the recognition we were getting for producing quality shows. Bigger venues, all of which seemed to be handled by Sankyo, were requesting our presence. How grand it all sounds.

In 1983, the best ten thousand dollars we ever spent was for the blood money Atsuko Iwata, niece of our first agent, Joe, demanded in return for giving our phone number to Kato San of Sankyo Promotions. A right bitch if ever there was one. Sankyo Promotions had seen our shows and the awards we were racking up. They knew we had, at one time, worked with Atsuko. We tried for years to get an Ito contract, Ito having one of the largest, and most highly respected venues in Japan. They were very anti-Australian as they had been bitten before by some crappy, fly-by-night shows. Atsuko called me in Perth, saying, 'Kato San was asking for your number, should I give it to him?'

'Of course,' I said, 'Yes, please do.' Her answer was, 'Sure. Okay, but I want ten grand.' Outrageous. Who has such money lying around waiting to be given away? We came to an agreement. Sankyo would deduct money each week from our six-month contract and pay her. She was in no way embarrassed about her deviousness or that Sankyo knew. As I said, World-Class Bitch. Today it sounds like a lot of money, in 1983 it was a huge price to pay.

So, after such a long time of trying, we were now with Japan's top agency. Sankyo Promotions were the Japan agents for the Beatles, and the Rolling Stones, amongst many other massive headliners, now they would be ours.

The contract in Ito led directly to a Walker Hill contract in Seoul, which lead to a second Walker Hill contract, et cetera. So, while Atsuko got a lot of money out of us, it ended up being money very well spent. The Sun Hatoya Hotel Ito, on the east coast, 100kms south of Tokyo, was an absolute prize contract. Every show producer in our class – that is to say, the highest class – naturally focused their eager little eyes on it. It was a brand spanking new hotel right on the beach with an outstanding, world-class showroom. Scenery was specially designed for each new show, and for each number in the show. Dressing rooms were modern and fitted out with every luxury. The dancers were treated with the utmost respect, and a six-month contract there fairly flew by. We were, over the years, as hungry as every other show to be offered this remarkable venue. Whilst our agent Hamada San had the very best venues up to a certain size, the really important places seemed to be in the hands of Sankyo Promotions. Getting the proverbial foot in the door was near impossible. Until the Atsuko episode.

Sun Hatoya was a privately owned hotel. The only owner we met was an elderly woman to whom we were introduced at the funeral ceremony for her husband. It was held in front of the original Hatoya Hotel, up through the city on a mountainside, which she and her husband also owned. She took the opportunity to lecture us, given we were all gathered in the same place for the ceremony. Stern old bird. Tough as nails. Spoke English very well and let us know, in no uncertain terms, what she expected from us, and just exactly what we could expect in return. Fair enough, I suppose, but odd at a funeral. This original hotel is where we lived, and from where we were transported to the beachside venue for performances and evening meals. When we first arrived, we were given rooms in the general guest part of the hotel.

The preceding show out of New York was still performing, and we took over their rooms in the entertainers' wing after they vacated. The rooms were comfortable but showing their age a bit. Watching this US show, I can't remember being particularly impressed. It was well known the owner of Sun Hatoya steadfastly refused to have an Australian production within cooee of the place. Only our superb reputation, and the reputation of Sankyo Promotions swung the deal for us. There was still some obvious reserve and those first days we were not treated as I expected we should be. The hotel manager was very toffy-nosed and treated me, in particular, with an undeserved dose of disdain. I often checked the soles of my shoes after getting to my room, just in case I'd walked a bit of doggy doo into the hotel lobby.

On the day the US show left, we were told by this manager person, we 'may move into the entertainers' accommodation directly after breakfast'. Not so fast, Buster. I know any and every show from the good old US of A was treated as though God himself had produced it, but we also possessed a certain reputation in both Asia and Europe, and I wasn't about to let this stuffed-shirt herd us into rooms without prior inspection or approval. When I informed him that I would review the rooms before anybody made the slightest move towards them, you could have cut the air with a very dull Samurai sword.

Off we went, this pompous penguin and I, on a grand inspection tour. Doors were insolently flung open, and I was waved into the first room as though I'd been upgraded from cattle class. I intended to be super, super, fussy but, I simply didn't need to be. The rooms were a disgrace. The preceding artists having vacated, a couple of maids waved a duster around, and changed the sheets. To my mind, that was it. The shoji screens, traditional Japanese rice paper screens, dividing the bedroom from the bathroom were all punctured, some had holes big enough to put your head through. The bathroom basins in every room were filthy, makeup stuck to the sides. Sitting rooms looked like they might well have been accommodating the homeless, and light fittings were either broken or missing entirely. Well, so much for the prestige of an American show. That was quite enough for me.

I slowly wandered from room to room, making the most extensive list possible. This list I handed to his nibs, and in the politest manner, informed him my dancers would shift into these rooms only after the repair and maintenance list was completed, and a further inspection was made. I can see this guy as easily inhabiting the role of Captain of a WWII Japanese POW camp. He glanced over the offending report in an arrogant manner, gave a mighty hurumphhhh, and took off down the passage. Twenty minutes or so later, I was informed by telephone that my dancers could stay where they were until the rooms had been attended to. Gotcha, imperious prick. We were still in the hotel rooms three days after we opened before I was asked to re-inspect the artists' accommodation.

What a difference, they looked absolutely brand-spanking new. I gave the dancers such a lecture about keeping them that way. I must admit, the manager certainly changed his entire attitude to us after reports regarding our show began flooding in. He started to fairly glow with pride whenever the dancers passed him, and a lovely deep bow was always forthcoming. Even I was given the seal of approval, and completely forgiven for any ruffled plumage. Quite something in Japan.

Our dancers were a particularly tall and glamorous lot, each and every one a lady, even the boys. High summer came and went, and the show was a resounding success. All too quickly, the six months were up. Our agent, Kato San was overjoyed, and brought many owners of big venues to see the show. One, in particular, was supremely impressed. Mr Lee, Showroom Director of Sheraton Walker Hill in Seoul, Korea. In no time at all, a contract for this most prestigious of show rooms was offered, and hastily, but not too hastily, accepted.

CHAPTER 24

IT'S NOT LONELY AT THE TOP

After the initial contact was made with Sheraton Walker Hill in Seoul, things moved quickly. For the first time we were to create an original show for a specific venue. So back we went to Perth to plan and to create something completely unique, a one off. We knew we must impress. Kato San, Mr Lee and a few others, flew to Perth to nut out exactly what type of show we needed to take to this magnificent venue. We went absolutely crazy turning out costume, set and prop designs, and ideas for routines. Information was provided telling us that all Walker Hill contracts required major scenery/costume changes every three minutes, and minor changes every thirty seconds.

We were as ready as we could be. Designs all approved, concepts by Luis raved over, all systems go. It was time to organise Australia-wide auditions. This show was to be Broadway Follies, three fifteen-minute routines, opening with a Broadway medley. There was a clever, quick change from black sequin jackets to red sequin jackets performed on stage in this number. I never met a person who ever noticed this change, some things can be done too well. The middle section was the Inca, and then the White Fox finale. This would not be possible in today's climate, as this finale included twenty thousand dollars' worth of silver fox tails embellishing the costumes and hats.

As ever, Luis and I made the costumes. Our house looked like a factory for the next few months, and we worked day and night. More diamanté crowns were to be made by Nakamura San in Tokyo. He was the very best in the business, after all. A twelve-month show in the mid-80s cost upwards of five million dollars before one penny of profit was made. We never, in thirty-three years, lost a single dollar. Not bad for two unschooled guys.

Finally, we were off to Walker Hill. The Sheraton complex sits on the site of the A-Cha Fortress from the Silla Dynasty (57BC–668AD). The walks I've taken around those mountains, with everything covered in two metres of snow. The views looking down the slopes, and across the frozen Han River were spectacular. Apart from the main eleven-storey tower, there are six houses or small, two-storey complexes of twenty or so rooms, each scattered around the 139-acre complex. One of these, Maxwell House, was allocated to us during our stay there. It is situated not far from the rear entrance to the backstage area, but in winter you needed a full snowsuit just to cross those few metres between buildings. Although hotel restaurant meals were included in the contract, most dancers preferred to use the communal Maxwell House kitchen, which I persuaded management to install on the first floor. Eating every day in a restaurant with a constant unchanging menu can get very dull, no matter how luxurious it sounds. Although the resort is on the outskirts of town, it was only a twenty-minute taxi or shuttle bus ride to downtown.

I was late arriving at the Sheraton as I was busily winding up one of our shows in Japan. On my arrival at the hotel a few days after the dancers, the first people I saw were Luis and Dale Campbell. Wearing my new, and I thought, very stylish, beige, ankle-length, voluminous, cowl necked cape-style raincoat I'd recently purchased in Tokyo, I stepped from the taxi as a gust of wind whipped it up behind me. A very theatrical and appropriate entrance, I thought. It must have made an impression because Dale told me it stuck in his mind forever. He had just finished a contract at the Broadbeach Hotel on Queensland's Gold Coast in the show *Blondes Have More Fun*. Hearing through the good old grapevine we still needed one male dancer, he'd contacted Luis directly on a recommendation from a friend, so the timing was perfect. His excellent reputation in the business meant Luis accepted him sight-unseen, something which mutually, has never been regretted. To join the rest of the cast in Perth, and with money so tight, poor Dale had to travel from the Gold Coast to Perth by Greyhound bus. This journey by bus to the most isolated city in the world meant a four and a half thousand-kilometre, four-day trip, including crossing the huge, arid, near-featureless desert of the Nullarbor Plain.

Many of the cast of the first Korean show, including Dale, were to stay with us for years to come. Getting ready for this show was like nothing we'd ever experienced. Two weeks of rehearsal at the venue were provided for in the contract. These rehearsals took place in the huge purpose-built room below the dressing rooms, an exact replica of the stage. Such a luxury. Opening night there was only one night of dress rehearsal on stage with sets and props. An ice show from New York was performing every night of the week. The crew would rapidly dismantle their sets, take them out to the back lot, strip off anything useful – the lights for example – and burn everything else. Sad, but there was no place to store old sets. The same would happen when we left. Only after the stage was stripped, and our sets hurriedly installed, would they call us for rehearsal, probably around three a.m. We would rehearse all night, sleep through the next day and open that evening.

I always kept an eye on Luis, he and time had a rather shallow relationship. He'd work the dancers to death if I didn't intervene. Around six a.m, the dancers were visibly tiring, so I called a halt. I expected food and beverages would be laid on by management after such an intensely long rehearsal, but it seemed not. I questioned Mr Lee regarding this, and he said, 'No, we never supply a meal during rehearsal'. Hmm, that's not right. You want the best show on earth, then look after your artists. I called room service and ordered a full breakfast for forty people, twenty-two of us, eighteen management staff, our agent and crew. Shortly, a great train of room service trolleys arrived down the centre aisle of the auditorium, each trolley set up with breakfast for four, complete with silver service coffee and starched napkins. Many mouths dropped open from the Walker Hill staff, including management. They dropped even farther when I invited everybody, not only the dancers, to eat up. I admit, my mouth dropped as well when I got the bill—it was over six hundred US dollars. What price a lesson in class? If you want to change things in Asia, don't get upset and yell. Face is the name of the game. On the changeover of the next show, which was us again, break time was called, and we were invited to repair to the Greenroom where a buffet feast had been set up, compliments of management.

Opening night all too quickly arrived and we were as ready as we ever would be. I was far too agitated to dress up and go out front, so I stayed backstage in case of an emergency. No need to worry, the show went off as smoothly as could possibly be hoped for. Luis's amazing choreography, rehearsed to perfection with the help of our assistant choreographer Jillian, and the enormous sets twinkling with hundreds of thousands of lights, an orchestra playing over the taped music, and our tall, extraordinarily beautiful dancers giving their all. The extravagant over the top diamanté and rhinestone-encrusted costumes twinkled and sparkled. I was never before so overcome with pride and emotion. I will never forget any of those magnificent artists.

Walker Hill provided an opening night celebration buffet in the Greenroom, evening wear requested. It was a grand affair. The dancers went to a lot of bother and looked devine. A table was laden with carefully arranged, scrumptious food, and an enormous central ice sculpture. There were many congratulatory speeches from both sides, and many tears were shed as we dedicated the evening to our dear friend Peggy who'd died the week before we left for Seoul. All in all, what could be called a bloody good night.

Seoul is a great city. There was certainly a lot to do. Itaewon was very much an area where American service personnel shopped, you could find everything there from a can opener to leatherwork ateliers able to whip you up a jacket or a whole suit in a day. We all took advantage of that. Nightlife abounded and we even found a gay bar frequented by US servicemen and women. Then there was Dongdaemun, home to many multi-storied warehouse markets jammed packed with clothes, fluffy toys, shoes, and every brand name on earth. A huge variety of brand names were manufactured in Seoul then—you could buy $250 Nike shoes for $10. These were supposedly the real deal, and I believe they were. The factories would make way too many and flog them off locally, so the story went. In Numdaemun there were lots of little bars, a beautiful garden called the Hidden Garden, and the National Museum, where a lot of empty plinths bore signs reading: 'This was so-and-so, stolen by the Japanese'. No end of shopping at Lotte department store, and anywhere else you could point a stick. Fun times in Seoul.

Air raid warnings. Let's not forget the air raid drills. Nobody had mentioned anything about these regular occurrences. The first time I experienced one was on a bus downtown. Off went an incessant wailing, the bus stopped precisely where it was, along with all the other traffic. People exited orderly from all vehicles, and the surrounding streets, and completely disappeared. I was left sitting in the bus completely alone. Ten or fifteen minutes later, it all happened in reverse. The siren sounded followed by the unhurried return of absolutely everybody, and we continued as though nothing happened. Only later, when I got back to the hotel, and was talking to Mrs Wong, the pharmacy owner in the hotel shopping strip, did I learn about these drills. They had been going on for decades apparently, all in preparedness for a sudden attack by North Korea. A friendly heads-up to the poor foreigner might have been a nice gesture.

We were making very good money in Korea. We needed it to pay for the colossal expenses incurred in putting on the show. Whenever Luis and I were making good profits, we liked to give back to the community which gave us those profits. Mrs Wong mentioned she provided free pharmaceutical-line medication to a small private orphanage a little way out of town. She agreed to take us there one Saturday. A married couple ran this little private orphanage. The husband worked as an accountant and the wife, along with help from two local ladies, ran the orphanage. This was not a purpose-designed and built institution but, rather, a large private house in need of a great deal of work. There were twenty children living with this loving, caring couple, ranging in age from toddlers to sixteen. On reaching the age of sixteen, work and a place to stay was found for the child leaving, and it was a sad but necessary parting. The couple existed on this man's earnings and charity alone with no help from the government whatsoever. Things were tight money-wise, but the love which permeated every corner of the house was palpable.

The day we arrived we were introduced to all the children. One little girl who was almost blind from malnutrition, gripped Luis by the hand, and he lifted her to his shoulders. We visited every weekend, bringing much-needed food, and equipment, and this was the pattern of things. Out she would dash, and up onto Luis's shoulders. This little girl's brother was also there, both of them were recent arrivals. Their parents had died in a car crash. An uncle had received money from the estate to care for the children, but completely ignored them until they were taken in by this private orphanage, on the verge of starvation. Bastard.

We learned a very valuable lesson from these people. We might have given a lot but, believe me, we got an awful lot back. One Saturday, we bought a huge, semi-commercial refrigerator, loaded it onto the back of a hired van, and delivered it with such a feeling of pride. Pride very quickly turned to humiliation and embarrassment; we learned a massive lesson. 'Thank you so very much for this beautiful refrigerator,' said the couple, 'but, we have no food to put in it.' That was profound. An entirely Western way of thinking turned on its head in an instant. How thoughtless of us. Back went the fridge, and instead, the following week we arrived with twenty winter coats, twenty pairs of gumboots, twenty rain hats, twenty scarves and twenty pairs of warm gloves. Food, we also learned, was to be bought and consumed daily. A lot of kimchi, spicy fermented cabbage, a Korean staple, was made, and carried to school in twenty plastic lunch boxes along with twenty rice containers.

When it came time to leave Seoul, we visited for the last time. This was not going to be easy. What a surprise there was in store for us. A makeshift stage and tent had been erected in the garden, and all twenty children had rehearsed a song, a dance, a story, and communal singing as a goodbye concert for us. A great length of paper was produced, rolled up scroll-fashion. Inside were little drawings and well wishes in English, from everybody. As I write this, tears are falling onto my keyboard.

CHAPTER 25

BIG BIGGER BEST

Three months into our Walker Hill contract, we were approached by Kato San with an astonishing proposal. Management was thrilled, not only with our show, but also with the way we handled our artists, and the respect shown us by them in return. Many problems can arise from such a big production on such a long contract. These problems, dancers leaving, getting into bother some way or another, ill health etcetera, always end up in massive headaches for management. Nothing of the sort had happened with our show. Mr Lee was genuinely impressed and asked whether we would be prepared to make a new show, and carry on for another six months. Oh, boy, would we! This was the first time any show was ever offered a back-to-back contract. Firstly, we must ask our artists. No surprise that out of twenty-two people, only four or five cared to leave. Even these few were only leaving because of prior commitments.

So, it was on. Back to the drawing board. Another show to produce. This was to be 'The Grand Moreno Show', not our preference for a name but Walker Hill was insistent. The new show would consist of a circus opening, complete with fat lady (Dale) descending mid-showroom in a chandelier, trampolines, and dancers stretched out in huge chrome wheels rolling across the stage; The Bond number, a tribute to the Bond movies complete with the nightclub scene where the DJ box transformed into a smoke-spewing escape rocket, and a gigantic black and gold hand gun on which Melissa, our stunning leading lady, would perform in a seductive trio with two guys. For a finale, a Tropical routine with a Brazilian flavour. I experienced a great deal of trouble in convincing the set builders that fruit designed to be four and five metres in height was going to look perfectly okay. They simply couldn't understand fruit being bigger than people. This show was largely made from scratch, and I travelled home to Perth to do several things. Firstly, I collected what we had in the way of existing Bond costumes. I also bought a large house, reconnected with my parents and invited them to live there.

Yes, I had forgiven, but not forgotten the acts of this man, who called himself my father. After I'd left for Perth in 1969, he went bankrupt, and took the cloth, ending up with a Church, and parish in Geelong. When his tenure was over, the church, being oh so Godly, heaved him out on his arse. My parents had nowhere to live, so Luis and I installed them in the new house, bought them a Jaguar to cruise around in, and paid all their expenses. They settled in as house sitters and stayed on for four years until my father's death in 1990. It was important for me to show him the way obligations to your family should be carried out. I flew backwards and forwards from Spain when he was diagnosed with throat cancer. On the last occasion, the time of him meeting his maker, I held this man in my arms waiting, waiting, for just two words. The words I'd wanted to hear since I first laid eyes on him again in 1964. That small but incredibly important apology for the extraordinarily hard times he put me through as a child. I closed his sightless eyes without ever hearing 'I'm sorry'.

On my way back to Seoul, I treated myself to a short holiday in Bangkok, where I bought an entire bunch of super-green bananas for the dancers, and an appropriate backpack to carry them. Bananas might seem a strange gift to purchase, but for some unexplained reason, bananas were illegal in Korea. You could buy them on the black market at little felonious fruit stalls at the going rate of a dollar per half banana. I thought, get them green, they will ripen during the trip. At customs in Seoul, an official found them, and gave me a wink-wink, and stuck his hand out for a bribe. Done. At least the kids got their bananas. For a time, I did a great deal of business in Japan, and I was commuting daily. I'd take off early in the morning by Southwest Airlines amid the howling and screaming babies going to the US for adoption. This flight was dubbed the Nursery Express and was a very trying trip. I'd attend business meetings all day and fly back in time for the show. Very wearying, but the agents needed to be kept up to date with the progress of the new production as it neared completion. These days it could easily be accomplished with video conference calls.

One night in mid-winter, I was dropped off by taxi at the bottom of the hill leading to the Sheraton a hundred metres away. There was often so much snow, taxis without chains couldn't make it up to the lobby. I paid the driver and was about to navigate my way by the streetlight and the light from the hotel's main entrance when off went the bloody air raid siren. Blackout. The road wound up and around in a tight curve, I couldn't see a thing. I was knee-deep in snowdrifts, plodding through a wooded area when I remembered I had my miniature portable TV with me. I'd used it in Tokyo to show Kato San video of our progress. Switching it on, I made my stumbling way to the hotel by its light, accompanied by the raucous voice of Joan Rivers appearing on *The Tonight Show* with Johnny Carson. I would probably have ended up in the clink if I'd have been caught or have guided a full-scale attack to the Sheraton if the air raid had been the real deal.

Opening night approached, and this time, instead of expecting the dancers to perform two shows then rehearse all night for the opening the following night, management did something previously unheard of, they closed the showroom for a night. The following day they took the entire cast to a fun park, and mock-up rural village outside of Seoul, and we had a bang-up meal before our only night off in a year. Bliss. The Grand Moreno Show – I hated the name which translated to the hardly glamorous 'The Great Brown Show' – opened with as much success as the previous show. Another lavish opening-night party was thrown, and we settled in for another six months.

This second six months truly seemed to fly by. Summer came and management – realising the girls couldn't wear traditional swimsuits because they made tan lines – closed the small Executive pool to all staff and gave it over for the exclusive use by the cast of the show. We even had our own lifeguard. He was both delightfully friendly and delighted at having to watch over so many beautiful topless showgirls. I think he was extremely disappointed that they never needed his life-saving services.

The time approached all too rapidly when people whom you have worked so closely with must say goodbye to each other. I'm sure Charles Dickens won't mind me twisting his magnificent opening line from *A Tale of Two Cities*: 'It was the best of times; it was the best of times.' I want to say it twice because that's how good it was. I kid you not, I was literally picking up hysterically crying dancers from the grass verge, and carrying them onto the bus. I have never before or since worked on a show where we all became so close. Never during the entire year, was a cross word ever heard. No cliques were created (they wouldn't dare) and true and close friendships were formed, and extend to this day. Bless good old Facebook; I can still see the messages flying back and forth between the members of the cast thirty-five years later. Pictures of adult children, even grandchildren are accompanied by well wishes and messages of love. Luis and I might not have children of our own, but we have these people, and they are indeed our family.

We rarely worked in Australia. Australian venues simply could not afford to run shows of our quality. One exception to this was a tiny cabaret/restaurant in little old Perth. Vince Todaro, self-proclaimed, but dubiously mafia-connected Capo of cabaret entertainment, and owner of La Tenda, offered us a three-month contract. This diminutive, slightly comical, little Italian man with his flawed English and dyed comb-over, was head over heels crazy about show business, and the undisputed king in his field. He did, however, possess a reputation amongst suppliers, and tradespeople of being a little lax when paying his bills. To the entertainers of Australia, he was wonderful. Vince always managed to have top headliners appearing at his venue, and as long as you gave what was expected, he never once played the tough-guy card.

No biggie for me if he'd tried, I'd handled the Mano Nero venue operators in Europe for years.

Just what the doctor ordered as far as we were concerned. We needed to be in Perth to get our next show ready to tour, and being able to keep our dancers employed meant we could keep them for the new tour as well. The three-month contract unexpectedly turned into a year. When the current show had to leave for Europe, we made another one to replace it. Vince was thrilled with the show and took enormous pleasure in having these fabulously beautiful women gracing his stage. The place was packed every night, and he must have been making a profit, or he could not have kept us there that long. The patrons were definitely not coming for the food. His reputation as a tight arse was well deserved, but on the odd occasion when he hadn't paid us on time, a quick conference in his office, listening to his financial woes, was always followed by the expected cheque. A strange little man, full of inconsistencies. Adorable one moment, then threatening to cut the fingers off a bad reviewer the next. Dining out at a rival Italian restaurant, Corzinos, on one occasion the owner said there was 'Chicken Todaro' on the menu. On enquiring what it was, he said, 'The chef drives past and fires it through the window.'

Once, there was a rather well-endowed female singer-cum-exotic dancer working at La Tenda named, for obvious reasons, Alexander the Great 48. There was a falling out and this extraordinarily big busted lady decided to escape through the skinny, tall, arrow-slit windows in the dressing room next to Vince's office—very much a 'camel passing through the eye of a needle' act. We are talking ground floor by the way and she'd arranged for her manager to wait outside. Window opened, costume case out, makeup case out, left leg out, left arm out, left tit out and there the escapade came to an impasse. Poor Ms 48 was stuck tight. Vince had to call the Fire Department to take the window out, frame and all. The papers made a field day out of it. I certainly saw a different Vince on that occasion. Oh, such outrage and fury from such a tiny man. Australian entertainers such as Ricky May, Barry Crocker and my darling Maria Venuti constantly performed at La Tenda. After Ricky's untimely death, Vince organised a benefit to aid his wife and young family and some of the biggest stars in Australia travelled across the country to pitch in.

I add here a very strange aside regarding Australian men. This never happened in any other country. Often, and I'm talking quite often, I would pass through the lobby bar après show, and men would strike up a conversation regarding the performance, how much they enjoyed it, and how very beautiful the girls were. Invariably the conversation would get to that question. 'Are the girls 'real girls', or are they men?' This is a peculiarly Australian question. Why on earth would men think to themselves—*well, these girls are too beautiful to be real women, they must be men*?

CHAPTER 26

SEDUCED BY SINGAPORE

During the time at La Tenda, we were often approached by dancers requesting an audition. Luis was not the type to turn down any young dancer, having been through the whole audition process himself, so whenever it was at all possible, auditions would be held. Some talented, and not so talented, dancers were put through their paces, and some went on our books for consideration for future productions. Two teenage boys approached us to audition, they were incredibly keen, and both dancers were given a thorough work-out by Luis. He was especially impressed, not only by the level of proficiency, but the obvious natural gifts of the taller boy. He was good looking, a bit thin, killer smile, and a great connection with an audience which wasn't even present.

Luis upped the ante and pushed these kids even further, both not only ran with it, but the enjoyment, and the competitive spirit between them was absolutely thrilling to watch. Although the shorter boy was not tall enough to dance next to our showgirls, the taller boy was so obviously destined for good if not great things. So it was, that the fabulously talented Todd McKenney moved onwards, and upwards to the dizzying heights he achieved in so many fields of entertainment. He is now an Australian icon. I had the pleasure of working with Todd in several of his shows some years later, but although always pleasant and friendly, he didn't remember me. Why should he?

During the late '70s we were offered way more work than we could handle. Shows could be sent out by themselves, but I was never keen on the idea. I liked a mature person to accompany young dancers with a show. There was nobody we trusted enough until discovering our dear friend Ron Deschamps was back in Australia, touring with Warner Brothers' *Bugs Bunny Follies* as Sylvester. Luis caught up with Ron in Melbourne and asked him to take on managing a tour of Japan for six months. Pitching the idea to him proved beneficial to us all, and so Ron was the first of a string of show managers to take out second, and on occasion third shows for us.

Ron was discovered in the YMCA. At least on that occasion, he was discovered dancing. In 1958, a young Ron volunteered his involvement with the Perth YMCA Ball and was learning, of all things, the Can Can. Nothing like starting out your career dancing one of the most difficult of routines. He must have shown promise, because the Ballet Mistress of the West Australian Ballet Company singled him out, suggesting he should start taking professional lessons. She introduced him to Madame Bousloff, who as you might remember, was the Founder and Artistic Director of the Company. Kira, who was Russian/French, was amused at the similarity of Ron's Swiss/French name, Ron Deschamps, meaning Ron of the Fields, and the ballet term Ronde de jambe, a round movement of the leg. This coincidence has tickled the fancy of any, and all of Ron's fellow dancers, and ballet chums, and has become something of a legend.

I still occasionally do a little work with the Australian Ballet Company and not long ago I heard one of the students talking in the dressing room. He was telling one of the other dancers his lecturer told them a story about a well-known male dancer whose name was Ron Deschamps, and he'd thought, 'What a load of crap, nobody could possibly believe a dancer would call himself that'. I took great delight in telling him, not only was it true but, Ron just happened to be sitting out front that very evening.

Ron did particularly well with his classes and impressed Kira so much, after only one year she invited him to perform with the Company. This is extraordinary, as any classical dancer will tell you. Starting training at eighteen (Ron was born on Australia Day 1940), bending twisting, and moulding an adult body to conform to the rigours of classical ballet is a process usually undertaken by boys aged eight to ten or barely into their teens. Ron continued to take classes whenever possible. Money was tight, so he was forced to take a precious year off and go to work with his father way up the West Australian coast on desolate Dirk Hartog Island off Shark Bay. Ron worked as a plumber's labourer and sheep musterer, throwing in a spot of crayfish fishing and fruit picking as well before heading back to Perth for more classes and some performances with the Company. Deciding in 1961 to continue his ballet training seriously, Ron hopped a bus for the three-day overland journey to Melbourne, where his classes were interspersed with tram conducting, and more fruit picking to pay the never-ending bills. His tenacity, and hard work paid off with invitations to work with the Elizabethan Opera, and a couple of musicals: *Finian's Rainbow* and *High Spirits*. Ron's classical work over the following five years included contracts with New Zealand Ballet, Queensland Ballet and the Scottish Ballet. He often branched out into commercial theatre working in London's West End as well. Ron went back and forth to Australia during this time working again with the WA Ballet Company, partnering such great Royal Ballet Ballerinas as Robin Haig and Elaine Fifield.

Our initial six-month deal with him ended up lasting seven years when he either toured with us or danced in, and managed other shows of ours. Altogether I think he racked up time in over fifteen countries. Sadly, we lost Ron's services when he bought his own company and did it all over again for the next three years. He is now retired and lives in country Victoria.

Having Ron with us meant we could split the company—I took one show to Singapore, and Ron took the other to Japan. When Luis and I first entered Singapore on the 'old Turkey' it was a thrilling and exotic country, unlike today. Now it has endless concrete, steel and glass canyons, and a monotonous vanilla personality. Today, most of the charm of Singapore has disappeared. Change Alley, where it was fun to be crushed in the crowd, bargaining for things you certainly neither wanted nor needed, is gone. The family-owned shop-houses on Orchard Road where you could make yourself incredibly ill on a monstrous, towering, heart attack-inducing sundae called a Knickerbocker Glory, gone. The old original China Town with its street of green shuttered apartments for old maids (i.e., any woman over thirty), gone. Sago Lane, the street of the dead where coffins, and the paper cars, houses, and other offerings to be burnt, and the shops selling joss money, gone. The old CK Tang Department store on Orchard Road was the most delightful place to spend an afternoon. The building itself had a certain Chinese flavour, and the goods for sale certainly did, also gone.

Some taxis had meters back then, but they were rarely turned on, or were left on from several fares ago. It was a case of state your destination, and haggle over the price before the trip. If you didn't, the fare at the other end might almost be more than the taxi was worth. That's gone too, but maybe it's a good thing. Sentosa Island with its quiet, secluded beaches and tropical charm, where we could sunbathe in g-strings and the girls could be topless, was once difficult to get to—and on weekdays almost deserted. Now it's a garish, plastic fun park with buses, golf carts and crowds 24/7. There is a four-lane bridge from the mainland, and a multi-storey state-of-the-art casino. Of course, this negative change is all from an outsider's viewpoint. I'm sure the Singaporeans revel in their sparkling new city with its mass rapid transit trains, and the very latest technology. But even they must miss the soul of the place sometimes.

From 1970, the Singapore government officially discouraged long hair wearing on males. In the late 60s, long hair, bell-bottoms, and psychedelic shirts were primarily associated with the hippie culture of the West. Students might be detained, and civil servants refusing to cut their hair were sacked. Groups of long-haired men were routinely rounded up and questioned by the police. Pop groups, including Japanese musician Kitaro, and British rock band Led Zeppelin, were barred from entering Singapore. Luis and I both had longish hair in those days, and we knew the authorities could either turn us away or lead us to the airport barber who would promptly give a ragged short back 'n sides, with a few lacerations to boot. So, with the help of a few tight curlers the night before, and the tucking of wayward strands under a cap we passed scrutiny, and officially entered the country.

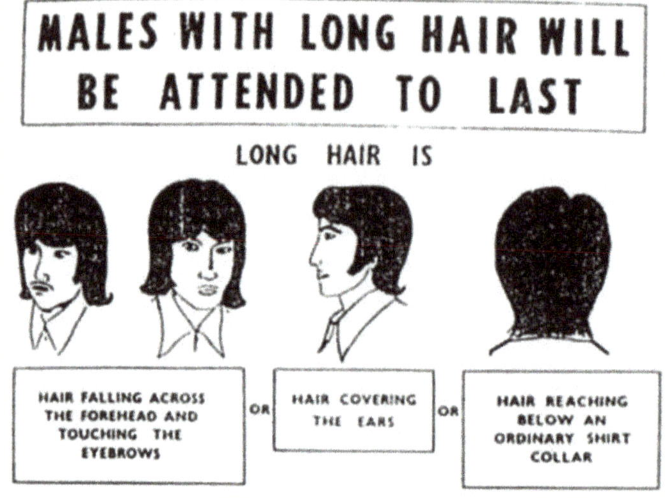

Photo credit: National Archives of Singapore

Excursions to Arab Street, Peoples Park, and China Town led to the most delicious fabric shops where laces, trims and feathers were plentiful, and cheap. A show producer's paradise. On later visits, we found a little cobbler near the infamous Bugis Street who rented a cubbyhole in a rundown temple. He handcrafted our show shoes and boots for years to come. This amazing man worked in the softest leathers and made such strong, hard-wearing shoes at a quarter of the cost of new off-the-shelf dance shoes. What a treasure of a find he was, and what a delightful person. He lived in the back of his minute workspace with his wife, and two children, and became a dear friend indeed.

Bugis Street in the early '70s was one of the great tourist attractions of Singapore along with duty-free shopping, a deciding factor in tourists choosing to visit Singapore – not that the Government would ever admit it. Made famous by the armed forces on R&R during the Vietnam War, this busy, grubby little daytime street by night turned into an open-air market and eating mall, with alfresco bars and cabaret shows. Bugis Street and its tiny offshoot lanes, featured for sale anything and everything the human mind, in all its deviousness, might be inclined to desire. Rickety street food tables surrounded by even more unstable stools were dotted amongst stalls and stands of cheap costume jewellery, souvenirs, fruit, table linen and endless bars.

The drag queens and trannies, strolling, or pushing, amongst all this brouhaha were the whole reason for the crowds. While some gorgeous numbers were flaunting their wares, others of the more tragic variety were not scarce either. Every so often these ladies of the night would stage impromptu shows on the roofs of the shop verandas, and the notorious, dingy public toilets fronting the street. Bugis Street was a free-for-all, and the more attractive girls did quite well. The deed could be done in any number of places, ranging from small, rented rooms, to an entire lane of specialised shacks only a block away, to the toilets themselves for the more desperate, or if one's pocket didn't reach to the former. All this has sadly gone now. Bugis Street is a rather upscale shopping mall with as much charm and character as…a shopping mall.

Our many subsequent visits to Singapore were for month-long, twice-nightly performances at the Tropicana Theatre Restaurant on Scotts Road. This venue was a first for Singapore and was the brainchild of Mr SC Shaw. SC, as we always called him, was an amazing entrepreneur. Although not from the famous Shaw family of Hong Kong, he did come from the same province in China. He'd made a financial killing in buying and selling building materials after WWII and saw the need for a Western-style entertainment complex to be built in Singapore. The ground, or first floor of the Tropicana was called the Treetops Bar, and the top floor of the four-storey building was fitted out as offices. The main dining room, where the shows were staged was a two-storey affair with the main dining room on the second floor and VIP seating in a mezzanine area directly opposite the stage.

Sightlines to the stage for the patrons had been meticulously worked out. The dance floor was close to eight metres long and was elevated during show time to become the stage. There was a central mechanical revolve, and the backdrop could be wound up electronically to reveal the different designs. This backdrop was a catastrophe if dancers were too close when it was rolling up, and many a disaster was averted by quick thinking, and clever little non-choreographed manoeuvres.

The bands rarely contained less than a dozen members and were recruited from all over the world. Tropicana very quickly became the place to be, and the place to be seen. Big names often performed there, and the roll call was impressive: Duke Ellington, Frank Sinatra, Lulu, Johnny Mathis, Pat Boone, Paco de Lucio, Count Basie, and many, many, other top names were contracted anywhere from two weeks to a month. The food was also a huge attraction, their famed dim sum was made very early in the morning and flown to Hong Kong and Taiwan for lunch that day. If I had an early start, on entering from the side lane kitchen entrance, I often stepped over dozens of uniformed schoolgirls seated on old milk crates wrapping the various dumplings on a board in front of them.

SC always treated his artists exceptionally well, and over the years we became great friends. He sometimes called me early in the morning after a show that had ended at midnight, 'Are you awake? Let's go shopping'. Off we'd go, on what SC called a 'typical day's shopping', during which he might buy two Mercedes Benz cars and a stretch limo. I brought my parents to Singapore for a holiday in the early '80s, and SC simply could not do enough for them, with box seats on the mezzanine each night and chauffeur-driven sightseeing trips during the day. Working at Tropicana meant you were the flavour of the month as far as the wealthy local socialites were concerned. Rarely a night would pass without one of our regular escorts waiting to whip us away to the latest disco, members-only lounge, the ever-so-slightly-illegal Pebbles gay bar or to some seedy, but excessively expensive joint. Of course, with our bevvy of tall, jet-setting showgirls to be wooed, the guys got a free ride.

As all things must, Tropicana had its beginning, a fabulous middle, and a declining end. The era was over and, although Tropicana was still making profits, it was time to go. Tropicana closed its doors in 1989 and was sold for seventy million dollars. What stands there now? What else but another shopping centre.

CHAPTER 27

THE LAND OF SMILES

After Singapore, our next port of call was often Bangkok. In the early days we always flew with Air Siam, an obscure airline owned by the Thai royal family, which operated from 1971 to 1975, and as far as I know, owned only a single aircraft. This seemed a relatively safe mode of transport because you would imagine if there was only one aircraft, it would be pretty well maintained. We never took off on time, a lot of tinkering was always going on. Quite often we would be requested to 'disembark through the forward door', and 'enjoy a light lunch in the airport lounge', while running repairs were carried out. Then on to Thailand, the country I fell most in love with, a love affair lasting to this day.

My first visit to Thailand in the early '70s was on an overnight stopover from Madrid to Perth. I arrived late afternoon and was shunted off to the White Rose Hotel. A smallish hotel with beautiful grounds, and a long, unpaved driveway planted with roses either side. I looked for this hotel many years later, and discovered it was now the Bangkok Art and Cultural Centre. Obviously, such lavish grounds in the centre of town were very valuable, far too valuable for such a modest hotel. I was excited to be spending even one night in such an exotic place as Bangkok, and I took off for the streets outside just minutes after checking in. I wasn't disappointed that evening nearly fifty years ago, and I have not been disappointed on my many, many, visits since. As a child, I'd read a book called The Purple Pagoda, that stuck in my mind. A childish, kiddie-winkie book, but the descriptions of whatever Asian country it was set in stayed with me, and those images connected with the sights and smells of Bangkok then, and still do. Thailand has its own fragrance. You can smell it on arrival at the airport. It's the smell of ripe tropical fruit mixed with rotting vegetation, and the cloying, heady, perfume of flowers. Granted, it struggles a bit in downtown Bangkok these days, but it is underlying, and persistent. No other country I have visited has this unique, evocative aroma.

That first evening, the streets seemed to have more people per square metre than I had ever seen. People, cars, tuk-tuks belching blue-grey smoke, noise, noise, noise. I loved it. First, I turned left, and walked over the Phanta Bridge of Saen Saep Khlong with its four concrete guardian elephant heads. Most of Bangkok's inner-city khlongs (canals) were still there then, and still used to ferry people and goods all over the city. The Venice of the East. It seemed so other-worldly, looking down from the bridge into the long, thin, colourful boats with their noisy, smoky outboard engines. This particular Khlong is one of the only remaining waterways in the city today, all the others having been covered over with roads. They are still there though, under the streets and footpaths. For years, a decent cloudburst would see these underground streams flood up into the city streets in less than an hour. People with their skirts and trousers hitched up, their shoes in their hands, would splash through the teeming water along with the swimming rats that had been flushed out. The drainage systems are improved now, and this no longer happens. As annoying and inconvenient as it was, it was very much a part of the character of the city. Over the forty years I visited Thailand, some visits were work with our shows, some just plain fun, and others for heart-breaking work with the desperately poor.

The Galaxy Theatre Restaurant was possibly Bangkok's most prestigious venue back in the '70s and '80s. Seating at least two hundred diners, there was a vast glassed-in mezzanine section of private rooms overlooking the stage. The royal family had a permanent reservation in the centre room, and the décor was fittingly lavish. We were performing there for a month. Two shows in the evenings, each show broken up with attractions and singers. The stage was monstrous, it had outstanding artists' facilities, and it was an easy, and very pleasant contract. There was one slight hitch. During the 1970s' the Vietnam War, coup d'états and seemingly endless political unrest, often put Bangkok under curfew when nobody could be on the streets between midnight and five am. The current curfew meant, should the show run overtime, which it often did, we would not be able to change, remove makeup, and be out before curfew. Not even to run across the road to our hotel. Consequently, on many nights we were stuck in the venue, or perhaps in a club or bar. It was not such a big a deal as the entire staff were in the same boat. The venue was a vast place, and altogether I suppose, there was a hundred employees, plus us. Management at the Galaxy was always very kind, we worked there on many occasions, food was laid on, and there was dancing to the resident band, who were happy to while away the hours playing for us.

On a few occasions, the band was joined by an exceptional trumpet player who would jam with them till the wee hours. The trumpet player was always treated with great deference, invariably out front and with a great deal of space around him, almost like an invisible buffer zone. It wasn't until near the end of the contract our agent told me, strictly entre nous, this gentleman was none other than His Most Royal Majesty King Bhumibol Adulyadej, the King of Thailand. Also known as Rama IX, the ninth Monarch of the Chakri Dynasty. The King was considered one of the best trumpet players in Thailand and the band leader was his maestro. There was undoubtedly a great deal of covert security around, but everyone just got on with whatever they were doing. I got to know His Royal Majesty, and his beautiful wife Her Royal Highness Queen Sirikit in later years when we were the official entertainment at some of his birthday celebrations.

Our first invitation to perform at the King's birthday event was a huge feather in our caps. After that, all doors were open, we could pretty much choose where and when we would perform. The first time, however, was a nerve-wracking event at the Dusit Thani Hotel when absolutely nothing went right. It was flood season, and we arrived late on a Friday, ready to perform on the following Sunday. Because our flight was late, customs refused to release our trunks, telling me to 'come back Monday'. No point telling them we were there to perform for His Royal Majesty; they simply wouldn't have believed me. The hotel was at panic stations, they contacted a royal aide who tried to get the airport unaccompanied baggage section opened, but he was seemingly not of high enough rank, and the airport remained closed. The King was up country with his senior aides, doing what he'd always done in times of flood. Talking to and reassuring the populace, even getting onto the back of a truck heaving out sandbags. I have witnessed him doing this, as preposterous as it may sound.

Right, nothing for it but to get to where the King was, and have some sort of document signed to allow us entry to the airport. Easier said than done. When Thailand floods, it really floods. A four-wheel-drive vehicle was found, and a young hotel representative, the driver, and I set out for the flood area in the north. The going was rough, with constant rain the entire trip. For years I had a newspaper photo of this young aide, and myself sitting on the roof of the truck, while elephants with chains on either side of the road pulled us through the floodwaters. The royal work party was finally in sight; I could plainly see His Royal Majesty in his shirt sleeves on the back of a massive flatbed truck doing what everybody else in the party was doing, working at damming the flood. My young aide introduced me to another aide who introduced me to yet another, and slowly but surely, we worked our way up the chain of command to someone who possessed the power to open Don Mueang, the old airport.

The all-important document in hand, we turned around, and made the return journey with all possible haste. By the time I got back, it was Sunday morning, the morning of the show. Some hotel management accompanied me and we took off for the airport at sparrow's fart. The entire baggage section was opened, I was waved in with a take whatever you like attitude. Trunks retrieved, we were back at Dusit in plenty of time for rehearsal, but it was a near thing.

We performed all over Bangkok at different official birthday venues that particular year. They start to meld into each other after so much time, and so many occasions performing the same show. One performance was at the racetrack of all places. This time I knew Their Majesties were there because I could see them. We were to perform in front of the Royal Box on a beautifully decorated portable stage out on the field, with a large tent erected behind as dressing room. Flowers and champagne were distributed for everybody, and we made our way back to the Dusit. Getting out of the bus clutching both flowers and champers was tricky. One of the girls, Faye, caught her heel in a wayward piece of aluminium and came crashing down onto the footpath face first. A girl after my own heart, the poor darling lay semi-conscious, half in, half out of the minibus, with the hand holding the magnum stuck safely straight up in the air.

CHAPTER 28

LOOKING DEEPER

Bangkok back then was not quite as seedy as it later became. Sure Thanon Patpong 1, or plain old Patpong, existed, but it was just a street with a few girly bars. There was none of the hassling and hustling, no night markets full of fake Rolexes. Bangkok's best English-language book shop was on the corner of Soi Patpong 2 and Thanon Patpong 1. One of the few supermarkets in Bangkok selling Western produce could be found on Thanon Patpong 2, opposite Soi Patpong 2. We once lived in an apartment on the first floor in Thanon Patpong 2, and it was relatively quiet.

Harry's Bar on Soi 2, which shared a common wall with Ciros Bar, was a favourite gay haunt for the entire cast. When the licence time for Harry's was up at one am, we all herded through the connecting door to Ciros, whose licence time was just beginning. Stuck there during curfew, we would party away through the small hours, and make our way home in full daylight. Ransang owned both bars; this way, he was able to stay open for longer hours. Vichai owned the bar upstairs, dubbed the Chicken Bar because it tended to have much younger guys, too young probably. Ransang and Vichai between them owned almost the entire tiny lane. Later, in the late '80s, it became a big nightclub area with DJ Station opposite where Harry's used to be. Ransang became a good, close friend over the many years, and Luis and I often ate in his small but beautiful apartment above the shop. He was an avid collector of Thai antiques; the entire house was full of unquestionable good taste. Ransang was the spitting image of actor Charles Bronson. So much so, he doubled for him in most of Bronson's movies, a nice little side business allowing him to buy even more antiques.

A few blocks down Silom Road on Soi 4 stood the then famous Rome Club, the Club 54 of Bangkok. A ground floor plus three huge mezzanine floors, Rome Club was mostly up market gay plus local Bangkok A listers. For Luis and me, our names were always on the door, and the mooching to be your plus one was heaven. The drag shows were the best in town, and the comedy routines, although completely mystifying to non-Thai speakers, brought the local guys to their knees in fits of laughter. Luis, being Spanish, was friendly with Manuel the Spanish co-owner. We made a few routines for their talented drag queens, and they were a fun, appreciative lot. In the '80s a fire gutted the place, and with probably rightful blame placed squarely on the drag queen's careless attitude to smoking in the dressing room. Bitterness saw the club reopened as a straight venue.

Some weekends, we would go to Pattaya for a swim or hire a small boat to take us to the nearby islands. Consisting mainly of small fishing villages, Ko Phan or Ko Lan were not tourist destinations then. Pattaya too, was not the rowdy meat market it is today. It was becoming significant to the tourists because of both its proximity to Bangkok and its reasonably clean beaches. There was no gay beach or Boys town, and it was just a nice place to get away from the city. There were a few big hotels, Royal Cliff probably being the best. At the foot of Royal Cliff was a small, typical Thai village with oiled teak houses and small gardens. Roger and Milo, two of my very dear friends lived there. These two American guys had been lovers for twenty years when I met them in Paris in the early '70s. They worked in the Lido and Moulin Rouge as sight acts or attractions, and presented the funniest magic act I have ever seen. When not working, they preferred to stay in their small house in Pattaya. They made a deal with the Royal Cliff Hotel whereby they would do the occasional show in exchange for eating in the restaurants gratis whenever they, and their guests chose. They were still there well into their eighties before deciding it was time to move back to the USA to be nearer medical help as they got older. Sadly, both have since passed away. Good, kind, sweet friends. I miss them dearly.

One morning while staying at Roger and Milo's, I decided to walk along the beach, passing under Royal Cliff, and on towards the small fishing village of Jomtien. A bit of a hike, and when it got way too hot, I found an upturned fishing boat, crawled under it, and slept. I awoke when the owner tipped his boat over to use it, giving both of us a bit of a shock. This man seemed friendly and totally unconcerned I was there. He invited me to eat with his little family on the beach. That was the start of a great friendship between us, and I was to observe over the years that deserted strip of coast turn into one of the busiest pieces of beach I've seen in the world. As the tourists started to discover this little beach gem, the family jumped at the opportunity to start a beach chair and umbrella service. Over the years, I watched them put their children through university with their constant hard work, and they expanded their holding to several umbrellas, and fifty or so deck chairs.

Sadly, the wife of my friend was hit and killed by a drunk driver twenty years ago, and the last time I went back, maybe ten years ago, the entire family had moved away. The beach now is a never-ending diorama of slowly roasting falangs (foreigners). The hundreds, no thousands, of deck chairs lined up in rows, shoulder to shoulder, facing the water like theatregoers waiting for some tremendous aquatic spectacular, go all the way down to the waterline. The farmland behind the beach is now chockers with high rise condos. Not somewhere I care to go back to.

During my many visits to Thailand, I worked with several small organisations which try to improve the lot of the urban poor. The people I was involved with were not part of the big international aid organisations but alternative, small private groups of well-meaning and caring professionals. They willingly gave up their precious vacation time to teach the very poor to husband their small incomes, and learn about nutrition and sanitation on little or no budget. I know everyone who has been to Thailand has seen the poor begging in the streets. Many tourists regard these people as part of the scenery, like some sort of Disney theme park, but rarely does anybody see the desperate people who live in the slums lining railway tracks, khlongs and the Chao Phraya River running through the city.

There is a section of slums along the Chao Phraya River called Yannawa. It is less than a kilometre from the famed Oriental Hotel, once considered to be the most expensive, and most famous hotel in the world. An impressive list of wealthy and extraordinarily wealthy people has stayed there, but I dare say that not one of them saw the utter poverty and misery of the many thousands of people who live those few hundred metres to the south. Entire families living in one or two-room shacks. Some of the shanty style dwellings actually hang out over the heavily polluted river on stilts, with all manner of foul, stinking garbage clinging to the banks or lazily floating by. It was not rare to glimpse a tiny human corpse.

The groups I worked with insisted volunteers live, eat, and work in the community. Each of us were assigned a family to live with. The 'family' I shared with lived in the top section of two Ford packing crates, that had been placed one on top of the other. Families were more than happy to share what little they had, and perhaps that is the most outstanding aspect of these people. The poor will give you whatever they have. Strange, because theft is rampant. It is said of the Thais, they are the friendliest, most smiling thieves on the planet. Sharing living arrangements with these families was an eye-opener. Sharing is the keyword. Nothing belongs to any one person. Everything belongs to everyone.

After my time ended there on that occasion, it was more than a year before I returned—only to find a huge swathe of the slums gone. In their place were brand new two- and three-story luxury homes with waterfront views. The law in Thailand was, and maybe still is, if a squatter remained on the same piece of property for five straight years, the property became lawfully theirs. Property owners felt obliged to move people on before their five years were up, and the moving on was accomplished in several ways. They could request that you move—not going to happen. Or they could post a public notice stating the site was to be bulldozed on such and such a day, regardless of who or what was still there. This latter method was used most often, or failing that, and the cheapest option, they would hire thugs to set a fire raging through the area, move if you could, burn if you couldn't. I was confronted with the effects of a burnout which had occurred several months before. I enquired where I might find my little family and a few friends. I was sent here and there with no luck until someone suggested I might find the daughter of the family I lived with, begging on a nearby street. I went in search and found her. To my horror, she was living on the street, sitting on a mat in filthy rags, a baby in her lap, and holding up pleading hands welded together by horrific, untended burns. The rest of the family had perished. I did all I could to help this poor girl, then through tears, I turned my back, and walked away. Cowardly, yes, but I felt totally defeated by man's callousness and greed. I have never gone back to that district. I understand it is now the playground of affluent urban Thais and not a trace of old Yannawa remains.

I will always remember Thailand as work, fun and heartbreak. The Thai people are still very dear to me, and Thailand is the only Asian country where I would care to live. In reality, however, I can't face knowing that beyond the beauty lies such utter inhumanity.

CHAPTER 29

22 SHOWS PER WEEK AND RATS

It's important that you don't try to follow this book chronologically. You might do yourself a mental mischief. Here I've condensed at least four trips to Taiwan, which in the '70s was not a dream destination. Quite the opposite. There are some places with which you have an immediate rapport, a kinship, a feeling deep inside, this is going to be good. Nothing but nothing like that happened with Taiwan. On the first trip, the dancers and I arrived in the early evening at Taipei's Taoyuan International Airport from Hong Kong via China Airlines. At the Arrivals Hall, we were met by the agent, a very charming and very attractive Debby Park. Mister Debby Park by the way. Debby promptly propelled us to another gate to board a domestic flight to Tainan in the south. This destination name, at the time, meant nothing to me. If only it had stayed that way.

When we disembarked in Tainan, the tone of things to come was immediately apparent. Tainan soon came to be associated with everything about a city that is filthy, disgusting, most definitely, and hopefully, forgettable. We were bundled into taxis with our suitcases hanging precariously out of the boot, and entered what I can only describe as a modern-day version of the chariot race from Ben Hur. I have never witnessed such driving. I was going to say everyone displayed a lack of driving skills but, on reflection, the skill level must have been remarkable indeed to negotiate the incredibly confusing tangle of traffic. The throng of cars in various stages of decay and a predominance of motorcycles of every description, large and small, new and old, all spewing out their own distinctive clouds of blue-grey, choking smoke.

On take-off from a green light, the air, quite suddenly, became so dense I was amazed anyone could see to drive. One sight about to become totally familiar, was that of entire families on one motorcycle. Dad driving, Mum on the back, side-saddle, of course, to preserve modesty, kid behind Mum, clinging on for dear life, and another standing between Dad's legs. Sometimes a baby on Mum's knees would be added to the mix, or perhaps the weekly shopping hanging off every protuberance. There seemed to be no road rules whatsoever, definitely a survival-of-the-fittest-or-nimblest scenario. Opposing lanes of traffic appeared to head straight for each other, dodge, weave, twist, turn and out the other side. Pedestrians played a type of Russian roulette in making their way from one side of a street to another. Not for the faint of heart.

The hotel, once we gratefully arrived, was modest, comfortable and staffed by the laziest, surliest, most unhelpful people I have ever dealt with. There was a station on each floor for a room boy to fetch drinking water (water needing to be boiled and cooled for drinking). I never once saw them awake. They were always sprawled out over the station counter sound asleep. The front desk staff were completely and utterly uninterested and disinterested, both at the same time. We were picked up the following morning to inspect the venue, the streets were hazy with vehicle fumes, and the art of dodging a great gobbet of spit was learned very quickly. A warning was heard when the spitter performed a thorough, loud, sinus-clearing drawback before launching the offending phlegmy globule. No aim being considered by these spitters, other than the aim of getting rid of it. Dancers are an agile lot, so there weren't too many hits before this little piece of choreography became familiar.

The venue was on the fifth floor of a rather down-at-heel building. Most buildings looked a little care-worn. I dare say a bit of a scrub-up would have made a world of difference, but I truly don't think aesthetics were on anyone's radar. Outside of the lift to the fifth floor there was a distinct odour of stale urine, the reason became clear all too quickly. Each floor had a doorless public toilet adjacent to the lift, the stench when the lift doors opened was overpowering. I've found this in most Asian countries. Urinating is a bit of a hit and miss affair, and nobody seems to be aware of the smell. Flushing seems to be something people can't get their heads around. The venue, a Music Hall is what I think it was called, consisted of rows and rows of rather shabby theatre seats, and a stage bereft of decor. Luis and I always had a thing about clean dressing rooms. Our usual procedure is to pre-inspect before the dancers get there, and to clean where necessary. Toilets get a good going-over, and a liberal dose of room deodoriser is applied all round. The rule is, enter dressing rooms which are spotless, and leave them in the same state for the following artists. These dressing rooms were grubby to say the least, so the first thing on our list was to give them a good cleaning. The taps over chipped and stained basins produced a transparent liquid, which we presumed to be a form of H2O, and dried and cracked remnants of yellowed soap were prised from their resting places.

Now to rehearse and unpack. Fine. Where are the show trunks? Oh, dear. Mr Park seems to have left them behind at the Taiwan airport. Sorry, Mr Manager, but we can't perform tonight because we have nothing to wear. A hasty, and what seemed very heated exchange took place between agent and manager. The Chinese always sound angry with each other. The conversation was translated and relayed to me. The contract start date was today, and there would be a show or we'd be cancelled. Okay, we can do that. We performed that night in a variety of our personal street clothes. There, you've seen your show.

Unpacking the newly arrived trunks the following afternoon, it was noticeable the one-and-a-half-metre gap between the stage and the first row of seats was now filled with another two rows of assorted dining chairs. Some impatient and slavering patrons, already seated and leaning on the stage with both arms, were set up for the view of their lives. Sorry, guys, that's not gonna happen. Me to agent, agent to management: 'Get those seats out of there right now or no show.' Management hurled a few furious hisses back. Agent to me: 'So sorry, Mr Thomas, but management says no show, no pay, and tear contract up now.' Oh, Mr Park, I've been in this game long enough to have the odd trick up my sleeve. 'Okay. All good. We will go and prepare.'

The show did go on in the afternoon to my instructions: 'Treat the back of the stage as the front, do the show with your backs to the audience.' Nobody could argue that the show didn't go on. That night, the extra seats were gone, and it was pretty much plain sailing from then on.

Taiwan, apart from the filth and mess, was a tough gig anyway. All contracts were three shows per day, admittedly only one hour duration, and four on Sunday making it twenty-two shows per week. Which meant, applying makeup around two pm, and removing it around midnight. Seven days per week of this treatment, and even the hardiest skin starts to react. Shows were broken up into three or four-number segments with ultra-glamorous Chinese singers and international attractions slotted in between and run approximately two hours apart. Still, there was not a lot of free time after tidying up and getting back to the hotel. We wore sunglasses during the day to save re-applying makeup. The girls felt they looked a bit tartish in full slap and lashes; the boys just felt fabulous.

People often said to me, 'Oh, Taiwan. How wonderful. Did you go here, see this, do that?' The answer is generally no. Firstly, there was not a great deal of time between shows. Apart from having to eat, playing tourist in full theatre slap in broad daylight is uncomfortable, and especially for the guys, largely inadvisable. Contracts per venue ran from one to two weeks, pack the costumes after the fourth show Sunday, and a bus would take us the several hours to the next city. If you couldn't sleep on the bus, then your day was pretty much ruined. After arriving at the new destination, there was little time to unpack personal gear, unpack the costumes, have a quick rehearsal, and go straight into the first show. Sounds such a glamorous life with all the travel, but believe me, even though we were all much younger, it certainly was quite tough.

I am an animal lover. I generally prefer the company of animals to humans, and my cats have all lived beyond twenty years. However, I draw the line at rats. I can take the odd rat here and there. In Bangkok's rainy season, for instance, you must cope, but here was different. I had never before, or since seen so many rats congregated in one place at one time. The garbage collection pattern in Tainan consisted of rubbish from all houses, shops, restaurants, whatever, being brought to the nearest intersection, and dumped smack in the middle. This mountain of garbage then became a central clearing point for some council truck. The height reached by this method was phenomenal, well over my head at times. Around the perimeter, in friendly alliance, were the fattest cats and rats in the world: cat, rat, cat, rat all the way, not a half metre between them. I quite forgot the atrocious smell in my fascination of this nightly ritual.

After Tainan, we travelled to, in no particular order, Kaohsiung, Taichung and Taipei. Kaohsiung was a tad cleaner, but getting to the theatre meant crossing the Love River (Ai River)—an incredibly misnamed foul stream, a stinkingly, polluted, barely flowing runnel. At least it was a proper theatre, wings, crossover, proscenium, the lot. During a performance in this theatre, there was an Anthea moment. I was to do a small duet with her, however on this occasion, I made my stage entrance expecting to see Anthea emerging from the wings on the other side. Not today. Anthea never appeared, so I proceeded to make up and improvise my own little routine, trying not to look the complete fool. A huge ask for somebody as poor a dancer as I was. Dancer? Even mover was a stretch, I was propelled by fear of ridicule mostly. During one little turn, I noticed Anthea peeking out from behind the blacks in the wings offstage. After my little impromptu solo was completed, Anthea said to me, 'Oh, that's lovely Tom. I've never seen it before.' I answered, with as much restraint as possible, 'No, dear, because you're in it.'

The city of Taichung was worlds removed from the other two, and quite a lovely place where people appeared much friendlier. There was a patron at Taichung Music Hall with a permanent booking for every show whenever we were in town, retired physician Doctor Lee. He clapped loudly out of time throughout each number. His habit was to come backstage after each performance to present the entire cast with cake, boxes of expensive fruit or, on one occasion, gold rings. A section of Taichung, not far from the venue was full of shirtless and weather-beaten old men working on the pavement in front of their shops. These chaps turned out the most exquisitely carved wooden furniture. We ordered a double-doored and heavily carved bar from one of them. I took great pleasure in watching this piece take shape on my daily visits. It still has in pride of place in my tiny home in Campbells Creek.

Lastly, there was Taipei, which was not as dirty or chaotic, but still the rat problem persisted. I'd lie in bed listening to rat races in the ceiling. On one occasion after the show, sitting on the edge of the stage waiting for Luis, I thought I saw the pattern of the carpet on the restaurant floor moving. I grabbed a work light, and what a sight. Wall to wall rats. Obviously, the cleaning was left until the following day, and the rats enjoyed a nightly feast of scraps. In the same venue, a small rat dropped out of a topless model's voluminous waist length wig onto her shoulder during a performance. It must have been sleeping in there. Not a very seductive sight, a topless showgirl in full and frenzied flight off stage.

Peculiarly, there were police previews to go through in Taipei, but not in other cities. Ten or so police arrived in uniform plus the management, and we would present the show. The police possessed full power to make cuts wherever they thought reasonable. A kiss on the cheek between Anthea and me in one particular number was cut. The topless models' nipples were fine, but their belly buttons had to be covered.

A very disturbing event took place in Taipei, my first and last encounter with violence on any scale, perhaps surprising when you consider all the dodgy places I have lived and worked. Night clubs are rarely situated in the most savoury end of town. I've walked through the Suzie Wong district of Hong Kong in the early hours of the morning, through Central Park in New York late at night and so on, but this was my first, and only experience, of its kind. It was nothing less than terrifying. One afternoon after a show, Luis and I had made an appointment with a recording studio to re-do one of the showreels. We flagged down a taxi and gave the driver the address. He immediately gunned the car into the traffic and proceeded to weave and dodge at breakneck speed. I am shockingly nervous in these situations, so I politely tapped the driver on the shoulder and asked him to slow down. Nothing, he continued this craziness. I tapped him again doing the hand down motion which is generally accepted as a slowing motion. He went even faster if it was possible. After several attempts he eventually complied, by doing the extreme opposite. He slowed to a walking pace, laughing like a lunatic. Enough is enough. We managed to get him to stop, threw some money at him, and got out. There was no way this nut job was going to leave it there.

We tried to wave down other cabs, but he drove alongside, in front and behind us, stopping all attempts to get the attention of other drivers. A taxi managed to get around him and pulled up in front, we quickly got in, showed the new driver the address and started to drive away. Quite suddenly, the crazy guy pulled sharply in front of our taxi, threw open his door, and jumped out waving a huge screwdriver with which he tried to stab our driver through the window. Before we knew it, cabs pulled up from nowhere. The drivers hauled the attacker off, and threw him to the ground, punching, kicking, and beating him. At this point, it was way too much for us, we scrambled out just as one of the drivers pulled a large piece of loose concrete from the kerb and held it ready to heave onto the head of the guy they were beating to a pulp. Luis and I looked at each other in absolute horror and hightailed it in the opposite direction. Frightening. Absolutely frightening. In all we were pleased to leave Taiwan and, after two or three of these little tours over several years, we decided never to go back.

There were fortunately other experiences of Taiwan which didn't involve rats and violence. During a tour of the National Museum in Taipei, I was fascinated by their bound-foot shoe collection. There was an old lady there with bound feet, and she would demonstrate the making of these tiny shoes, and the method of binding. The ghastly process of binding began as young as age five or six, and each girl is expected to make her own shoes. Fine hand stitching was highly prized. The old woman would unbind her tiny, perfect three-inch lotus feet to show the results of this disgusting mutilating, torturous tradition. After noticing me several times, and noting my interest, this kind lady gave me a pair of her shoes. I have a small collection still, and this first pair is treasured. There must have been other interesting occasions, but I've managed to erase most of Taiwan from the hard drive in my mind.

CHAPTER 30

PHARAOHS AT THE BOTTOM OF THE GARDEN

One of the highlights of my life was spending the equivalent of a year in Egypt. The period of twelve months was broken into four, three-month visits over the course of a few years, but that made it seem delightfully longer than it actually was. Two of our shows were touring Japan, and both were due to go to Hong Kong then onto Bangkok, whereupon the best dancers from each show would be chosen and amalgamated into one big show for Cairo. I was unbelievably excited the day we flew to Cairo. Throughout my entire life, I'd wanted to be an Egyptologist. As a young person from a poor family in Australia, higher education remained my unrealised dream. Dreams were only for the well-heeled.

Landing late in the evening, and seeing armed guards, I mean heavily armed guards, was very confronting. The atmosphere in the airport already told us this was Egypt. There was sand everywhere, on the tarmac, on the stairs, and all over the baggage collection area. No carousels, just a somewhat shaky, looping old belt popping out of rubber doors at one end, disappearing through more doors at the other. The wait was eternal. We amused ourselves by trying to remember the different cats riding on the belt and the luggage. So many cats. Our hotel rooms were still occupied by the current show so the first night was spent in a small, bungalow-style house in Zamalek on the other side of the Nile from the downtown section.

I was up and out very early to soak up as much atmosphere as I could. The house we were in looked remarkably Australian. Single story, with a veranda across the front, an English-style cottage garden, and a post-and-wire fence and gate. Everything – plants, veranda, footpath – was covered in powdery, cream-coloured dust, a typical Cairo trademark. The street and footpath were unpaved, there was not a great deal of activity yet, but I did find a shop, more a hole in a wall really, nearby and bought a dusty packet of biscuits from a gellabiya-clad, beturbaned gentleman. It was such an exotic sight; I was in love with Egypt in five minutes flat.

Our agents, Bella Chillian, her partner Dick Mahadesian and assistants arrived around noon. We were bundled into taxis and headed out along Al Ahram Road to the Mena House Hotel. Bella was the daughter of Serge Chilian, an Armenian refugee. Serge started his theatrical agency in Cairo after fleeing the Armenian genocide. This man became as famous and loved as the artists he represented. Bella was always mindful of his remarkable reputation when selecting people to represent. We felt extremely fortunate to have this top-shelf agency behind us. The drive itself was astonishingly different from a trip through any major city. Every sight was distinct. The dust-covered cars, the local dress, the constant honking of car horns, the different modes of transport. Small, medium and large wagons drawn by donkey, camel and horse, herds of sheep, goats and camels competing for road space, the not unpleasant smell of camel shit. Chaos, but chaos that was strangely ordered and wonderful.

Thirty or so minutes later emerged an unmistakably recognisable vision, the top of a pyramid above the beige urban vista in front of me. Nobody hinted our hotel, the fabulously historic Mena House, was literally at the foot of the Giza pyramids, or that the pyramids nestled on the very edge of suburban Cairo. The first sight of Mena House was something else as well. It was a grand Arabic-style building with sweeping curved driveway, and gellabiya-uniformed doormen. The lobby was all gleaming brass and traditional carved wood mashrabiya latticework, like something from *A Thousand and One Nights*. Past the main building complex, along the driveway with its gardens and pool, were our rooms in the newly constructed Garden Wing. The Mena House pool, Egypt's first, opened in 1890, and became part of the folklore surrounding this most celebrated of hotels. The pool was emptied, and filled by hand daily using the pristine drinking water from the hotel. Constructed in 1869, the Mena House is probably the most famous of the historic hotels in Egypt, if not the world. Originally built as a two-storey royal lodge, it was enlarged when Empress Eugenie, wife of Napoleon III and Empress of France, visited Cairo for the opening of the Suez Canal. The road from Cairo to Giza was constructed specifically for this visit, making the pyramids much more accessible. The hotel was requisitioned to house Australian troops for both World Wars. During 1979, Mena House was the venue for the Mena House Conference where President Sadat met with President Carter and Menachem Begin, Prime Minister of Israel. While we were there, the hotel and grounds attracted security of the highest order, with heavily armed soldiers positioned outside every few metres around the high stone perimeter wall. Among the notables who have stayed at Mena House are Arthur Conan Doyle, the creator of Sherlock Holmes; Prince Albert Victor of Wales, in 1909, the future King George V, who was said to like to tee off his first hole from the top of the Cheops Pyramid, and Queen Mary; Winston Churchill; King Farouk of Egypt; Agatha Christie; Roger Moore; Cecil B. DeMille; Charlie Chaplin; General Rommel and, later, Field Marshal Montgomery, the list goes on and on. Many films have also used Mena House as a location. Truly, a hotel with a more glorious history would be hard to find.

I should mention the process of claiming the trunks from customs, if only for its uniqueness. The day following our arrival, William, Bella's assistant, took me to the airport in Heliopolis to retrieve our trunks, but first he told me to grab a jacket. A jacket? It's bloody boiling outside, but okay, let's not make waves this early in the piece. I'd performed this little task in a dozen or more countries so, went along expecting a variation of the usual theme. Paperwork in hand, we first rocked up at the excess baggage office only to be handed another enormous sheaf of papers. These volumes were then taken to a strange, isolated little shed-like building sitting quite forlorn in the sand some fifty metres off to the side of the main airport.

Here, William knocked on the small window and handed the whopping bundle of paper to whomever was in residence. Then, backing up several metres from the door, he picked up two discarded sticks and handed one to me saying, 'Now you'll need your jacket'. With this, he squatted in the sand and made a small tent over his head with the stick propping up his jacket. Not slow on the uptake I immediately did the same. William, in his wisdom, had done this many times and knew the drill. We were in for a wait. Possibly, the person inside needed a decent amount of time to process it, or at least, make it apparent that all the paperwork had been meticulously studied and stamped before handing it back. Once this was completed, the rest was a breeze. A certain amount of baksheesh crossed palms, none too discretely, and we headed off back to the hotel to wait for the trunks to be delivered.

During the winter months we performed inside, at the Abu Nawas restaurant. Abu Nawas was a more intimate setting, and Cairo's elite often attended. Some guests, however, were not so elite. The staff of the Australian Embassy would often be there. On their first visit to one of our shows, the Ambassador's wife kept shouting, 'Garn,' over Luis's end of performance introduction speech followed by, 'You're not Aussies,' as she waved an arm in a plaster-cast over her head. 'Oh, yes we are, madame,' Luis, oh so politely responded. 'Nah, course ya not. Garn, sing Waltzin Matilda.' So, Luis led the embarrassed dancers in a wobbly chorus of our most famous song. More or less satisfied, Madame sank back into her chair until the next visit when it would happen all over again. Thankfully, other guests with a tad more decorum attended. Omar Sharif was a regular and was charm itself. Luis always made a point of publicly greeting him at the end of the show, and there were many photos taken of them giving each other a friendly hug at his table. On the morning of 11 July 2015, Luis contacted me to say that this kind, handsome cinema idol had died at 83.

In the summer at Mena House, we worked outside on a stage built over one side of the pool. This stage was big enough to take the whole company spread out, and with plenty of height, literally the sky was the limit. Directly behind the stage were the pyramids, probably one hundred metres away, they were lit during the show, surely one of the most exotic stage sets in the world. What a backdrop.

Nothing about a contract at Mena House was dull. Every day was a pleasure, and on the last two contracts, we were lucky enough to have one of the Oberoi family members as our General Manager, the delightful Mr Kaval Nain Oberoi. The Oberoi Group had taken over Mena House in 1972. A funny, kind, generous man, and a true gentleman. The magnificent Churchill Suite and Montgomery Suites had much cared for marble terraces, sand being carefully removed by hand each day before mopping so as not to scratch the precious stone. Kaval Nain would often requisition one of these suites for our entertainment, and he would join us for rather grand soirees in sumptuous, regal splendour. Food was brought in from the kitchens and spread-out buffet style, and booze flowed as freely as the Nile.

Mena House has its own stables. We were allowed full use of the horses whenever we chose, along with the swimming pool, golf course, tennis courts and restaurants. A horse ride could be organised after the show in the cool of the evening with supper beforehand. If you preferred, you could always take a leisurely, very early morning ride to one of the oldest monuments in Egypt and find yourself in Memphis, the site of the step pyramid, several kilometres away. A young boy rode behind us on a donkey, carrying the girls' handbags, and staff were sent out beforehand to set up a picnic breakfast, perhaps on a five-thousand-year-old carved rock. A delightful afternoon jaunt was a camel ride out past the pyramids to the Oasis Café.

This little Oasis was an illegal café built a kilometre or so off in the desert past the pyramids. It was a ramshackle hut with a palm frond roof, large, open, sandy courtyard, with palm frond shade and mismatched rickety tables and chairs. Light Arabic snacks, tea and coffee, could be enjoyed while fronting one of the most magnificent views in the world, all three pyramids, with hazy Cairo in the distance. This delightful little sanctuary was deemed unsightly by the Mubarak government, spoilt the view of desert from the pyramids and so was bulldozed down. Now there is an extraordinarily ugly 20 kilometre, four-metre-high chain link and concrete fence around the pyramids. Complete with infrared sensors and motion detectors, tourists must enter through a ghastly brick building with metal detectors and X-ray machines. Approximately 200 closed circuit cameras record the slightest movement and guards in a control room scan every foot on 24 screens. I deem that unsightly, it spoils the view from all directions.

For me, with my Egyptologist aspirations, the whole idea of living on the doorstep of the pyramids was wondrous. I never tired of sitting with a book on a dusty, rocky outcrop facing Mena village. Cairo in the distance on my left, and on my right the timeless and mysterious Sphinx, with a small, steep, battered road leading to the Cheops pyramid, between us. My heart flutters now, remembering it.

We were treated as honoured guests, not just the entertainment. I promise you the life of the average touring showgirl was often far from this level of pampering. Mind you, we gave the very best in glamorous, classy, sophisticated entertainment in return. Panache was the name of the game, and we played it well. Our international reputation for presenting beautiful women, sumptuous costumes, Parisian-style cabaret shows, comportment and respect was most definitely hard-won.

CHAPTER 31

BELLY DANCERS 'N BOVVER BOYS

Though living and touring in Egypt was extremely comfortable, it was a little like being inside a gilded cage. We couldn't make a single move without somebody, or everybody knowing, and at times the armed guards on the perimeter walls could be quite intimidating. As delightful and luxurious as it was, when we returned for our second contract in 1980, we readily accepted accommodation in the form of a grand three-story villa complete with staff for the dancers, and an apartment for Luis and me a few palm-strewn blocks from Mena House.

There were a few occasions in Cairo which definitely shook me up. During the early days of our first visit, I took a leisurely solitary walk along the Nile from the Meridian hotel towards the Nile Hilton. The path along the Nile side wasn't up to much, broken and scattered with rubbish for the most part. I found it strange that there is this magnificent, wide, historic, river with colourful feluccas sailing up and down flowing right through the heart of the city, so tranquil, yet rarely did you see anybody walking alongside it. Across the road, yes, but right beside the river, not so much. I love to walk, especially where nobody else wants to. I approached the level of the Nile Hilton, just past the Kasr Al Nile Bridge linking the now famous El Tahrir Square, when I noticed a great pile of newspapers beside the river.

Me being me, I simply had to see what was underneath. Oh lordy, it was a stinking, swollen human corpse. Evidently, the poor devil had drowned, been hauled out, and covered over. That sweet, putrid, cloying smell has stayed with me forever. I can smell a dead mouse from a hundred yards. I crossed the road to the Hilton and reported what I'd seen to the doorman. He seemed most unconcerned, and from what I gathered, attributed it to the will of Allah with a barely audible 'InShaAllah'.

Another occurrence was decidedly scarier. I was walking perhaps where I shouldn't have been once again. I'd gone into a poor part of town, which is not hard to do in Cairo, the poverty was appalling. Tourists manage not to see these parts of any city, but they are what makes up the character and I think they should be seen. Not with camera in hand, your best clothes and a nosey attitude, mind you, but more a casual, dressed down passing through, eyes straight ahead, and an air of going about your business. You can see a lot that way, more than you will see on any tourist route. Taking in everything around without causing offence, blending in like a chameleon is the aim.

I was on one of these discovery jaunts when I seemed to pick up a friend. A very tall, powerfully built young man started walking beside me, chatting, wanting a cigarette, a 'Mister where you from?' sort of character. I answered politely but made it clear I was not interested in a chat or anything else when suddenly I had another friend. One each side of me they persisted, almost trying to guide my direction. The old radar kicked in, and I gently but determinedly steered a course for the more crowded streets. My two new friends were equally as determined and, with a hand on each of my arms, gently but quite forcibly, guided me into a coffee shop. Not a coffee shops westerners would be familiar with; this was an Egyptian coffee shop.

A crumbling façade led through a stained, smelly passageway into a large open-air, dirt-floored courtyard. Local men with their strong coffees and bubble pipes, sat on an assortment of chairs and at tables which had seen better days. Nobody took the slightest bit of notice of this foreigner and his two burly escorts. Coffee and pastries were ordered in Arabic, and we settled into a forced comradeship. My mind was racing. Who knew what these two roughs were about? No good, that's a certainty. Okay, think calmly, I need to take a piss. 'Where are the toilets?' Surely getting away for a minute or so will present itself with a solution. With that, my two friends asked me for money to pay the bill and led me to the toilets where they lounged against the filthy passage walls, waiting. These guys were clever.

Zipped up and nervous as hell, I walked out and headed for the exit, my buddies adhering to me all the way. Wandering through streets visibly thinning out, I made a quick left at a busier intersection where taxis were waiting, engines idling. Diving for the first in line, I slammed the door shut and screamed at the driver, 'GO, GO, GO.' This driver had the smarts, I tell you. He gunned the poor old rust bucket and shot across the intersection with my two 'best mates' in hot pursuit. They were yelling and banging on the boot of the car, but we were away in seconds, leaving them standing in a cloud of yellow haze. The driver asked me if I knew these men, I said, 'No, I've never seen them before. They were following me.' He said, 'You are very lucky. They are very bad, bad, men.' I never found out exactly what sort of bad, bad, men, but I tell you, I didn't give a fiddler's fuck. Just get me outta there. It was a while before I could summon up the courage to go off the beaten track again.

Buildings which have seen a good deal of history seem to exude a magnetism. You find yourself drawn to them for no apparent reason. They can be plain and featureless, or sometimes have a grand architectural façade peculiar to themselves. Whatever the case, they seem to absorb a certain amount of the integral character and history of a city and give off an aura drawing you in. Groppi's, is just such a place, situated a short distance from Tahrir Square, on the five-way intersection, Talaat Harb Square. We knew absolutely nothing of this place when Luis and I first walked past, but for all the above reasons we were attracted to this quaint, Art Deco building with its narrow, porticoed entrance and fine, colourful floral-style mosaics.

A semicircular shop-like foyer with glass pastry cases filled with exquisitely tempting chocolates, cakes, pastries and ice-creams led into an ill lit café/ tearoom simply oozing old-world charm. Waiters in their distinctive sky-blue gellabiyas and little white fez caps buzzed about. I recall two old dears in a corner who could have been extras on a WWII movie set with their overly made-up faces and crimped 40s hairstyles. Where on earth were we? This place is fantastic. Only later did we learn about the internationally famous Groppi.

This monument to history was designed and built by Swiss businessman and pastry chef Giacomo Groppi in Cairo in 1892 and quickly gained its reputation as a place where superb pastries and coffee were served along with a considerable dollop of discretion. At Groppi's, overheard conversations were immediately forgotten. Groppi's became the place to meet, discuss, plan and plot. Businessmen, politicians, European nobles, officers who were Nazis, British and the local Cairene dissidents plotting their latest coup, all rubbed shoulders with British dukes and French bourgeoisie. Debates on the future of all of them took place there in Groppi's washed down with tiny cups of incredibly strong coffee and mouthwatering confections.

It's over forty years since I've been in Cairo, but from all accounts, little is left of those days of Egypt's glorious Belle Époque. The wonderful feeling of nostalgia at Groppi's never diminished. It became a bit of a ritual for Luis and me to pop in for a coffee and some forbidden sweet treat every time we went into Cairo. Perhaps only what is remembered in biographies, novels and thousands of feet of forgotten film now remains. Groppi's went through the ups and downs of Egypt's growing pains, burnt out and rebuilt, forced closures and grand reopenings. The fourth and last generation Groppi sold out to Abdul-Aziz Lokma, founder of the Lokma group, in 1981. So ended nearly a hundred years of continuous family ownership and a massive slice of the character and charm of old Cairo.

A frivolous and much-loved number in our show was the appearance of a gorilla on stage—often me. There were some hilarious and worrying moments in that gorilla suit over the years. Of course, the costume itself was extremely well done and was complete with a fibreglass chest and moulded rubber face, hands and feet. Quite realistic. The routine started with a supremely sexy singer in a revealingly slashed cocktail dress. Performing this in Cairo, I would be lowered in a cage by a crane onto the stage behind the singer. The cage would stop about a metre from the floor, where I would rattle the bars and grunt, then continue to the floor. The singer would walk around the cage, teasing the poor beast, and showing various expanses of flesh. This frustrated the gorilla, causing him/me to break out. Every alternate bar of the cage was rubber. I, the gorilla, would then abandon my fascination with the singer and cruise the front of the stage, eyeballing the audience.

I would search for a likely subject to jump towards and harass. Often, especially on weekends, bridal parties would be celebrating there. Brides were particularly tempting targets and always guaranteed the perfect mix of fright, and just enough decorum. I heaved myself off the metre-high stage, goading my subjects into squeals and sometimes some very hefty slaps from them. Often, I'd steal fruit from the table and take it back to the dressing room. Bananas, for example, were an expensive luxury in Cairo.

One evening, out by the pool, I picked my victims. Right, I thought, they are my target for tonight. A rather posh-looking couple of ladies, fairly dazzling with expensive bling and designer dresses. I had no sooner got to their table when I felt myself lifted off my feet and half-carried, half-dragged to the back of the venue where I was shoved up against a wall with a handgun stuck in my face. Much haranguing in the local lingo ensued while I tried to explain that, hello, I was really a harmless poof in a costume. They held me in that position for the rest of the show and I watched the finale go on without me. It was unbelievably hot in the suit, and I thought I might well drown in my own perspiration.

After the manager was called for, the harmless nature of the stunt was explained satisfactorily, and I was let go. It turned out I had chosen two very, very, high profile and well-guarded notables as my targets. They were none other than the First Lady of Egypt, Jehan Sadat and her sister-in-law. This remarkable woman, Jehan Sadat, was respected throughout Egypt and beyond and touched the lives of millions. She played a crucial role in reforming Egypt's civil rights laws during the late 1970s—frequently referred to as Jehan's Laws. She also helped change the lives of Arab women and the world's image of Arab women. Both women were positively charming about the gorilla incident and the following week, I had a sweet little note delivered to me backstage saying, 'I'm back, in the centre and in white. Looking forward to being harrassed.

~Mdm Sadat'. I did indeed choose them, Mr Sadat's sister and another friend that night, but it was a mild, fawning, wimpy, gentle assault.

We loved having guest artists, any guest artist. It meant we got the night off. One night it was Julio Inglesias. The evening Julio was to perform, the girls were heading off to Juliana's Club at the Nile Hilton. They were so looking forward to it. Otherwise, we usually had only Friday nights off – which is Muslim Holy Day – so no Juliana's. Kaval Nain introduced me to Julio and his son Enrique. Julio told me he understood how disappointed the girls would be if they couldn't see his sold-out performance. So, he had arranged for chairs to be put on the flat, low roof covering the restaurant and audience in front of the stage, the stage being open-air. Well, just how do I take this bit of news? On the one hand, I guess it's very thoughtful but, on the other, the ego of the guy. Now, what do I do? Tell him thanks but no thanks, the girls are going partying, or leave the chairs empty and insult him? I'll never see him again, so if the truth hurts, so be it. He was not pleased—I passed him in the lobby later the next day, and got a curt nod.

Fifi Abdou was the highest paid belly dancer in the Arab world. This voluptuous woman commanded enormous sums of money to perform. She was reckoned by many to be one of the wealthiest women in Egypt. Fifi had the reputation of being an absolute ball-breaker in business, more than a few of her ten or so musicians were rightly terrified of her. In the early '80s, when we often worked together, it was said she was receiving anything from two to ten thousand dollars per show, often working two or even three venues in the same night. Watching Fifi dance was fascinating. Obviously, I never knew – and still don't know – the intricacies and improvisations of the belly-dance world. It seemed to me in Fifi's case, there was an awful lot of not much happening besides Fifi's total absorption and enthrallment with her huge knockers. She was forever checking them out for lengthy periods, adjusting, and shoving them around. Maybe it's all part of the seduction, but whatever it was, she was brilliant at it. I never saw her in the same costume twice. It was said she had over five thousand of them, with the most expensive worth a cool forty thousand dollars. Seems an awful lot for not much if you ask me. Good newspaper copy though. In 1996, Fifi was robbed and it was reported that the thieves had made off with a hundred thousand dollars' worth of jewellery.

I often wondered how these women fared after the stricter Islamic tenets crept into mainstream Egyptian life. I learned from one of our former dancers still living in Cairo, that in 1991, Fifi was charged with depraved movements by a Cairo court and sentenced to three months in jail. Whether she actually served any time I don't know. She was always pleasant to me. I hope she is respected and left in peace.

CHAPTER 32

WAR WOUNDS

One morning in 1981, I woke to what felt like an earthquake. The whole building was shaking, and there was a tremendous roar outside. Padding naked to our third-floor lounge room window, I decided to see what was going on. Out there, I saw a massive helicopter gunship travelling low over the roofs of the houses leading into Cairo. While I was standing there, the shaking began again as another one passed low overhead. It really did convulse the entire place. I heard the chandelier clinking and clanking, and as I turned to look up at it, it fell right on top of me, one of the longer pieces of crystal piercing my stomach. In the shock of the moment, and quite unthinkingly, I started to pull it out. It had penetrated a long way. I was amazed I could see down into the deep, silvery hole it made, and at the lack of blood. That was short-lived, the blood soon began to flow, copiously. Of course, getting a doctor at that particular time was impossible. Every medical person in Cairo was attending the carnage of the Anwar Sadat assassination downtown, which is where those gunships were headed. One of the dancers had some volunteer nursing experience that was as close as I could get to professional help. She did a very tidy job of sewing me up with needle and thread from the company sewing box and making a bandage from toilet paper and sticky tape. I can go right back to that dreadful day every time I feel or see that jagged little scar. My only war wound, and it had to be something as gay as a crystal chandelier shard.

We only learned of the tragic assassination later in the day, and I was shocked and horrified. The TV news was ghastly to watch. So much carnage and death, so much panic and sadness happening just a few kilometres away. Sadat's actions were not universally popular in the Arab world. On 6 October 1981, as he stood and watched the annual parade celebrating the anniversary of Egypt's 1973 war with Israel, he saluted his killers as they leapt from vehicles, thinking they were part of the parade. That tragic day was the start of the end of Cairo as we knew it. The assassins' bullets terminated the life of a man brave enough to go into Israel in 1977, the camp of his enemy, and negotiate a peace lasting until his death. It also ended the hope of the non-Muslim world that peace in the Middle East was possible, and achievable without bloodshed. The Nobel Peace Prize was awarded to both him and Israeli Prime Minister Menachem Begin for those 1977 negotiations. Sadat's bullet-riddled body was rushed to the Maadi Military Hospital where he was proclaimed dead. Ten others died that fateful day, and another 28 were injured. President Sadat had always refused to wear a bullet-proof vest, proclaiming confidently, 'I am among my sons.'

In the following days there was a palpable hush over Cairo. Bewildered faces mingled with shocked ones. You could only imagine what people were thinking. Egypt enjoyed such peace, freedom, and comparative prosperity during the Sadat era. Very soon, the streets started to become dangerous, and a breakdown in law and order quickly ensued. Forty days of national mourning was declared, and with entertainment banned, performing was out of the question.

Our management was very understanding of our situation, and they offered us two possible solutions. We could be paid out, and terminate the contract right away, which meant having no work in front of us for a few months until we were due in San Remo, Italy. Or, at management's expense, we could go to the Aswan Oberoi Aswan, in Upper Egypt. We could stay at their sister hotel, situated in perfect safety on Elephantine Island on the Nile, for the duration of the mourning period, then come back and complete the final month of the contract. A quick conference with the dancers, and it was mutually agreed, option two with a month's holiday was the way to go. I witnessed the fastest packing I'd ever seen.

We took the evening sleeper train to Luxor first, opting for a few days there to take in all this amazingly historical town had to offer. We rented bicycles and pedalled our way from breathtaking monument to breathtaking monument. Luxor has no motorised traffic, only bicycles, horse- or donkey-drawn vehicles and camels. Sounds old worldly and delightful, and it was, except by noon, sun on the manure and puddles of urine caused a stink decidedly Ancient Egyptian. Makes you wonder what those Victorian dresses were dragged through. A short ferry ride to the opposite side of the Nile takes you to the Valley of the Kings. I often think how fortunate we were, because throughout those wonderful forty days, there were no tourists. To have a tourist-free run of these sights has got to be a rarity, and a privilege. Tut's tomb was nothing short of awesome. There was a local chap outside the tomb offering to look after cameras as they were not permitted inside. Ever distrustful, I decided to conceal mine and hope for the best. Being alone inside the tomb, I was confident I could bend that rule ever so slightly, and sneak off one or two shots when the most extraordinary thing happened. As I was lining up my first photo, my camera literally exploded. I mean, it just flew to pieces. Springs, lenses and bits and bobs of my lovely Zenit flew all over the tomb. I've pondered the fabled mummy's curse in a different light ever since.

From the minute we stepped off the train, Aswan was captivating. Slow-moving, laid back, and with the big bonus of being free of rubbernecking-tourists. The only way of getting to the hotel was by the hotel ferry or a private felucca. The latter are small, one-man-operated, triangular lateen-rigged sailboats, and the fare charged was minimal. The hotel itself was a small tower of guest rooms and suites with a couple of restaurants and a pool. As the tourists had buried their jewels and fled and we were the only people staying there, the management allotted us a suite each. What luxury. A fully-staffed hotel, all for us. Meals were an absolute treat, with freshly caught Nile perch on the menu every day. What a way to live. Gertrude Stein once said, 'I've been rich, I've been poor. Rich is better.'

The precious time at Aswan will forever stay in my mind as one of the most peaceful times of my life. Nothing to do all day, every day except for whatever took my fancy. I spent a lot of the time exploring Elephantine Island, an historic island in its own right. It was once the home of Lord Kitchener, and his house is still on the southern end. The small, one-man feluccas were sturdy little sailboats operated by young, supremely muscled, Nubian men. Many of them were university students on holiday who lived in a small Nubian village downstream on the west bank. These young guys were all very tall, very dark, very well built and very, very, handsome. Wearing long, white, fine cotton gellabiyas, they stood with their legs akimbo, slightly apart at just the right angle to the sun, so the entire outline of their bodies could be seen in stark relief. Most wore no underwear, and their more than adequate charms could easily be seen dangling in the breeze. This deliberate and sometimes lucrative ploy encouraged wealthy, older American female tourists to take a lengthy boat ride down the Nile. Tall thick reed growths were numerous through that section of the river, and there were plenty of convenient little boat ways worn into them. These poor boys started to become very frustrated by the lack of tourists. I'm sure our little group of beautiful showgirls, and men, did all they could to normalise the situation. The boat boys were thoroughly delightful and very friendly, taking us downriver to their traditional style village on several occasions. The families were kind and welcoming, and we enjoyed many a superb meal there.

Once, I requested to be dropped on the west bank for the afternoon, so I could go exploring. The west bank was thickly verdant for fifty to a hundred metres in, then nothing but sand, rock cliffs and virtually uninhabited except for the Nubian village farther down. I had often noticed a little square building sitting on top of a high sandy hill a little way downstream and I wanted to go look at it. The bank was thick with reeds, grass and trees. Still, I made my way to where the sand started not far in from the bank. It was easy going until I was below the now not-so-little pink marble building and started a challenging climb up to it. I had barely reached it, and was making my way to the opposite side when a very superior, English-accented voice said, 'May I help you?' Certainly, the last thing I expected. I turned in the direction of the voice, and not ten metres away, on the south downward slope, was the perfect Downton Abbey butler. I thought it's unquestionably time to get out of the sun. But no, this was a real-deal butler who was also, in fact, a real-deal gardener.

I told him I was simply being nosey, adding that I was staying at the hotel and the circumstances leading to my stay. He was charm itself. This was the tomb of Aga Khan III, spiritual leader of the Ismailis, a Shi'ite sect of Islam. The Aga Khan was an extraordinarily wealthy and extremely large man. On his birthday in 1945, he was weighed in diamonds, which he then distributed to his followers. He died and was entombed on this hill in the late '50s. On the orders of La Begum, the Aga Khan's widow, and this man's employer, he was to place a red rose inside the tomb every day when La Begum was not in residence. These roses, by the way, were often especially flown in from Paris. La Begum, a celebrated French beauty born Yvonne Blanche Labrousse who, in 1929, was named Miss France. She met and married the Aga Khan, the love of her life, in Cairo in 1944. What a delightful story. He added that La Begum was in residence only three months of the year and would be arriving within the week.

The following week, I was surprised to receive a beautifully handwritten note from La Begum inviting me to afternoon tea. I was thrilled to accept, and a few days later was back on the little felucca, this time dropped at a small, private mooring. I followed the butler/gardener up along a path through palms and high grasses to an entirely dream-like oasis with a smallish white house set in the middle. La Begum greeted me, and although flattered by her invitation, I quickly realised she was interested in getting as much firsthand information as she could about the state of affairs in Cairo, and what was happening in general. This delightful lady, then in her early seventies, was old world glamour itself and to my mind, still very beautiful indeed. Afternoon tea was ordered, and I had the first of several fascinating chats with this legendary woman. La Begum died in 2000 at the good age of 94.

The forty days went by all too quickly. So easy to get used to doing nothing in such an exotic place. So easy not to have performances to think about. News from Cairo said all was pretty much back to normal, and we were booked on the overnight train in a few days' time. The trip back was uneventful, saying goodbye to our new friends on Elephantine Island was as difficult as always, with promises and good intentions, the usual 'We must write,' or 'We will visit'. This is always a huge problem with living and working on tour. You meet so many lovely people, but back then, it was almost impossible to keep in contact.

Our agent during our second Egypt contract was the prominent Parisienne agent of the time, Roland Bertin. A great, bloated toad of a man who managed to make an appearance only when picking up his commission. Never a phone call, never a letter from this delightful man. No praise for an exceptional run, no hasty, concerned telegram during times of local unrest, no visit from him or his staff. We may as well have been contracted to a phantom. Our third contract in Cairo was handled by myself directly with the hotel manager, Kaval Nain Oberoi. The usual contractual deal with agents is, should you appear in the same venue within one year of a previous engagement, the original agent is entitled to a full fee. For our third contract in Egypt, I pointedly made very sure this did not occur, we were indeed past the one year. Not much, but a bit. The bastard sued us anyhow. The first I learned of it was a piece in a Cairo newspaper saying a lawsuit was taking place between us, and I owed US$100,000 in commission fees. One hundred thousand dollars! Do you realise this figure is supposed to be ten percent of our contract? Do you honestly imagine we were earning a million dollars for three months work in a hotel? Needless to say, the hotel staff and a few friends who read the story started bowing down before me. 'Oh, Mr Thomas,' they would say, 'you very rich man.' Yeah, right.

I was livid with rage, but our local lawyer advised not contesting as it seemed Monsieur Bertin was not French after all but, originally hailed from downtown Cairo. The advice was, for a foreigner to fight a local Egyptian in an Egyptian court was tantamount to suicide. Well, bugger off you lot. I'm not giving in to blackmail. So, fight it we did. We fought it for five long, expensive years, and we won. Yes, two young guys from Australia (Luis was a naturalised Aussie before we left for Spain) unschooled in law, managed to tell them just where to get off. Not long after this little victory, the charming M Bertin went to meet his maker. Not a moment too soon I say.

A battle with a shitty agent is not a note to finish up on. My time in Egypt was, and is, one of the most meaningful episodes of my life. I have often longed to go back, reconnect with the marvel of the first visit. Our darling leading lady Bonnie, who still lives there with the husband she met during our last visit, told me not to bother. The Cairo of that time and the Cairo of today are vastly different. 'Keep your wonderful memories,' she tells me, and she is right. The Mena House gardens have been remodelled, the old pool has gone, and been replaced with two or three new ones. Gone as well is the outdoor restaurant and stage where we performed. Could I perhaps go for a nostalgic wander around the pyramids at night? Sneak into the little-known tombs and partial excavations, run my hands over the ancient, monolithic rocks of the pyramids themselves? Might I recall heated but civil arguments with Director of Antiquities Zahi Hawass? If you've ever watched the most insignificant doco on ancient Egypt, you will have seen this most conceited of men. No licence for filming was ever given without the inclusion of an appearance by this pompous man whom I privately called Mastryoshka, so full of himself was he.

No, is the answer to all this. My beautiful pyramids are now surrounded by those aforementioned high, ugly, concrete walls.

CHICAGO TRIBUNE. August 12, 2008

Tourists have long been awed by Egypt's famed Giza pyramids and irritated by having to fend off peddlers relentlessly offering camel rides and trinkets.

But the hustlers were gone Monday as Egypt started an elaborate project to modernize the area and make it friendlier to tourists. Security also is improving, with a 12-mile chain-link fence featuring cameras, alarms and motion detectors.

> *'It was a zoo,' said Zahi Hawass, Egypt's chief archeologist, recalling the past free-for-all. 'Now we are protecting both the tourists and the ancient monuments.'*
>
> *Tourists undergo a constant barrage from peddlers selling souvenir statues, T-shirts and other trinkets. Visitors are sometimes followed by men on camels selling rides or photos—and rarely taking no for an answer.*
>
> *New technology aims to curb shenanigans by both peddlers and tourists, who can ramble freely around the pyramid grounds. Tourists enter through a new brick entrance building, with half a dozen gates equipped with metal detectors and X-ray machines.*

Never will I forget or allow myself to negate the importance of Egypt. Tits and feathers are a bloody huge leap from Egyptology but, in the convoluted ways of life I made it to Egypt, I appreciated it, and I loved it.

CHAPTER 33

DIVINE DAMASCUS

Syria today is immersed in years of civil war, rife with horrendous atrocities. When we performed there in 1979, it was one of the most delightful countries I had ever visited.

The Syrian people were extraordinarily friendly and the streets seemed safe, although it was disconcerting to see so many people with firearms. Even youths were carrying Kalashnikovs or AK 47s. Who knows the difference? A gun is a gun to me. There was a seven pm curfew as far as walking was concerned. That was strange in itself. Seemed you could go anywhere at all in a vehicle, just not on foot. I had occasion to collect some newly recorded show music one evening and couldn't find a cab. With some apprehension I decided to hoof it, warily hightailing the few blocks there and back. I felt so exposed. Maybe it wasn't so peaceful after all.

We were offered the Damascus contract as part of the entertainment line-up for a Russian Evening to be presented by the Meridian Hotel. The evening was to be on a grand scale with international guest artists including Eruption, The Gibson Brothers, Les Claudettes and us. Nobody under sixty has heard of any of these people. A 747 aircraft loaded with Russian food was also to be flown in, so you can see it was no simple affair.

Our cast arrived a few weeks early because we were expected to produce a new Russian-style show complete with new costumes, and the hotel footing the bill. Which they did—costumes, music, the works. We were a little concerned at first about availability of the fabrics, sequins and beads we needed to make new costumes. A trip to Al Hamidiyah Souk (bazaar) located inside the old walled city of Damascus next to the Citadel soon put our minds at rest. For anyone making costumes, that souk was a dream come true: bead shops, sequin shops, fabrics, feathers, leathers and furs. We sold the costumes plus everything concerned with the business a few years ago, and found still unopened two- and three-kilo bags of all manner of bling. We'd gone a little overboard when stocking up.

The souk runs in and around Straight Street which is mentioned in the Bible. It's said to be the oldest, continuously running souk in the Middle East. I could certainly feel some age to it. Once, while ferreting around upstairs in a drapery shop, I saw shelving strung between old Roman pillars. It fascinated me such history could be treated so casually. What was equally impressive about this medieval warren of little streets was that Jewish, Christian and Muslim shops all coexisted, not only peacefully, but both neighbourly and friendly. A Jewish owner would send us to a Muslim-owned shop, or a Muslim owner would direct us to a Christian-owned shop. A far cry from today. Poor Syria. It must be remembered that Syria was and is a secular state. Not a Muslim state as most people believe.

We had free run of the hotel. The rooms were large and pleasant, and all meals were taken in the restaurant which offered full Western as well as Middle Eastern menus. We were very comfortable. We were also entertained daily during meals by a singer accompanying himself on a piano. This gentleman possessed the outstanding ability to completely mangle every song he attempted. He would pass through the restaurant, asking what people would like to hear. Our clever girls always said, '*If You Go Away*', but he never got it, and he never did. The Argentinian band from the showroom called him Manitos de Platanos, meaning little banana fingers—a play on words prompted by the name of one of Spain's greatest guitarists Manitos de Plata (little fingers of silver). This strange little man also had cassette tapes for sale stacked on his piano. The dusty stack never seemed to diminish, and the clever Argentinian boys put it about that he was going to do a benefit concert for the deaf.

In the meantime, we performed our regular show each evening in the main restaurant and rehearsed and made costumes during the day. The stage was built especially for us, it was not big but adequate. The problem was the dressing rooms. Three guest rooms were reserved for this purpose directly below the restaurant, one for the boys, one for the girls and one for the costumes. A nearby door off the sizeable balcony behind the stage was used to reach these rooms. The balcony led directly onto the stage through glass doors and was sealed off for our use. Our shows rely entirely on quick costume changes, there is no time to go up and down stairs. The balcony was certainly big enough for the purpose, but this was November, full winter, and Damascus in winter is possibly the coldest place I've endured. No snow, but the wind whistling off the mountains behind the city was bloody freezing.

Management didn't seem to get it, the dancers had to strip down to almost naked, and re-dress in this refrigerator. I suggested a compromise: we would use the balcony for changing if they shifted their desks out there during the day and worked naked. I guess that got through, and they solved this problem by curtaining off the entire balcony with canvas and some overhead heating. Warmer. Not much warmer, but definitely better.

A few funny incidents took place in that restaurant. Well, funny in retrospect, but not quite so humorous in actuality. As always, the incidents occurred because of, or during the gorilla routine. Why does that number attract so much attention? Firstly, management called to tell me that a general in the Syrian Army would be attending that evening's performance, he would be sitting in such and such a place, and the monkey was 'under no circumstances to go anywhere near him'. Turns out he was afraid of this costumed creature. Some General! Obviously not a front-liner on the battlefield.

The second occasion was on New Year's Eve. The restaurant décor had a stretched beige sail-like fabric ceiling that curved down to each of the four supporting centre pillars and curved up again between them. During the monkey routine, just as I managed to get our stunning leading lady Colleen stripped to her g-string before picking her up to whisk her off stage, an enormous hulk of a man lumbered onto the stage and began to pummel me in a heroic attempt to save the poor damsel from that vile creature. Before I knew it, I was gripped in an agonisingly crushing bear hug, really feeling that I might pass out. I managed a glimpse at Colleen, left arm modestly across her bare bosom and right hand swinging the heavily glass beaded bra as a weapon, whacking the man over the skull in an effort to secure my release. Luckily, Luis and Ron were sufficiently clad to rush to my rescue from the dressing room and hustle the indignant brute off the stage.

After the show, I questioned management about why security had not stepped in. Their answer was, 'Oh, security was too busy putting out the fire.' What fire? Some revelling bright spark had decided to set the paper streamers dangling from the support pillars alight, and the ensuing flames had reached the fabric ceiling, setting it alight as well. We certainly didn't see any of that nor, seemingly, did any of the guests. There was, however, a large scorch mark on the ceiling at the back of the room. Demonstrates how positively riveting our show was.

Our hotel in Damascus was the only place open 24/7, so the restaurant was a great place to hang out. Other similar shows in town came there to eat after their performances, and being full of glamorous showgirls, the restaurant was an absolute magnet for the Damascus social set. In those days the Middle East was as open and free as Europe, and cabaret shows abounded. The waiters were very good to us and would set up one huge, long table able to accommodate not only our people but eight new friends from a Spanish-owned show. These delightful dancers performed in another venue not far away called Waadi Aghdar (Green Valley) on the Shara Beirut (Beirut Road).

Beirut, by the way, was a hundred kilometres straight ahead! I took that road every two weeks, hiring a taxi to take me to Beirut to cash our US$ cheque from the hotel. I always insisted on US$, and no bank in Damascus could cash the fortnightly cheques. The cabs were all black, most having lighting in the back window that would shame any disco. I would make the two-hour drive huddling on the back seat of one of these weird cabs. The taxis were all Mercedes Benz that had seen better days, some even had bunches of black ostrich feathers proudly blowing in the wind on each corner outside. Bit funereal that little touch, and I hoped not prophetic. Once across the border, I would get as close to the floor as possible as we ducked and weaved around bomb craters and rusting burnt out car bodies. Poor Beirut was so very battle-scarred from the Israeli attacks they called Operation Peace for Galilee. It got a lot worse and has never really recovered.

We met the members of the Spanish show in our restaurant late one night. One particularly tall woman caught my attention. I said to Luis, 'I'm sure I have seen this woman before, many times, in fact.' Of course, showgirls look very different without the heavy stage makeup, but there was something unmistakable about her. Her very bearing was unique. I had seen a topless model in many shows in the past who I found breathtaking. Her stage persona was of the straight-backed, gliding style with a sort of misty, faraway but all-encompassing gaze set in an exquisitely beautiful face. I'd always yearned to meet this vision and now I was positive this was her. Luis gave me a shove and said, 'Well, go introduce yourself and find out.'

I am essentially a very shy person but I summoned up all my social courage and went to speak to her. She was indeed the same woman I'd admired all those years. Her name was Agneta or Aggie, and we became the firmest of friends in the weeks, then years, to follow. Incidentally, that sort of misty faraway but all-encompassing gaze was the result of Aggie's poor eyesight. She usually wore very strong glasses but of course, went without them on stage. Agneta was wandering around blind, just hoping beyond hope that everyone else on stage was where they ought to be.

Aggie is Swedish, a unique person, extraordinarily beautiful on and off stage, inside and out, very tall and willowy with the most beautiful eyes. Her English is of the blue blooded, aristocratic variety. She was not a trained dancer, but in those days, the models did not have to be classically trained. They just had to be glamorous, musical, tall and have a perfect bust. In addition to all these attributes, Aggie is a fine, intelligent, sensitive woman with a real skill for photography. Stray animals, cats in particular, were her weakness, and she had an incredibly wicked sense of humour. Aggie's entre into showbiz is a great little story. While working as a receptionist at a Stockholm hotel, she noticed the visiting Lido Bluebells ate gratis at the cafeteria. She thought she fitted in quite well with the physical look of the dancers so tagged along for the free food. After a day or two Margaret Kelly (owner of the Bluebells) asked her if she was with the troupe. Aggie confessed she was not. Margaret said 'Well, you had better join or pay for that meal'. How wonderful. Aggie went on to have a very long showbiz career.

One morning when I was still heavily asleep, there was a loud, insistent knocking at the door, which I groggily opened. There was Aggie, looking distraught and holding a woven basket of the Red Riding Hood variety, which appeared to be full of foxtails. Aggie told me the venue where she worked had a mother cat with kittens under the stage. It wasn't unusual for this cat to wander across the stage during the show with one of its offspring clutched in its mouth. The night before, Aggie had found one of the kittens in the dressing room, and being unable to locate the mother, had taken it home. This morning she had got up to pee and observed that the cat was stretched out full length on her bed and appeared to be dead. Picking it up in tears, she noticing it was as stiff as a board but still breathing. She stuffed the poor thing into the basket, covered it with foxtails filched from one of her costumes to keep it warm, and rushed to me. She positively insisted that I get dressed and go with her in search of a vet.

Some hours, and several taxi rides to leads that went nowhere, we arrived in a part of town that looked as though we might end up on the white slave market. Aggie approached some children playing on the street and with practised gesturing and a quick display of the state of the poor kitten, made them understand we needed a vet. One of the children grabbed her arm and led us deeper into this decidedly mediaeval part of town, up an outside wooden stairway and stopped us in front of a metal-studded wooden door, indicating that we should knock. Immediately, a little barred hatch set into the door opened, and a woman asked what we wanted. Aggie simply displayed the kitten, and after much withdrawing of bolts on the other side of the door, we were waved inside. This, it seemed, was the vet's wife, and after seating us in the living room went off, we hoped, to get her husband. The vet appeared, looking much as I had when Aggie arrived at my door. He had been asleep and was dressed in a long nightshirt. Shoving his hand into the basket, the vet announced in broken English that the patient was dead. Aggie removed a foxtail from his hand and uncovered the still prostrate kitten. The vet took hold of the little body and went back the way he had come. We sat and waited. Sometime later he appeared with the kitten and a bottle of pills. He told us the patient, he only ever referred to the kitten as the patient, must have three tablets per day, if, after three days, the patient had not recovered, the patient would indeed be dead.

By this time, it was dark, and we grabbed a cab and rushed back to our respective accommodation to prepare for showtime. Two days later, Aggie was overjoyed to announce that the patient had recovered and was rushing around doing kitty things all over her apartment. A further two days later, Aggie told me the patient had given her a little gift. She unwound her scarf to reveal little burn-like marks: Ringworm! Not the best of looks for a nearly naked showgirl, but with the clever application of makeup, Aggie got away with it and left us each evening after supper saying, 'I'll give you a ring tomorrow'. Yeah hon, not likely.

A dancer's professional life is generally short. Still, occasionally there are the lucky ones who maintain their bodies and looks and go way past the shelf life of the average professional. Aggie was one of these people. She must have been around forty when we met and went on for years after that. In people's minds showgirls lead exciting, glamorous lives that are one party after another. Well, not so, particularly in the case of a touring dancer. Yes, entertainers do visit exotic countries, meet new and interesting people, are invited to a lot of parties and glam events. But, and it is a big but, living out of a suitcase, eating in restaurants, living in hotel rooms, constantly saying goodbye as you go from one city to another is not always enviable.

Aggie had had her share of tucks and trims. Her boobs went under the knife several times, and each time takes its toll. The last time Aggie had undergone this ordeal, she decided to have the nipples placed just slightly higher than usual, with the result that when she was wearing something low-cut in streetwear, they often peeked out. We were all aware of this and would give Aggie the Foo sign. Everyone knew Foo, the little graffiti cartoon universally appearing on walls and unlikely places, the tiny hands clutching a straight horizontal line and the bald round head with big eyes peering over the top. So, the Foo sign was to clutch an imaginary wall at eye height and peer over it at Aggie. This bought on a quick turn aside, and a furtive poking of nipple back down out of sight. Of course, it was only natural that eventually Aggie would meet her prince and want to settle down. As with so many showgirls, Aggie's prince was a musician. After all, we work together, sit between shows together and often are the only other English-speaking people around. Aggie's particular prince was the charming Ezio, an Italian from Milano. I have had to go back and change my darling Aggie into 'was'. Sadly she died of a heart attack during the time I was writing this book.

The big Russian-themed night was drawing closer, and the costumes were finished: scarlet military-style jackets for the boys with fur hussar-type hats, and slashed, black baggy trousers trimmed in gold, and tucked into knee-high red leather boots. For the girls, fur-trimmed hussar-style hats, aqua military jackets slung off the shoulder, aqua bras and slashed, gold-trimmed trousers, tucked into knee-length aqua leather boots. Very dashing, and all paid for by the hotel. Rehearsals were over and the routines polished. The hotel had the top-floor ballroom beautifully decorated in gold and midnight blue, resembling a Tsar's palace, and the other guest artists were arriving daily.

Eruption: those old enough will remember their international chart breakers like *I Can't Stand the Rain* and *One Way Ticket*. I believe they carried on after their successes for some time, changing members along the way. When we later went to Iraq, customs thought the cassettes the girls brought with them were Boney M cassettes and unspooled all the tape onto the floor right there. Boney M were personae non-grata due to their song *By the Rivers of Babylon*.

The Gibson Brothers: *Que Sera Mi Vida* is the only song I recall making a big splash, but the brothers had more going for them. They were three good-lookin' black boys, and their arrival at the hotel nearly cancelled our show that night. No names will be mentioned, but you know who you are. The cute blonde that ran across the hall into Ron's room overlooking the lobby entrance, to get onto his balcony for a closer perv and B A N G … straight into the sliding glass door. Well, nothing broken, door or girl, but the nose was quite a different shape for a while. The Brothers went on for many years with concerts and TV appearances.

Les Clodettes: were the backup singers for Claude-François. He wasn't a big hit in Australia but had been a huge star in Europe. Poor Claude managed to top himself by trying to change a light globe while showering. Obviously, the light globe was brighter than Claude. The girls went on without him, and I have to say, they were super-hot-looking ladies with the smallest g-strings I have ever seen. And that's saying something.

So, that was the line-up, top singing acts from around the world and us. Mammoth amounts of money spent, all tickets sold out, show rehearsed, ready to roll and wham! Russia invaded Afghanistan and the show was cancelled. What an anticlimax to an event that had been so meticulously planned, and what earth-shattering and devastating consequences that invasion would have for the Middle East for the next forty-five years and counting. Things were decidedly dicky. We were advised by some American military personnel who were staying in the hotel, and with whom we had become friendly, to go to our embassy immediately as the Americans were organising and advising standby evacuation of all unnecessary US nationals.

That's exactly what I did. I took myself off that very day to the Australian Embassy to find an armoured tank covered in camouflage net parked under the trees outside and a note on the door virtually saying 'back after hostilities'. How very sad it is today, to read the news regarding poor Syria. The faces of so many Middle Eastern countries have changed beyond recognition. Such devastation, and hardship for citizens who only want to get on with their lives. Religion plays havoc with innocents who know no better.

Once again, the Yanks as well as the Swedes, strangely enough, came to our rescue with a full evacuation plan if needed. Fortunately, it wasn't. Our contract was up, and we already had seats booked on Olympic Air to fly to Athens for the next leg of our tour.

CHAPTER 34

THE CRADLE OF CIVILISATION ROCKS

Goodbyes over, we were off to Athens and the Spanish group were heading to Cyprus. I'd never been to Greece, and for someone who'd always wanted to be an archaeologist, the very thought of going to work in the 'cradle of Western civilisation' was sensational beyond words. As it turned out, we were to be working in a nightclub smack dab in the middle of Syntagma (Constitution) Square, in the very heart of Athens opposite the Royal Palace. We arrived at night and met our agent Jack Palass for the first time. It's not unusual for agents to pass an artist or artists on to another agent if there is no immediate work. The downside is you pay two agents fees, the upside is you have ongoing work. Jack Palass turned out to be thoroughly adorable, a trait not often found amongst the agent species. We were taken to the Achilleus Hotel on Stadium Street, only a block to the Club on Othonos Street, alongside Syntagma Square. Next morning, when I opened my window to take a peek at our new surroundings, I was stunned to see not far away and on the right, the magnificence of the Acropolis. What a sight, what an overwhelming sensation. Just imagine, I would be living with that astonishing historical monument a glance away. A quick reconnoitre of our new surroundings found little shops full of Greek yoghurt and honey and baklava and all sorts of treats for breakfast.

Luis and I were off to the club to meet the owner, check the dressing rooms and unpack before calling the dancers for rehearsal. The venue was not big, the room was not built to have entertainment on this scale. It did have a semi circular stage easy enough to fit the show on, and a large, long dressing room directly off the stage-right exit. The owner was a very worldly, cultivated sort who, although making us feel very welcome, had that just-under-the-surface authority of a man who is accustomed to being obeyed. Men like that were common in our business. After all, this is the world of the nightclub, what other sort of things went down in these places was anyone's guess. As long as you minded your own beeswax, and didn't poke your nose where it didn't belong, you were treated with great respect and kindness.

For instance, the price you were paid on a contract might look unbelievably lucrative. That's exactly what it was: unbelievable. There were all sorts of hidden cash deductions to be made, starting with the agent's, or agents' fee. Often there were nicely rounded little sums to be donated to the local Mafia. Sometimes, as was the case in Rome, a cut, or donation to the Juvenile Police. A representative of that extremely shadowy little faction would pop in on pay nights. Sometimes a generous slice for management or some middleman. Having said this, after emoluments, the take was pretty much the same for all venues. I'd been in the business for so long, I knew to the dollar what I needed and what I would get in my hand. Two different half-hour shows per night were contracted, and after a quick placement rehearsal, it would be pretty plain sailing.

Opening night went without the slightest hitch except for one distressing surprise. None of us had ever worked in or even been to Greece before, and when the plates started flying, the shards and chips stinging bare legs, we thought the absolute worst. 'Oh, my God, they hate us.' Quite the contrary: they loved us. What an extraordinary way to show approval. It certainly took some getting used to, and it was something of a relief to know that these plates were manufactured from plaster for that express purpose. Patrons buy huge stacks of them, hold the stack at the bottom with one hand and hack at the top with the edge of another plate held vertically like an axe, before heaving the entire shattered remains onto the stage. What a mess. The smashing of plates is a time-honoured tradition, but the origins of the practice are murky, ranging from fun and appreciation to warding off evil spirits and offering good luck. Whatever, it gave us all a turn, a plentiful supply of bandaids was kept on hand from then on.

Other artists were also working at the club. These were very high class, exceedingly well regarded and well rewarded, strippers from all parts of the globe. They started their shows late, after our second show. These girls were expected to remove their hugely expensive costumes and get down to the buff, and they did it with such panache. I always had a ball watching while waiting for Luis and the dancers to remove their makeup and change. They were so professional and knew, oh so well, what to expose and when to expose it. Great ladies. Loved them all.

We arrived in Athens at a time when the government was experimenting with energy consumption cuts. Discos, restaurants and all nightlife (without Mafia ties) were obliged to close at midnight. After a show, everybody is hungry, so we went as a group looking for an illegal eatery we were told about, the 'knock twice and ask for Athena' type. We found it a few blocks away at the foot of the Acropolis in Plaka. It was very much a cloak-and-dagger affair, and after mentioning who sent us, the door opened a crack to admit us to a room with a sawdust-strewn floor, a few rustic tables and chairs and huge barrels of wine anchored high on the walls. The doorless kitchen was on the left as you entered. There was no menu—just an invitation to the kitchen and the lifting of pot lids emitting the most enticing smells, then the pointing of a finger at what smelled the best, and that was it. Wine was a help-yourself affair from the barrels, and one price fits all. Oh, the feasts we had in that place during our time in that fantastic city. Not long after, these futile government energy-saving efforts were relegated to the past.

Next morning, we had the best surprise. Jack called and told us our dear friends from Damascus had their show in Cyprus cancelled due to disturbances between the Greeks and the Turks. What else is new in Cyprus? Not only would they be arriving that day by ship, they would be working two doors down from us.

The day of their arrival, the entire cast took off to Piraeus to watch them dock and welcome them to Greece. When we got to their berth, there was just an empty pier, and we were told they were late but would probably be there within the hour. There were some great-looking cafés around, so we ate and waited. Before too long, we could see their ship approaching, and not long after we could make them out, all up front of the ship, waving like crazy, Jack having primed them to expect us. Berthed next to them was a US aircraft carrier, it says much for Aggie's reputation as they docked, a great cry of 'AGGIE' went up. Ohhhh, Agg darling. How embarrassing.

At the end of our month-long sojourn in Athens, we were off to Crete next for a month at a hotel resort on Apollonia beach not far outside Heraklion. The flight from Athens to Crete was very short, and Jack came with us to settle us in. The resort/hotel was five-star stuff, and we were presented with two accommodation choices, rooms in the hotel or an entire house, complete with staff a kilometre or so towards Heraklion in a vineyard by the beach. Oh, we jumped at the house offer. Life in hotel rooms can be very claustrophobic and restrictive, no matter how glam the hotel. The house was old enough to have character but new enough that all the things that should work – like plumbing and electricity – did work. Behind the house and to each side were vineyards full of ripe grapes, and directly in front, across a small road, the beach—not a pristine beach with squeaky white sand and palm trees, but a beach none the less. The hotel was prepared to send a bus for us going and coming from work. Still, most nights we decided to hoof it cross country through the vineyards, gorging ourselves as we went on sweet grapes direct from the vine.

I cannot recall for the life of me what that showroom looked like, but it must have been adequate, or I most certainly would remember. I do recall we shared the stage with a magician and his wife-assistant, Harry and Anka. Anka, an apt name for a lady who lived on a yacht. Harry (Jamaican) and Anka (Dutch) would work only where there was a port and a mooring for their yacht. This couple were very worldly and well-travelled. They often invited Luis and me onboard for meals, their vessel was super cosy with masses of room for their big white doves' cage on the deck. Harry used the birds in his act, they were part of the family. Bizarrely, they kept two boa constrictors as guard dogs.

These massive, fat snakes had free range of the yacht and you can bet they kept any and all ne'er-do-wells at bay. It mesmerised me to watch Anka feed them. She would hold the body under her arm with the head in her hand and push steak mince down its gullet with a pencil, all the while carrying on a perfectly normal conversation. I was always transfixed by this little operation, almost as much as when she would massage and pick away at the skin around the snake's head in an effort to help it shed. Strange, unique, wonderful people. Harry was the son of a Jamaican prime minister. I can't remember his last name, so that's not much help. He was considered the black sheep of the family, preferring his life on the road, or waves, with his magic. Anka was a statuesque, glamorous creature with a gift for languages. At the time we met, she spoke upwards of ten, she said she could make herself understood in a new language within two weeks and had it down in two months. Remarkable.

There was much to see and do besides basking on the beach in Crete. Apart from the old city of Heraklion and the museum, there was Knossos to visit. The Palace of Knossos, the ancient capital city of the Minoan civilisation, was the home of King Minos, the legend of Theseus, the Labyrinth and the Minotaur. I spent many hours there and marvelled each time I saw the still fresh-looking three and a half thousand-year-old frescoes of the Bull Jumpers, the Porpoises, the beautiful Court Ladies and the lithe Boy with the Feathered Headdress. Excavated and reconstructed by archaeologist Arthur Evans, the site remains a bone of contention between people in the know, and a huge amount of scepticism was voiced. Opinion generally falls between pure fantasy and a reasonable facsimile. Regardless, there is enough to fascinate and awe. This magnificent, ancient civilisation was thought to be equal to that of the Egyptians of the period, with whom they traded.

In no time at all, the Crete contract was over, and it was back to Athens to perform in an outdoor summer theatre in an enormous park near the Athens Museum. For some reason, the name 'Alsos' pops into my head. With promises to Harry and Anka – oh those promises over the years to watch out for each other – we left Heraklion. Me by ferry with the baggage and the dancers by plane.

Back in Athens, the ever-thoughtful Jack had very kindly reserved the same rooms for us so we could feel at least a little continuity in our gipsy-like lives. Jack was an artist all his life before becoming an agent (a juggler I think), so he knew very well how to treat other artists. The following day we visited the outdoor stage where we would be performing. We were a bit flabbergasted at the size of the audience we would be playing to twice nightly. It was a sold-out capacity audience of three thousand people. Not just three thousand people, each show would have a completely different audience. That's six thousand people per night. With only one night off, we would be seen by thirty-six thousand Athenians each week.

It was now full summer, and the shows were very slick and fast-moving. Dancers get hot, even in winter, and the Athens heat didn't cool down a great deal at night. Costumes soon became permanently damp and it was becoming a problem, as was the makeup running down faces. We must have sorted it out because we finished the month-long engagement without anyone fainting from the odour, and makeup can be applied more sparingly to such beautiful women; just double up on the lashes for the people in the cheap seats at the back.

Kalamaki Beach is one of Athens' most popular beaches, but two good reasons stopped us from ever visiting it. One was it was closed due to pollution, the other is that the girls need to wear only a tiny g-string and go topless so as not to get tan marks that would show up on stage. Not easy being a showgirl. However, the dancers had plenty of gorgeous male friends from our last trip and they were only too happy to arrange cars and take us forty-five minutes or so out of Athens to a very rocky coastline that was remarkably private. Glorious days were spent there with some delicious picnic food and wine chilling in the water moored by a cord wrapped around the neck of the bottle. Some of these guys were most certainly god-like—Greek god-like, even.

Once, our male dancer Ron got a little more sun than was good for him. That night at work, he was so fiercely burnt he couldn't bear the costumes touching his skin. One of the Greek singers suggested darting over to the deli and grabbing the biggest jar of yoghurt I could lay my hands on. The entire contents were rubbed gently over Ron's body. The idea being, to sit and wait. Less than an hour later, the only visible sign of yoghurt on his body was a fine white powder which, when lightly and gingerly brushed off, left Ron red but totally without pain. It's a little secret I've passed on more than a few times since.

Another month had gone by so quickly. Apart from thinking about moving on again, I couldn't help wondering what had happened to Harry and Anka. I knew through Jack they were supposed to be sailing to Athens shortly after Crete, but nobody had heard from them. Walking through Plaka a couple of days before leaving, I heard my name. There in front of me, not fifteen metres away, were those two wayward seafarers. What on earth did they look like? Always smartly dressed, this time they were both wearing grubby shorts and tee-shirts and looked ghastly. I rushed to greet them, and we headed to a nearby coffee shop where the whole near-tragic tale came out. Having left Crete after two weeks sailing around the island, they headed for Athens. Noticing the yacht was riding too low, they discovered to their horror, a leak in the hull that proved resistant to all their mending efforts. Slowly but surely, their home was sinking, and being entirely out of normal sea lanes they could not expect any help. Just as their predicament was at its worst, the yacht barely afloat, a small cargo ship appeared. It was empty and captained by a man heading home for vacation. Harry and Anka were overcome with emotion at this point in the story and it took some time for them to feel composed enough to continue. The ship pulled alongside, literally as their boat sank, and from the ship's deck they watched it disappear beneath the waves.

They had lost everything. The doves had sadly been set free in the hope they might reach land and they lost sight of them after they had circled overhead in a little flock for quite a long time. The two boa constrictors had presumably gone into hiding in some pockets of air they had found. Harry thought that the saltwater had probably done them in and they were already dead. All their clothes and belongings except for what they wore had gone down with the yacht. The captain changed course and very kindly took them to Piraeus where they were given shelter at a seamen's mission. Definitely the stuff of tears and valium.

Heartbroken, they had tried to contact Harry's father for money. I gave them what little cash I had and we agreed to meet the next day when I was able to give them a good deal more as well as a lot of clothing. We left after a few days. I never did hear what happened to this delightful freedom-loving couple after that.

Opening my hotel room window and seeing the Acropolis at the end of the street is a vision that stays with me. Athens, the city which in 507 B.C. gave us demokratia, democracy, rule by the people. It is a working concept so very important to the free world. How thrilling to work and live in that history-soaked city.

CHAPTER 35

DON'T DIE, MR TITO

Early in 1980 we were leaving Athens. There were terrible problems that year with airline strikes and our next opening date in Spilimbergo, an hour from Venice in the north of Italy, was imminent. With the help of Jack Palass, the hunt was on for a bus that could fit us all in with two seats each for comfort plus the trunks, personal luggage and a couple of drivers to get us from Athens, through Yugoslavia – the Socialist Federal Republic of Yugoslavia, to give it its mouthful of a correct name – and down to Spilimbergo, nonstop. It was a dicey time because President Tito was deathly ill and not every bus driver wanted to take the risk of him dying while they were on the way there or back. The death of any Communist president could lead to unpredictable unrest, and it would be anybody's guess whether borders would be closed. Eventually, I found the owner of a bus who was willing, for a hefty fee, to make the run.

On the evening of the last show in Athens, the bus arrived at the venue, and we started loading. The drivers offered us the use of sleeping bags in case the heating system was not sufficient. It was winter after all, and we could expect the Yugoslavian leg to be through deep snow. It was going to be tight, but after carefully stacking the trunks, there were just enough seats left. The dancers had gone to the restaurant nearby to pick up food previously ordered for the trip, and to get a last snack before the twenty-four-hour journey. I went to call them back for boarding, and when I returned to the bus, a half dozen strangers were sitting in our seats. A lot of hand-waving and shooing, and the bus driver made it known to us through broken English that these were some of his family members coming along for the ride. Yeah, right. Out, out, out. Off we went, up through Thessaloniki, skirting Belgrade and Zagreb, entering Italy northeast of Udine. A long trip, and the more haste, the better. Don't croak, Mr Tito, please.

During the night it became very, very cold. The sleeping bags were an excellent idea, and combined with the bus heating system, it was quite cosy. Quite suddenly it became very cold and I could hear complaints and shouts of 'turn the heat up' coming from all over. Except, for one little voice that said, 'I don't know what you're all going on about. I'm lovely and warm. In fact, I'm too hot.' Our resident firebug was at it again. Anthea had decided the floor was comfortable and had managed to jam the foot end of her sleeping bag down the main heating duct. Not only had she blocked off the heat to the rest of the bus, but her sleeping bag was smouldering and on the verge of bursting into flames.

In Yugoslavia we passed through a few little towns or weigh stations, which offered not much in the way of facilities. Loo breaks were taken on a 'need-to-go' basis and behind the bus was as good a place as any. Ron seemed to be getting a tummy bug, and his need to go was becoming more frequent. Poor Ron, he left some lovely little frozen presents in the snow throughout the trip, a nice surprise for spring. When dawn broke, we could see the landscape we were passing through was truly magical. Townsfolk were out and about in horse-drawn sleighs complete with bells, and what looked like delightful, hand-crafted, colourful blankets over their knees. Now at least there was the opportunity to stop for food and a real toilet. Poor Ron was still not doing well.

Sleeping on a bus, in fact, bus travel, in general, was never comfortable for me and I woke to the slightest noise or bump. You know how it is, you feel a bump and ignore it, hoping sleep will come. Bump, ignore, bump, bump, ignore. Suddenly there were way too many bumps to ignore, and I opened my bleary, sore eyes to the sight of the two drivers passing a bottle of brandy back and forth between them. I was out of that seat in a flash yelling and, using the internationally recognised hand down motion for 'slow down', I got them to pull over to the side of the road. As far as I could make out, they believed brandy would keep them awake. I've got a better idea guys—I'm going to sit behind you with the bottle and at the slightest hint of a nodding head, I'm going to whack that head with the bottle. Think that'll keep you awake? There were no further incidents except Ron's worsening tummy, and we got to the Italian border near Austria with Tito still alive.

Tito died very soon after in May, the aftermath burdened with tensions, state paralysis, irreconcilable ethnic differences, and recriminations resulting in shocking death counts and injuries. The States of Bosnia and Herzegovina, Croatia, Macedonia, Montenegro, Serbia, and Slovenia have since been created or recreated. How sad to think of the dreadful fighting and destruction that beautiful country went through not many years later. Is this becoming a pattern? Do our visits have a negative effect on Governments?

With Spilimbergo still a couple of hours from the Italian border, it had been an uncomfortable but pleasant enough trip through some magnificent mountains, quaint rustic towns and marvellous rural winter scenery. Spilimbergo is a small town a little over an hour northeast of Venice. Very old, with buildings such as the Torre Orientale (Eastern Tower), which was part of the first circle of walls, dating from 1304, and a few palaces including the Casa Dipinta (Painted house), painted in frescoed scenes of Hercules, from the sixteenth century. We were there in the depths of winter with snow, ice and slush everywhere. It offered a seemingly unsophisticated mentality with the only nightlife available being the club we were about to work in. An hour's stroll takes you over the entire town, so the thought of a month there wasn't very appealing. We stayed at the Albergo Michielini between the centre of the old town and the railway station. The passageway and rooms were so unattractive and the ambience so quiet that the dancers began referring to their rooms as Ward 23 or 17. I can't blame them. After Athens, this was definitely not a highlight.

Our first sight of the venue came the following day when an old VW Kombi van picked us up for rehearsal. We wondered where on earth they were taking us because we saw nothing along the way, but farm houses and stretches of snowy fields. The club, Scaccomatto was bang in the middle of a snow covered clearing in a field of barley some ten kilometres south of Spilimbergo. How this nightclub came to be there or the reason for its immense popularity I'll never know. The exterior of the club was bare red brick, pretty much a rectangle with no redeeming architectural features whatsoever. Gloom was most definitely setting in. Once inside, the transformation seemed impossible. Three sizable dressing rooms right off stage left, a good eight metre by eight-metre stage split into two levels, and a huge dance floor with comfortable-looking armchairs and sofas in small, intimate groups for the audience. A monstrous, L-shaped bar and a generous, welcoming entrance hall. A pleasant surprise, to say the least. Business must be good, and money must be plentiful to be able to afford a show the size of ours. The Bluebells from the Lido in Paris had appeared there not long before.

The trunks were brought over the previous night so I unpacked while the dancers rehearsed. Lots of hanging space and a lovely high ceiling, so no problem with the tallest hats. We still hadn't met either owner or management, but that was of no concern. Tomorrow we would open and, all being well, there was plenty of time for introductions. Rehearsals and unpacking finished; the decrepit VW took us back to the hotel. Meals in the hotel dining room were unfussy, home-cooked, inexpensive and excellent quality. Night-time pick-up hour came and we were rugged up and waiting in the lobby. Two ten kilometre trips so far today in this old, draughty, rust bucket had prepared us for a bumpy, even colder trip at night.

Entering the club through the back door with direct access to the dressing rooms, we were greeted by the two other artists appearing with us. One was a world-class, award-winning magician, working exclusively with clocks and watches. Swedish, if I remember correctly. Nice guy, I looked forward to seeing his act. The other was an older, chubby Italian man who was a female impersonator called Madame Maurice. Now, this I couldn't wait to see. He seemed pleasant enough, spoke no English, but we felt the vibes, and it was all good. Just as we settled in the owners came back to be introduced. A cordial enough couple, not overly friendly but certainly correct and professional. They welcomed us to Scaccomatto and Spilimbergo, enquired whether we had been treated well, and informed us that we needed to go to Klagenfurt in Austria the following day to have work permits stamped. Great, a two-hour drive there and another two back in that dreadful rust bucket. They then excused themselves. Well, I've met friendlier venue owners, but we would give them our best and see if the ice broke a little.

The first of our two nightly shows started on time, no problems, good sound, and the lighting cues followed meticulously. The magician did things with clocks and watches that were nothing short of miraculous, and Madame Maurice, fully made up and frocked, and after seeing how beautiful the girls backstage were, decided she was too emotional to go on. Shortly, after a few tears and some very dramatic and racking sobs, Madame Maurice recovered sufficiently to burst through the curtains and tell the audience that the 'kangaroos' backstage were positively the most gorgeous-looking people she had ever worked with. You go, Madame Maurice, you sell us to those two cold-fish owners. Madame Maurice's act was incredibly energetic for a man his size and age. He sang live, no lip-syncing, his cracked and croaky voice made the act all the funnier. During *New York, New York,* the last New York disappeared entirely. His last song was, what else but, *I Am What I Am*, performed with a huge jar of cold cream held aloft in his left hand, into which he made constant sorties with his right hand, rubbing vigorously at his heavily made-up face, revealing the man underneath. The grand, final gesture was a superb flourishing of his wig as he leapt down from one stage level to the other without fracturing a hip. Bravo Madame Maurice.

After a week or so, on our day off, we were relaxed enough to take day or overnight trips, to Venice or Udine. Venice was of course, just too breathtaking. We went there often—it was so magnificent and hard to take in. We even worked there a couple of times in an underground disco, not in the furtive or illegal sense, just located underground on the mainland part of greater Venice, of course, not in the lagoon.

Sometimes, if you had a good show, venue managements would get offers for you to work either before or after your regular show at another venue.

These gigs, or galas, paid well, and we would all come out of it somewhat better off. Still, the packing and unpacking, the drive there and back, plus a show in a place you had never seen before were hard work and we didn't do it often. Years later, after we had been to Spilimbergo three or four times, management sold us on for a gala, and we took the wrong show music. Luis was all for apologising and calling it quits, but I wanted to put the show on with the wrong music, doing the choreography for that show but wearing the costumes we had brought. I won, and the dancers could not keep a straight face. In the show we took, there was a Commando number where the costumes were all camouflage design with netting, huge pockets, guns and strategic rips and tears. The correct music was all thump-bang stuff, and it was quite popular. That's what the management at this venue had seen at Scaccamatto, and that's what they wanted. The music we had with us, however, was all a bit traditional showgirl with lots of high kicks. We did the show, and I told everyone to rush with the packing and get into the bus before the venue owners came to their senses. On approaching management for the money, they rather dazedly handed a fat envelope over saying, 'Strange. It looked so different in Scaccomatto.' I told them it had a lot to do with lighting and ran for the door.

The owners of Scaccomatto were very impressed with the shows and long since revealed themselves to be caring and friendly. Gone was the frosty attitude. On later tours, the owners put the dancers up in a vast villa they owned in town and Luis and I stayed in the hotel to give them some peace. We ended up going back there each time we toured Italy, all great friends and one happy family. They also supplied us with our own minibus, a brand new one. Goodbye to the draughty, clapped out, old VW. I always drove it and we had use of it whenever we wanted. Travelling from the club to Spilimbergo could be a bit harrowing in winter. We were always on the road late at night, and unless there had been cars in front, there were no tracks in the snow to guide us. Not too bad going but coming home was always a problem. Luis and the male dancers would take turns walking in front of the bus with a steel rod, feeling through the fresh snow for the edges of the road. It took forever.

Spilimbergo, or 'Spilly' as we all called it, started off a little frigid but became a much looked forward to leg of our Italian tours. The nearness to Venice meant spending every day discovering that city's magnificence if we cared to, and we often did. All in all, Spilly became a home away from home. A most welcome luxury, when home is so very far away.

TOP Flash Gordon.
BOTTOM Leading lady Donna with magicians Ger and Roland.

The popular pink, used as an opening or finale.

Leading lady Giselle with Luis, San Remo Song Festival, 1982.

Our Korean orphans getting their new raincoats.

TOP Leading lady Annie (centre), Tropical finale.
BOTTOM Inca, the biggest set ever built in Asia at that time.

The author, Luis, cast and production team, Sinbad on Ice, Dubai.

TOP The author's Genie design for Aladdin on Ice.
BOTTOM Russian fantasy, Aladdin on Ice.

The author and Luis, backstage, Aladdin on Ice.

CHAPTER 36

CONQUERING ITALY

Tortona is in the north of Italy, about midway between Milano and Genoa. Founded between 118 and 123 BC, it is one of the oldest Roman colony towns and was first known as Derthona, and later the garrison town of Deltona. There was even less to do in Tortona than in Spilimbergo, and apart from a visit to Santuario Della Madonna Della Guardia with its imposing golden statue of the Madonna with Child on top of the bell tower, you certainly needed to have a hobby in this middle-of-nowhere town. Or perhaps, a hospitalised sick friend who needed visiting regularly.

A week into the Tortona run everything was going well enough for me to jump onto a plane and head for Athens to pick up the silver fox furs I had negotiated to buy for a reasonable price. Twenty thousand dollars' worth. They were eventually to become the centrepiece of our famous White Finale and elicited standing ovations for many years. The furs were delivered to my old room in the Achilleus Hotel and I set about hand sewing bits together, rubbing make-up on different parts and sticking grubby name labels on. All this work was to claim them as used costuming on re-entering Australia, should Customs show an interest. The third day there was an urgent call from Luis, 'Get your arse over here quickly, Ron is in hospital with hepatitis, and you have to replace him tonight'. So, onto the next flight out, with the furs in tow, to Tortona. I have never claimed to be more than a slightly adequate dancer, picking up choreography is not my greatest talent. However, needs must, and I got stuck into learning the two shows. I learned a couple of routines per day and was popped into the show bit by bit, mostly dancing opposite darling Anthea. Luis said: 'If you're unsure, follow Anthea'. At the end of my first full show, Luis came back saying to Anthea 'What on earth were you doing out there tonight? You were all over the place.' Anthea replied in complete innocence, 'I was following Tom'.

Poor Ron, still sick and getting sicker, was turning what an interior designer might describe as a colour something between chartreuse and mikado yellow. Ron's diagnosis of a nasty case of hepatitis was a result of, the doctors said, from eating bad shellfish, or perhaps contact with an unclean female. Even though our Ronny can be a bit of a dark horse, we think it just might have been the shellfish. So that took care of what to do in Tortona. We visited him regularly, and although he was in quarantine, we were allowed to stand outside his window and chat. Thankfully, he was on the ground floor. Ron amused his fellow patients and the nurses by embroidering a tablecloth and six napkins with beautiful grapes and leaves, he became a bit of a star at the Tortona Municipal Hospital. After two long weeks in that charmless town, we were on our way to Modena.

Now there's a place I'd heard about. Modena, the home of, in no particular order, balsamic vinegar, Enzo Ferrari and Luciano Pavarotti, whose childhood home is now a museum. This ancient mediaeval town centre with its twelfth-century Duomo, its Torre Della Ghirlandina gothic bell tower and the enormous Piazza Grande, kept me captivated for the month we were there. The city of Parma was nearby as well as the beautiful, historic city of Bologna, the seventh-largest city in Italy. With a history dating back to 1000 BC, it is steeped in antiquity with its museums, leaning towers, and the oldest university in the world, founded in 1175.

Ron was out of hospital but in no fit state to work and needed a lot of rest and a bit of loving care. We all tried so hard to look after him, dear man, and Ron being Ron, responded incredibly quickly and was back in the show by the following month. The club we worked in was the Shilling, and it was quite a classy joint with good-size dressing rooms and a private artists' entrance. It was modern, chic with fashionable décor and an average size stage. The cars pulling up at night revealed the patrons were a well-heeled lot. They were well behaved, appreciative of the show and our beautiful women. At times, knowing very well our girls never entered the showroom unless performing, management was nevertheless obligated to communicate the numerous customer requests to join them after the show. Turning down these alluring offers was generally taken well and without insult. On one occasion, a gentleman insisted on sending back a few of bottles of champagne for the dancers. Okay, fine, no problem there. Three bottles were accompanied by a tray of glasses, and the bubbles went down the hatch with many thanks. I dressed and went out front to thank the gent for his kindness. I was delivering my little speech when he asked me to bring the girls out to thank him personally. To this I replied that was against our policy. 'Oh,' he said, 'so they don't mind drinking my champagne, but don't have the decency to come out and thank me.' With that, I asked a passing waiter how much the bottles cost and was told … gulp, six hundred dollars. I signed a chit so the man was repaid for his generosity and the money taken from our contract. Bottles were sent back unopened after that.

Genoa was on our tour list only once, directly after the first visit to Milano. Genoa, or Genova, derives its name from the Latin genu or knee. Look at the map, and you'll see it is precisely where the knee is on boot-shaped Italy. Poor Genoa was fought over for centuries and occupied by the Greeks, French, Austrians, Romans and anybody else passing through who fancied it. Today it is Italy's sixth biggest city and a major port and ship-building centre. We worked just south of the port where the high cliffs give a breathtaking view over the city and down the stunningly rugged coast to Portofino. Luis's parents joined us in Genoa, we packed many a picnic and took buses along the coast to the old fishing villages and storybook coves along the Amalfi Coast.

These small towns seem to belong on a film set with their faded and weathered pink, yellow, and orange stuccoed buildings clinging to the vertical cliffs and creeping right down to the water's edge with upturned fishing boats clustered around their feet. A short walk from Genoa's port is the house where Christopher Columbus was allegedly born. Located outside the twin crenellated circular towers of the old city gate, it almost disappears into the undergrowth behind it, with ivy crawling over everything but the first-floor window and the front door. The debate about whether or not this really is his birthplace has as many arguments as the pronunciation and spelling of his name: Christopher Columbus, Cristophe Columbia, Cristobal Colon, Cristoforo Columbo, Kristoffer Kolumbus, Christoph Kolumbus, and Christoffel Columbus. It is pretty much established now that 'CC' was born in the town of Cuba, Portugal. The month-long stay was not long enough to appreciate the history of the place or visit all the many museums. We left Genoa for Athens by ship, looking forward to the few days at sea. Luis's parents stayed on in Athens with us for a while before flying back to Madrid. Always great to have them with us for even a short a time.

San Remo is a short train ride away from Monaco and Nice, so there was always more to do and see than time to do it. In 1956, the San Remo Song Festival had inspired the creation of the Eurovision Song Contest. When we performed there for the 1981 San Remo Song Festival, they were going all out with their guest artists. The roll call was a singing stars' Who's Who. First and foremost there was us, of course—obviously the main drawcard of the season, the guest artists included The Village People, Gloria Gaynor, Bob Dylan, Marianne Faithful, Amanda Lear and some minor groups or solo artists we never got to see or work with. We usually opened for each artist, one per night. The associated worldwide MundoVision hook-up for the festival was causing a lot of trouble. MundoVision Corporation of America is a Spanish-language television broadcaster headquartered in Houston Texas, with the capability of broadcasting on global hook-up. Technology then was not what it is today, and these hook-ups were full of glitches. This country would not be available, that country wasn't ready. Often there were hours and hours of delays. Sometimes they could give us an approximate time frame, others not, and it was a matter of reading or knitting or finding some way to kill time while we waited interminably. There were benefits of course, occasional days and nights free were not going to be argued with.

Coming back from a day trip to Monaco one evening, Luis and I were sharing a compartment on the train with a young American girl who, after passing through formalities at the France/Italy border was visibly upset. Luis kindly asked her what was wrong, and the poor darling burst into sobs. The Italian border officials had rifled through her handbag, making a great deal of fuss over her tampons, pretending not to know what they were, holding them aloft and asking her to explain. Women are fair game to these big macho Italian guys. Where's the problem in causing an innocent foreigner a great deal of embarrassment if it helps pass the time? Bastards. We cluck-clucked and soothed her as much as we could. She told us she was an associate of Hall and Oats, a singing duo entering in the Song Festival. There was a problem with their master recording of the song they were to sing, and she was delivering a copy. 'Would you like to hear it?' We can say we were among the first people to hear that very successful number one hit, *Private Eyes*. At San Remo, we took her to the Ariston Theatre. Until 1976, the festival took place in the San Remo casino, but from 1977, all the following programs were held in the Teatro Ariston. Being official entertainers, we possessed Valid all Areas passes, so were able to get her inside to find Daryl and John. What great and memorable hits those two talented guys had: *Rich Girl*, *Kiss Is on My List*, *Maneater* and, of course, *Private Eyes*—highlighted by Billboard magazine naming them 'The most successful duo of the rock era'.

The Village People were super friendly, and we hit the town each night with free entry and free drinks in the two best bars in San Remo. Both venues would line up drinks waiting for us, vying for our patronage. A couple of the dancers, female dancers, note, made particularly good friends with the group's two straight guys, and all parties sported smiling and happy faces. Who could forget Gloria Gaynor and her hits *I Will Survive*, *Never Can Say Goodbye* and *I Am What I Am*. I have little to say about Ms Gaynor. During rehearsal periods her manager cleared the floor in front of the stage, sat Ms Gaynor down and surrounded her with a circle of chairs facing inwards. We perceived this as a subtle sign she was not to be approached. I wonder if it was her manager's doing, afraid we would mob her, or she wanted to be left alone. Either way, it seemed a little sad and unnecessary.

We had the dubious honour of rehearsing with Marianne Faithful, beautiful young girl she may have been, but by then was anything but beautiful inside and out. Her attitude in rehearsal was completely unprofessional, mouthing the words of her song in a manner that said, 'I'm bored shitless. Get on with it.' She was quite frankly, nothing but a pain in the arse. Bob Dylan appeared at a few rehearsals with his little son, but we never spoke. He seemed very quiet and serious. Amanda Lear, on the other hand, was very chatty and so, so easy to get on with. Famously born on 18 June or 18 November in 1939, 1942, 1946 or 1950, pick one, she was promoting her latest album *Diamonds for Breakfast*. Lear, singer, model and actress, was never big in Australia, but in Europe, she was an enigmatic superstar; to date, she has sold over twenty-five million singles and fifteen million albums worldwide.

Amanda was an absolute gay icon, and friend to Mick Jagger, Twiggy, David Bowie, Sacha Distel, and according to people in the know, Salvador Dali's muse. It's certainly true she ended up with quite a few of Dali's works, most of which went up in a fire when her home in the south of France burnt down in December 2000, taking with it her husband/manager, bisexual French aristocrat Alain-Philippe Malagnac. Amanda was eternally enshrouded in mystery. The press and street rumours said she was French, British, Russian and even Vietnamese. It was considered common knowledge she was once been a man and worked in a transvestite revue in Paris. In 2011, an Italian newspaper ran an article which included a copy of Lear's birth certificate, stating she was born Alain Maurice Louis René Tap on 18 June 1939 in Saigon, and featured a photograph of her as a young man. Lear never denied these stories, and it certainly did her career no harm. She even posed nude in Playboy. I remember all the gays scrutinising the photos, and deciding whatever she'd had done, it was a good job. Any publicity is good publicity was her motto. It was rumoured Dali paid for her sex change. I don't know what became of her although I hear she's still releasing records. I do remember she was politeness itself backstage and wasn't the least outrageous. As far as I know, she was never into the drug scene, so I suppose she retired somewhere quite well off and happy. I hope so.

The 1981 San Remo Song Festival was drawing to a close and it only remained for the winner to be announced. Giselle, our stunningly beautiful Sophia Loren look-alike, was posed in full costume next to the safe containing the winner's name. The name was read out to the world on the fickle MundoVision hook-up. What a great palaver. We knew who'd won long before the festival was over, but this little charade had to be performed.

The San Remo Song Festival still runs, stronger than ever I believe. How fortunate to have been guest performers there since 1971, and how wonderful to spend time in that quaint other worldly place where old money mixes with new, and the blue-blooded citizens take Sunday strolls in their finery with their equally well-bred dogs like a scene out of *Easter Parade*.

CHAPTER 37

LA BELLA ROMA AND A BIT OF MANO NERA

Who on this planet of ours would not love the opportunity to live and work in Rome? Four times we were fortunate enough to do exactly that. Paradise, a nightclub on Via Mario de Fiori, just off the Spanish Steps, was owned and run by Signore Bornigio, a charming and generous rogue with Mafia connections. There was no such thing as an Italian nightspot owner without links to la mano nera. Our first contract at Paradise was in 1982, and at the time we all lived nearby in the Hotel Julia on Via Rasella, off Piazza Barberini. Nice and close for getting to work, but smallish rooms, and a walk-up, there was no lift.

We needed a bit of space for maintaining and cleaning costumes. During our later contracts, Luis and I shared an apartment with Dale in Municipio II, outside the walled area of old Rome, above Villa Borghese. The apartment was owned by, and next door to, Signore Bornigio. This area is very much a suburban one and was gratefully, tourist-free. The tourists in Rome can become too, too much to bear. A couple of kilometres' walk, then through the beautifully peaceful Borghese Gardens and we were at the club. The girls continued to stay at Hotel Julia because it was so central, a few minutes stroll in any direction took them to the Trevi Fountain, Piazza Navona, the remarkable ruins of the Forum, shopping on Via Venti Settembre or the fabulous, and fabulously expensive, boutiques of Via Veneto. All this and getting paid to do it.

As I mentioned earlier when talking about Athens, it became important to not fool yourself into believing the amount stated in your contract is really yours. Rome, and actually all of Italy, was notorious for this. The amount of money deducted or handed out to the different people and groups who live off these shavings is preposterous. Of course, it is parasitic and unlawful, but it's the way it has always been, and the way it is. So, pay up and get on with it. The police take a significant slice, in particular the Juvenile Police. I had no idea whether they were a recognised government department or not, but they were first at the door on pay nights.

These young guys were never in uniform and were alleged to be clandestine police who infiltrated youth groups in discotheques, streets, coffee bars, shopping areas, and any place where teens generally hung out. I can tell you one thing about this group. Although the girls lived only a few streets away from the venue, they got home safely each night because of the payments to this little faction. They would tail and loiter invisibly wherever the girls might be, keeping away all and every nut, pervert, and yobbo—and Rome was chockablock with loonies. There were young guys on the streets very late at night who wanted to bother girls, drove in circles around them, chanted crazy things and were generally being pests. I saw it every night. But none of that happened after you paid your dues. Maybe those nuts and the Juvenile Police were one and the same troop. Who knows? Pay up and get on with it.

The Visa Department is another excellent example. Our papers were to be stamped after a week or so in each city. The queues in these offices had to be seen to be believed but, my philanthropic endowments got us to the front, seated, stamped and out, quick as a blink. Sure, you can say paying up fans the flames, exacerbates the corruption, the bribery problem. Maybe so, but I was not on a clean-up mission. I was just a show producer trying to travel around easily and safely with my precious dancers.

The first time in Rome, we arrived fresh from Iraq. We thought we'd become blasé about living in a war zone, but the subconscious mind plays tricks on you. I still found myself automatically ducking into the comparative safety of a doorway whenever a commercial jet passed overhead. I guess things take a little time. I might have looked decidedly weird to passers-by, but then I don't think anybody takes the slightest bit of notice of the strange antics of tourists in Rome. My sudden leaps for cover most likely went unnoticed.

Our first ever inspection of Paradise took place early in the afternoon the day after our arrival the night before. As usual, Luis and I went to 'kick the tyres' of the venue before the dancers arrived, make sure the dressing rooms were clean and tidy, allocate them, mop the stage, give the loos the once over and so on. There wasn't a great deal to do—a good sweep out, a bit of dusting, clean the mirrors and poke a nose into the toilets. These needed an hour's scrubbing, disinfecting, spraying and several cans of Harpic before they came up to scratch, fresh and ready for rehearsal. The stage at Paradise was a miniature traditional theatre, complete with red velvet curtains. The backstage entry led directly off the dressing rooms and was more than adequate. The stage was very high, raised about a metre with good-size wings and a crossover, an ideal place to perform. No problems with tall feathers or bulky costumes. It also offered a great lighting system and state-of-the-art sound.

Signore Bornigio was very strict but very correct. On this and later visits, he always loved having us there, and treated us with enormous respect. He owned a magnificent country home on a significant estate outside of Rome, and on Sundays he would put on wonderful afternoons full of food, rest, and games. Trestles covered with white butcher paper would be set out under the wide, sweet smelling pepper trees, laden with monstrous bowls of pasta he had cooked himself. There were salads of every type, freshly baked crunchy bread, and a whole wheel of Parmesan cheese. Superb Italian wines were laid on and there was nothing to do but feast, feast, feast. Blankets on the lawns were available for an hour or so nap, then the games would begin.

Lawn volleyball under hose sprinklers was a fun and welcome distraction on those sizzling Roman summer days. The house itself was a faded pink stuccoed two-storey affair with typically Italian drainpipe terra cotta tiles on the roof. Sr Bornigio's sister was a recognised and prolific artist. Her magnificent paintings featured wistful, melancholy clowns as the focal point and these beautiful works covered the walls. A couple of weeks before we left in 1986, someone broke into this peaceful place, and viciously slashed all her paintings. A true crime, it broke my heart. People involved in Mafia business have enemies, and I'm sure, ways of dealing with them. Sr Bornigio owned another venue a little way down from our apartment. This one was smaller, and mainly a nightclub/discotheque. He had two sons in their twenties, both as handsome as any of the busts in the Rome Museum. One was on the door at Paradise and one at this other club, alternating week by week. One Saturday night, the young son at the nearby club was brutally kneecapped. Not for the fainthearted, this lifestyle of infighting and paybacks.

The staff at Paradise had not changed in the four or five years we appeared there, which in itself says something about the owner. Working on the door was a large, tall, generously proportioned and not particularly attractive woman called Marietta, who simply couldn't wait to inform us she was a post-op transsexual. Having lived my whole adult life in the theatre, this little piece of news was nothing to write home about. To her, however, it was big, big, news which must be imparted, complete with visuals. It became such a battle to evade her. A glimpse of her hovering backstage would see doors hurriedly closed, and a great scuttling for cover. I had the good fortune to altogether avoid seeing the lifting of skirts, and the knickerless flashings of her good self, but others didn't—some quite lost their appetites for days afterwards.

On occasion, door duties were shared with a White Russian called Milka, well known by the staff for her ability to tell fortunes. I'm not a great believer in all that nonsense but, she absolutely insisted on reading for us all. She read cards, and as much as I loathe to admit it, she was dead right with her readings for Dale, Luis and myself at least. Quite spooky. Of course, it meant nothing at the time of the reading because, after all, it is the future. Some of the predictions came to pass within a year or two of our readings, and my bout with cancer at age fifty-seven was unbelievably spot-on. The only prediction of mine left yet to happen is my death at eighty-two. Tick-tock.

While we were appearing at Paradise, Sr Bornigio used his influence to get a bit of free advertising, having us appear on TV. Mostly we appeared on *Domenica In*, a TV variety show, presented by the fabulous Pippo Baudo, which ran for a lengthy six hours on Sundays and was on air for many years.

These little appearances could be quite exhausting because rehearsal would take place before the live show in the morning and then usually involve some hours of waiting to perform.

All contracts have provision for promotional appearances, so there was not much we could do but go with the flow. We were treated extraordinarily well after all, so didn't complain. On these little TV promotional jaunts, we worked with some tremendous international guest artists. One in particular has stuck in my mind, a certain dark-skinned Jamaican problem child who was to precede us, promoting her new album *Living My Life* singing a single, *The Apple Stretching*. This bête noire gave everyone the run-around when she went missing right before her scheduled on-camera time. On her five-minute call, a frantic director was searching for her everywhere when one of the dancers thought we might try looking in the lift. There was Grace Jones herself, on the floor, slumped against the wall and looking in no fit state to perform. Too late for cancellation and last-minute changes. She was lifted, unceremoniously draped on a grand piano, her head propped onto her hand, her musketeer-style hat jammed on her head and wheeled onto the stage where it was hoped she would be present enough to lip-synch the words to her own song. I didn't stick around to find out.

We did all the usual first-time tourist stuff in Rome, lining up forever to see the Sistine Chapel, discovering the Forum, picking our way over the Colosseum and visiting the Vatican. The Vatican impressed and amused me. It was bloody hot, and I was wearing a tank top. The priest/guard at the door advised me it was considered offensive to have the tops of my arms bare inside St Peters, and I 'could purchase a T-shirt at their nearby stall'. These stalls, judging by the queue of people, waiting to part with a few thousand lire to cover their repugnant nakedness before their maker, make quite a tidy little tax-free profit for that particular brand of Christianity. Wearing my newly purchased t-shirt and now suitably and modestly attired, I returned to the entrance. As I was about to pass the priest/guard, two girls were leaving dressed in mini sundresses with barely visible spaghetti straps straining to hold their overflowing mammaries. Turning to the priest/guard, I enquired whether 'God is a tit man'.

One evening I was lying on my bed reading before getting ready for work. I started to experience not pain, but an uncomfortable feeling in my left arm. Ignoring it, I carried on reading. Quite suddenly, my arm began to curl up in little jerks. First the elbow, then the wrist, followed by the fingers until my entire arm was contracted in the extreme, my fingers all curled claw-like, as though someone had pulled all the tendons tight. Now the pain started, a deep, throbbing pain, and with it, the muscles of my arm and the centre of my palm bulged and hardened. The pain by now was excruciating. Luis was still home, and he very quickly bundled me into a cab, telling the driver to get us to an emergency centre. The closest hospital turned out to be the Vatican Hospital. It must have been a quiet night for Rome because they attended to me immediately. I used to think Spain was backward in the medical department. Nothing could compare with this antiquated facility and its treatment. My Italian was not bad but, definitely not up to the rapid-fire technical-term-laden bursts fired at me that evening. Luis did his best but, even he was struggling.

One bright young chap in a white coat, the white coat is the thing – I mean, surely, it's a health professional – grabbed my arm tightly and forcefully bent it and my fingers open. At the same time, another white-coated individual strapped the entire limb to a wooden board. Oh, the pain! I swear I was about to pass out. I guess I was extremely vocal because that little decision was abandoned and the arm released to spring straight back to its curved state. Before I knew it, I was being undressed, admitted, pushed into a bed and trundled into a six-bed ward. Luis had to dash to get to work but promised to visit the next day.

Now the true extent of their backwardness started to reveal itself. Firstly, I still hadn't been given anything for the agonising pain. I guess I must have been upsetting the other patients because I do remember the gentleman next to me yelling for a nurse, telling her to give me something, and she did. An intravenous drip was prepared but, via no such thing as a peripheral cannula, the little tap-like valve used since 1950 in more advanced institutions for the pre-deceased. No, the preferred method in Rome was a quick slash with something sharp, and a large needle with tubing attached shoved up the vein. Not even the forearm but the upper arm. I had three to four bottles of something per day while I was in the bloody place, each time it was the slash and poke system in a different spot. My poor arms looked like those of a self-harmer or a drug addict. On one occasion some dreadfully careless, inept nurse fed the needle straight through the vein and into the muscle, which filled up with fluid, and looked like a hot water bottle hanging from my arm.

Meals in this hideous joint were thrust into the middle of the ward on a huge trolley, and it was the job of the mobile patients to feed the bedridden. Each day, I was diagnosed with something completely different. One day it was polio, the next it was something else entirely. Enough was enough. When informed after breakfast one morning I was to have my head shaved I heaved myself out of bed, and trailing tubes, bottle, and various bits of hardware, found a phone and called Luis. 'Bring clothes. Get me outta here'. I 'escaped' the Vatican Hospital and further torture, boarded the first plane to Australia, and was diagnosed in a day or so, as having suffered a mild stroke. That Pope John Paul II managed to recuperate after being shot, might have been luck, but how he managed to survive the ministrations of that very same Vatican Hospital, I simply don't know.

Oh, the tourists! The tourists. It is quite impossible to stay sane in Rome during the peak tourist season, June through August. The heat is bad enough, but add foolish, annoying tourists and it becomes too much to expect anyone to cope with. Dale, Luis and I learned of a nude beach some distance from Rome, Il Buco, or the hole. This nude/gay beach was outside of Ostia, about twenty-five kilometres from Rome. It doesn't sound very far, but we were more than happy to do the two-hour trip there and back each day just to get away. The trip involved walking to our local tram stop, a tram to Termini Station, Metro from Termini Station to Piramide Station, local train to the last stop, Ostia Antica, bus along the beach for a couple of kilometres, then a hundred-metre walk to Il Buco. Which turned out to be actually a hole in the fence and foliage along the road. A fifty-metre wander along the winding sandy pathway, through the dense bush, being very careful not to get sidetracked by the guys cruising along the way, and there you were, at a beach which was a far, far, cry from Bondi but completely tourist-free. There is absolutely nothing at this beach except coarse sand, the most polluted water outside of a sewage tank, and a tiny shack serving outrageously expensive food. Warning. Do not go into that water.

Well, tourists or not, we counted ourselves fortunate in the extreme to be able to work and live in this very historical centre of Western civilisation. Rome was good for us in more ways than one: it gave our company great prestige. To have added Rome to our list of conquered cities was a plus no matter how you looked at it.

CHAPTER 38

AN OFFER TOO GOOD

Saint Vincent in the Valle d'Aosta in northern Italy, is picture-postcard perfect. The Casino De La Vallee is small but elegant. Our only time there was in 1986, and it was then that Antonio Gallardo, the Spanish producer/agent, came to see the production. The show was quite a small one, but he knew us by reputation and immediately offered us a year in Gran Palace Lloret de Mar, an hour north of Barcelona. We still had Milano and Geneva ahead of us on our schedule, but the timing was perfect, and all the dancers were happy to extend their contracts.

Saint-Vincent was a pleasant place to live and work. Winter was coming on, and there was just enough chill in the air to get a taste of the area at its best. Warmish days and cold brisk nights gave us an excuse to have a couple of warm-milk-and-rums on the way home. The casino stage was at floor level and it wasn't the greatest venue to work in, but a charming place none the less. The town is typically alpine with steep roofs, and what I can only describe as a Swiss feel to it with brown, oiled-wood houses, fretwork cut-outs and window boxes full of colour. It also featured friendly locals, and the most dangerous pastry shops you have ever seen. Oh, the money we spent in those cake shops. A feast for the eyes and tasting every bit as delicious. Our hotel was a few streets away from the main road, up a small incline to Via Mus, then along a couple more to the casino on Via Marconi. Our bedroom balcony overlooked the edge of town, and in the distance the Strada Statale 26, the freeway to France. Further on was the Fiume Dora Baltea, a tributary of the Po River, then over the flatland before the mountains to the west.

The focal point of this breathtaking view was Castello di Ussel, between the river and the mountains. This castle was far from a ruin and looked very much like someone had dropped it there for our viewing pleasure. There was not a great deal of work to do after we settled in so, visiting this little castle was on our list. On a sunny, mild day, the week after opening, a group of us jumped into a taxi and pointed castle-wards. The closer we got, the prettier this fortress/manor-house became. After getting as near as we could, we instructed the driver not to wait, intending to walk the few kilometres back. The cab had no sooner turned around and left, than a large black saloon car pulled up, and a very smart-looking woman got out. We were not quite sure whether we were trespassing, but her friendly wave said not. The woman introduced herself, in flawless American-accented English, as the owner, Baroness Bich, wife of Barone Marcel Bich, founder and owner of the BIC Company. This woman was welcoming and not in the least concerned that we were sticky-beaking. She invited us in for coffee and kindly showed us over the castle which, for part of the year at least, was her home. How lucky. How kind.

Chatillon Castello di Ussel is the first example of a mono-block castle in Aosta Valley. Unlike most other Aosta Valley castles, which evolved over different construction periods, the castle of Ussel was built from a single plan around 1343 by Ebalo di Challant and once used as a prison. The pinks, browns and beiges of the stone inlay floors looked as though they were installed yesterday, as did the frescoes covering the walls. We were shown the secret escape passage behind the fireplace, reached after a sharp turn before the back wall, and after passing through the fireplace itself. Hairy to say the least if the fire was lit. The room at the back is quite large and leads to escape tunnels in case of attack. At the time of our visit, when the couple were not in residence, the castle was used for temporary art exhibitions. The castle was donated to the Aosta Valley Region by the Barone and Baroness in 1984. The handover period took several years to complete.

Many other day excursions were made from Saint-Vincent. The city of Aosta was barely thirty minutes away, and shopping in the twisty, winding streets of this old city is nothing short of fabulous. Fashion boutiques abound, a one-off piece could be bought in the off season for quite a reasonable price. I found a stone-washed olive and yellow oilskin jacket for less than a hundred dollars and treasured it for years. That jacket was stolen once in Bangkok. Ron and I were walking along the street near my hotel, and he said, 'Oh look, what a fabulous jacket that guy has on.' I looked and recognised my jacket which had disappeared from my room a week or two earlier. I ran straight up to the guy, pulled the jacket down over his shoulders to pin his arms and yelled at him in Thai that he was wearing my jacket and I wanted it back. My Thai was quite proficient then. He didn't turn a hair, simply asked to retrieve his bundle of cigars from out of the top pocket. I turned, jacket in hand, and returned to Ron, who was open-mouthed in astonishment. I don't think I've been so butch before or since.

Of course, the proximity to Mont Blanc from Saint-Vincent makes a visit to that 4,810m-high white mountain a must and we made the journey on a bright sunny day. The bus trip was less than an hour, the view through the windows as this mountain came into sight was breathtaking. The town at the foot of the mountain was decidedly disappointing, being mainly full of tourist souvenir shops. However, the twenty-minute ride in the Aiguille du Midi cable car, the highest in Europe climbing more than twenty-seven hundred metres, is staggering. When we arrived at the topmost viewing platform, the air was super chilly, but the sun was out, and the day was bright and clear. The swiftness of changing conditions at that height was brought home quite suddenly. The day turned from ideal to a freezing, turbulent run-for-your-life in less than a minute. What was clearly and spectacularly visible one moment, disappeared behind a bone-chilling, blustering, impenetrable grey fog the next. We left on the downward journey more enlightened.

Poor Mont Blanc, or Monte Bianco, depending on which map you're reading, has long been a bone of contention between France and Italy. The area has changed hands many times, even the Austrians laying claim to it. The current situation sees administration of the mountain shared between the Italian town of Courmayeur and the French town of Saint Gervais Les Bains. Although the Franco-Italian border was last redefined in 1963, the commission – made up of both Italians and the French – have ignored the Mont Blanc issue. That's one way to deal with the problem, I guess.

Our show in Saint-Vincent came directly before another Milano contract. After the Spain offer, I flew back to Australia to pack two big shows for Gran Palace. I was there about a month and packed some of the best and biggest numbers we possessed. The show was to be expanded by six additional people—four girls and two boys. There was to be a two-week rehearsal period, so counting Milano, Geneva, and what was left of the Saint-Vincent contract, there were approximately three months to go. Plenty of time to send the trunks by sea.

After the jaunt home to Perth getting the costumes packed for Spain, I went straight back to Milano where the show had commenced performing. There were two clubs owned by the same company in Milano, the Porta d'Oro on the Piazza Armando Diaz near the Duomo and the other, Astoria, on the Piazza del Duomo, directly in front and to the right of the Duomo. We had performed at both. They are hugely upmarket addresses and suitably expensive places to perform. The owner was always very good to us, often loaning us out for the odd gala. Both Milano clubs had smallish dance floors used as the stage but offered good-size dressing rooms. The size made it difficult to stage our shows, but they were hugely prestigious places to work. Living in proximity of the Duomo is to be right in the heart of Milano, with its history and shopping. All the big Italian fashion houses have outlets nearby, and the girls kept their eyes open for a bargain. I was always fascinated by the awesome cathedral that is the Duomo. On our first visit there some years previously, I painted a watercolour of the green-patinated bronze doors featuring their many-panelled depiction of the Creation. All of the downtown streets either radiate out from or encircle the Cathedral of Milano. Construction began in 1386 and took more than six hundred years to complete. Most people would say it is still not complete, and the ongoing maintenance costs require constant fundraising. The means of acquiring these funds are many and varied and the latest, in 2012, was perhaps the most innovative. The public was invited to financially adopt one of the 3,400 statues, more than 700 high-relief marble figures, and 135 gargoyles that grace it. The history of this impressive structure is as colourful and interesting as six hundred years of constant wars and the resulting changing borders could make any place, including, the crowning of Napoleon Bonaparte on 20 May 1805 as King of Italy. I believe one of the hundreds of statues standing on the spires is of Napoleon.

Once again, we counted our blessings in the offers of contracts in such glamorous locales, in the heart of places that people pay years of precious savings to visit. Mind you, Milano, as with every other big city, has its crime and dangers. Once on a previous visit, I left the Pensione Anna, (famous for her pasta—nobody ever missed a meal) with several thousand dollars safely zipped into my coat pocket to walk to a travel agency a few blocks away. On reaching into my pocket to pay for the ten or twelve air tickets for the onward leg of our tour, I found the bottom of the pocket had been sliced open, and the money gone. How on earth does somebody know that any particular person, at this particular time, is carrying such a large sum of money in that particular pocket? Who says crime doesn't pay? Weeks of our profit gone.

The Italian tours were always welcome for many reasons. For one, Italy is one of the world's greatest tourist destinations, and we were being paid to live, work, and rub shoulders amongst some of the western world's greatest treasures. That in itself, was reason enough to be grateful, and I believe we were. Sadly, this huge drawcard is also what brings over ninety million, thoroughly annoying tourists to the country annually. The crush, the rudeness, the queues, the me-first attitudes. The Italians who live through these migrations develop a temperament and coldness that I guess helps them manage, and maintain their sanity. Rightly so—but being treated as though you are part of these day-tripping hoards is wearing and at times downright unpleasant.

Italy was generally followed by a stint in Switzerland, and by the time that leg was nearing completion, we all looked forward to the relative friendliness of Geneva and living in apartments for a while rather than in hotel rooms.

CHAPTER 39

RUBBING SHOULDERS WITH THE RICH

Geneva—dates and times are definitely running into one another in my memory, so forgive any overlapping. Let's call this early '80s; I'm pretty sure it was after Milano in '82, directly before Iraq. Geneva's oldest and most exclusive nightclub—the Pussycat Club, opened in 1968 near the wealthy Old Town on *Rue Glacis de Rive 17,* a steep, hilly street just off the *Pont du Mont Blanc.* At the time of writing, this premier nightspot, catering to an older clientele, has presented artists from around the world for over fifty years. As in Athens, there was a more general audience for our shows, followed by highly paid strippers appearing late evening/early morning. I hate using the term strippers, but what else can I call them? These beautiful, exotic women were paid immense sums of money to perform, and in turn, attracted the biggest of big spenders. I recall one young lady arriving nightly in her brand-new Rolls Royce. They wore expensive costumes and worked with equally extravagant props. Occasionally I would stay behind to watch, but more often, I just wanted to get home and sleep.

In Geneva, the accommodation was of the artist's choice and they paid for it themselves. Wages on a Swiss contract reflect this, but generally, they stay where other artists stay. On this occasion, they were split half/half on either side of Lake Geneva. Luis and I were upstairs behind the club, above the shop as it were. It was the time of the inline rollerblade craze, so we all bought them and skated to each other's apartments. Luis was a former Spanish Junior Champion roller skater, so he managed particularly well. I, on the other hand, was a complete novice. I used the downward sloping hill of *Rue Glacis de*

Rive to get a bit of steam up—hopefully enough to get me across to the Lake Geneva bridge. Sometimes, if I noticed a bit too much traffic to cross the road at the bottom safely, I'd grab the traffic light pole, the momentum would swing me around like a Hill's Hoist. Luis used to kill himself laughing. I thought I cut quite a figure.

After Italy, we liked Switzerland for its cleanliness and friendliness. A good time was always had. It was during this particular contract that we were offered a contract in Iraq. We thought the show needed a bit of a tart-up, so I flew back to Australia to pick up more of our stored costumes which were kept on the ground floor of the 'big house'. I inspected them for damage, and mended, cleaned and repacked them for travel. By the time I got back to Geneva, there were only days left before we'd be departing for Iraq.

Apart from our appearances at the Pussycat Club, we also worked contracts at Maxim's on the other side of the Lake, in the more downtown area of *Place des Alpes*. Maxim's was owned by the fabulous Bob Azzam, a funny, warm, hospitable man who loved the good life. Maxim's was an enormously expensive place to visit, with an elegant décor that bordered on quirky and included nude shop mannequins covered in crazed mirror dotted about the place. This venue played host to some of the biggest names in show business. Bob, although born in Egypt, was a British Royal Navy electrical engineer. After leaving the Navy, he was given the dream job of designing the complete wiring plans of a Saudi Arabian Premier's two-hundred-room palace. However, collecting on the bill turned into such a nightmare, and he lost so much money, he decided to turn to music, his life's love. Bob, a beautiful singer himself, organised a small band and started picking up work almost immediately. While working in Lebanon in 1958, civil war broke out and he just managed to board the last ship out. His big break came with a song called *Mustapha* in the 1960s, which spent fourteen weeks in the UK top singles charts. Europe went crazy for him, and there was no looking back.

At Maxims, Bob set aside accommodation for us to choose from. The dancers opted for cute little studio flats just a block up from the venue. Luis and I lived in one of Bob's own apartments on the *Avenue de la Paix* opposite the *Palais des Nations* (United Nations)—a bit of a hike, but a great part of town. The apartment was on the top floor of a typical Swiss block of three stories. Quaint, as these places are, it had dormer-style windows under sloping roofs, and in each room, you stood with your head at a different angle. I'd bang my head on the ceiling if I sat up in bed. There was an adorable, tiny, one-by-one-metre balcony overlooking the park, Lake Como and the United Nations. I'd often go to the dancers' apartments during the day to grab Dale for a walk, and it amused me when the tarts on the street in front of his building were able to tell me whether he was in. There was one particular girl, or woman – she was well past her prime – who would grab my coat and do up the top button, admonishing me, telling me to be careful not to catch a chill. I thought this very sweet, but also amusing coming from someone dressed in a multi-coloured fun fur stopping at crotch level then nothing until her high-buttoned ankle boots. These girls were fun and chatty and not like the drug-hooked dregs that took their places years later.

Maxims was easy work in a laid-back atmosphere. Bob was a tough man, but if your shows filled his venue, you were treated extremely well indeed. Bob had a particularly wealthy Greek client who loved to buy out Maxims for himself. He would come in, eat, play the piano to himself, watch the show and leave. One evening he asked Bob if the dancers might join him for a birthday drink. Bob knew our policy, a*rtists don't socialise in the venue no matter what was on offer,* and was hesitant. This man was always the perfect gentleman, and seeing that he was quite alone, we relented on this occasion. We all joined this generous man, who opened bottle after bottle of champagne at a thousand dollars a pop. Oh, how the rich live.

Bob was also a wealthy man, who but a wealthy man would have an enormous Mercedes Benz tastelessly covered in mother of pearl? He frequently visited friends in Megeve, fifty or so kilometres from Geneva, in the French Alps. These friends were mostly clients of Maxims. When Bob had a very prestigious show at Maxims, he would try to have it invited to perform in the Rothschild's private nightclub. The Rothschilds virtually own the town of Megeve, which started as just a few private chalets in 1910. The Baroness

Noémie de Rothschild and her family began spending winter vacations there after St Moritz became too popular and lost its charm, with mere millionaire riff-raff clogging up the ski runs. In 1921, she built and opened a hotel which quickly became fashionable with her well-heeled friends, and by the 1950s, Megeve was the in place for the French aristocracy and the ridiculously wealthy.

An invitation duly arrived via Bob, transportation was arranged, and off we went. After a comparatively short drive, we arrived in this picture-postcard town. It had perfect little – and not so little – chalets, horse-drawn sleighs, even a small open-air skating rink. Snow covered everything, and snugly bundled-up people with skis slung over their shoulders wandered about the town. We were split into two groups, the dancers in one hotel brimming over with character, and Luis and me in a smaller carbon copy farther along. A time was set to meet for dinner, courtesy of the Rothschilds, and we started settling in to get every minute out of this little sneak peek at how the other half – make that one per cent – lives. The appointed time came, and we all met in the lobby of the dancers' hotel. Bob greeted us, and off we marched like a group of happy school children to meet our host.

We were herded through the front door of a small but rather grand hotel, and introductions were made to this particular member of the exalted Rothschild family. He was charm itself, showed us this and that aspect of his hotel, told us the capacity and who designed it, and finally, led us to the restaurant. By then, we were famished. Minutes later, a uniformed waiter set down in front of us sparse communal plates of cold savouries, such as rollmops and pickled fish. Why is it that people in cold countries eat cold food and people in hot countries eat food hot enough to burn your throat out? We made polite but urgent lunges for our share of what was clearly an entrée but, no sooner had we gobbled down this little offering we were rounded up and shunted out the door to visit another hotel belonging to the family. The same thing, charm and grace, heaps of helpful information about this little money-spinner, then to the dining room, only to have clones of the food offered at the previous place set in front of us. Except this time, we didn't even get a chance for a bite before we were herded off to yet another fine family establishment. At least at this final place the portions were a decent size, so we threw manners to the wind and hastily devoured the lot. Reasoning that this was as close to dinner as we were going to get, we ignored any remaining hunger pangs, and it was off to the nightclub.

This private nightclub is an invitation-only affair, and in the ski season it is packed to bursting with more obscenely affluent folk than you'll ever see in a single spot anywhere. Not a big fancily decorated place, quite plain really, it relied on the faces of the rich and famous to supply the wow factor. The big bar is an integral part of the entertainment, and is immediately inside the door to the left, it has a good two metres of space between it and the wall behind. Well known personalities, movie stars, and celebs are traditionally invited to serve behind this bar for a short period, and then write their names on the wall behind it. The wall is a veritable who's who of some of the most famous people in the world. Reading it, I could see Elizabeth Taylor, Zsa Zsa Gabor, Lee Marvin and dozens and dozens of other familiar names.

Drinks flowed free and freely, and it was evident we must get our show underway before the dancers were legless. We had only two routines with us, there was no stage. Space was cleared on the dance floor, and no lighting except an old teetering follow spot on a tripod which I operated. Strange really, you would imagine these prosperous folks might like to hang out in a joint with all the trappings of wealth such as a hydraulic stage and state-of-the-art lighting. Still, it seemed this sort of down on the farm ambience plus the close proximity to others of the same pedigree and affluence, was just what the social register ordered. A makeshift dressing room was rigged up behind a cloth around a corner booth, so on with the show. Considering the incredibly slippery floor, and the amount of alcohol surreptitiously consumed beforehand, I was surprised to see almost all the dancers stayed on their feet throughout, and gave such a great performance, except that is, for one person. Luis who doesn't drink but can't handle a slippery floor, spent much of the time horizontal. All in all, it went incredibly well, and we were such a hit, the crowd screamed the roof down. Back into civvies, pack the few costumes, pull the screen down, and it was party time. What a night it was, I think Luis might have ended up the only sober person in the entire room. An hour or so after the show, Luis and I were requested to do our stint serving behind the bar and take our turn to sign the wall. An announcement was made so we had an audience, and a great round of applause went up as we added our names to that list of celebrity heavyweights. I managed to squeeze mine in above Liz Taylor's.

Shortly after the signing, as far as Luis was concerned, things started getting out of hand. Dale mounted the bar and danced flamenco, not bad considering we had yet to go to Spain, and Luis's mouth fell open like a stroke victim when one of the girls fell on the dance floor, dragging a few other revellers down with her. Luis, full of dignity and in high dudgeon, clapped his hands and began rounding everybody up, thanking all and sundry for a marvellous evening.

The night, or by then early morning, was over, and it was back to our respective hotels, ready for an early call for the skiing trip organised for us. I set my alarm, slept, woke, tucked into a lovely hot breakfast, and we made our way to the dancers' hotel which was the meeting point. Not a soul around, nobody answering the telephone. Finding this odd, we started going around the rooms to collect everybody. Surprise, surprise, not one single dancer had stirred, and not one single person was in the right room. We cancelled the ski trip with embarrassed apologies and haughtily set out to explore the town. Back in Geneva, all was forgiven, and much gossipy conversation uncovered some hilarious goings-on after Luis and I went to bed. Thanks, Bob, for making our time in Geneva so pleasant. Sadly, dear Bob passed away in 2004 at the age of 90.

CHAPTER 40

BAGDHAD AND 1001 FRIGHTS

It was 1982 when we were offered the contract to perform at the official opening of the new Sheraton Ishtar Hotel in Baghdad. Although not particularly keen – after all, Iraq was at war with Iran at the time – we talked it over with our agent and the Manager of Sheraton and were somehow convinced all was well. What could happen in a month anyway? Baghdad had been offered to us several times in the past. There is a big showroom there called Moulin Rouge which is nothing to do with the Paris Moulin, they'd just filched the name. During an Athens contract, the owner of this Iraq venue had approached us and made all sorts of attractive offers and proposals—one being that he fly me out to take an all-expenses-paid look to check out his locale. If we didn't like it, no ill feelings.

I'd spoken to dancers from other shows who'd worked there, and found no one was particularly enthusiastic, so a polite 'thanks, but no thanks', was my answer on that occasion. I have always possessed a built-in radar when it comes to regarding someone's character. I meet a person, I either like them, or I don't, trust them or I don't. This particular gent from Moulin Rouge didn't sit well with me, those tiny hairs on the back of the neck and all that. Although he was offering huge sums of money, I couldn't say yes. I have agreed to international contracts on a simple handshake with no regrets whatsoever. Best stick with my old gut feeling.

This Sheraton contract offer was different. Firstly, I knew the manager, having worked together in the past at various Sheraton venues. Klaus was Sheraton's New Hotel Specialist Manager. He would go around the world getting new hotels up and ready to be opened. We met him in Cairo, and although he was a bit on the overpowering side, he was honest and professional. He gave me convincing assurances regarding our safety, and all in all, sold the gig to us very well. I met with the dancers, no contract was ever undertaken without consensus from the artists, and the deal was signed.

We flew Geneva–Baghdad on Iraqi Airways and arrived around ten pm. The flight was perfectly normal until we got into Iraqi airspace. The aircraft was then blacked out, window shades pulled down, and we picked up a jet fighter escort on each wing. Hmm, nobody had mentioned this would happen. The touchdown was smooth, and we went through to luggage collection and customs clearance. This was the first hint that things were, let's say, done differently here. The customs guys were all friendly smiles but interested in one thing only, music cassette tapes. Everything was gone through in the most detailed search imaginable looking for cassette tapes. Should a tape be discovered, it was scrutinised thoroughly, and either replaced or, the customs officer would shriek.

Great howling streams of Arabic would be spewed at both the offending tape and its owner, followed immediately by the frantic, frenzied un-spooling of cassette tape onto the floor. This, however, is not the end. With much continued windmilling of arms and screeching, the outraged unspooler would commence an energetic jumping and stomping on the great, tangled heap of tape. After any and each of these episodes, all would be quiet charm, and the suitcase rifling continued. Meanwhile, not having a clue about the actual transgression these tapes committed, the girls were standing in open-mouthed disbelief and outrage that their precious music was being destroyed. Only later did we learn they were looking for music recorded by, written by, produced by anyone who had even stood next a Jew.

First thing to be done after a headcount was to enquire about the costumes. Nobody, it seemed, had the slightest idea of where to go or who to see about excess baggage. I did manage to make myself understood to a couple of people who looked vaguely official and was told no excess baggage was ever allowed to be claimed on arrival because of extensive customs checks, I should come back tomorrow. Okay, we've heard it all before. We were in no hurry, the hotel was not to be opened for at least a week, I was content to go with the rest of the company to the hotel. It had been a long day, after all. Limos to the hotel poured oil on disgruntled waters, and the first glimpse of our glamorous accommodation for the next month soothed even the most ruffled feathers. The hotel lifts were pointed out when we were still some distance away. These two lifts started in the lobby, rose to the glass lobby roof three floors up, then popped out to continue their twenty-floor journey on the outside of the building. Each lift had a very bright, comet-like light circling it vertically around the outside, these could be seen for kilometres and were truly spectacular.

Although nearing midnight when we finally arrived, the hotel's departmental managers were lined up to greet us, and we were welcomed to Baghdad. The hotel was huge, the lobby alone taking up what looked like the size of half a football field. Its cavernous height extended to the third floor with the second- and third-floor guest rooms off mezzanine walkways overlooking the lobby in a horseshoe shape around the void. The lobby ceiling was made entirely of glass in flat planes rising like a shallow upturned diamond, with the central tower lifts in the middle at the rear. Just spectacular. The hotel was located in the downtown region of Baghdad, (as much as there was a downtown) and is separated from the Tigris River by Abu Nawas Road. The Ishtar Sheraton was the tallest building in Baghdad with the Meridian Hotel directly across Firdos Square being the next most elevated, and the News of the World building behind Meridian came in third.

First thing on the agenda was room allocation followed by an orientation session with the manager before turning in. This orientation session turned out to be the second unnerving experience since our arrival.

'Yes, we are most definitely in a war zone.' Right, got that.

'Yes, there are daily attacks by air from Iran, generally starting at 7:00 am but, don't worry; they rarely hit anything'. Right, sorta got that as well.

'Yes, you will be required to repair to the air-raid shelter in the sub-basement on the sounding of the air raid warning.' Don't recall mention of it in Geneva.

'The air raid warning goes off as the attacking aircraft are spotted over Basra, four hundred and forty kilometres away, and it takes approximately twenty minutes for the enemy to get here. Do not use the lifts.' Right, having been allocated rooms on the 18th floor, that's quite a hike. No lift. Alright, got that.

'Please keep a packed overnight bag by your bed and sleep in clothes suitable for travelling.' This is getting hairier by the minute.

'Contingency plans have been made with the US Government for your evacuation overland to Syria should the unlikely need arise.' The US Government? What about the Australian Government?

'Any questions?' Yes, quite a few, actually.

'No, okay. Sleep well, we will see you in the morning.' Gone. Sleep well. Yeah, right.

True to his word, the air raid warning went off on the dot of seven the next morning. I was out of my bed, and on the landing of the floor below before I remembered Luis and the dancers. C'mon, you lot down, down, down we go. We found the air raid shelter and settled in with a hundred or so hotel staff, and construction workers for a nervous wait until the all-clear was given. Jayne, one of the dancers, kept complaining she was being felt up. When I looked at her, I said, 'Well, no wonder, darling, you are supposed to be in travelling gear, not a sheer, crotch-length, baby-doll nightie.'

That morning over breakfast, I was talking to a Times reporter who asked what floor we'd been allocated. I told him the eighteenth, and he laughed. 'Tell them you want floors two or three (American style counting) overlooking the lobby—they are VIP and bomb-proofed.' By midday, we were in rooms on the second floor. Those seven a.m. air raids were as regular as clockwork. We soon became accustomed to them, and actually quite blasé about it all. Nobody ever bothered with the air raid shelter run again as far as I knew.

The tallest building in Baghdad, the Sheraton was used by Iranian pilots as a marker, up the Tigris, turn right at the Sheraton. That same Times reporter would often show me photos from the front, terrible images of the worst carnage imaginable. I recall seeing photos of drowned bodies where dams were deliberately opened as Iranian troops crossed below. These were not fighting men but children who all had little plastic keys around their necks, keys given to them by the Iranian government as the Key to Paradise, an inducement to enable them to wrest children from their parents' arms. They were used as cannon fodder in the front lines. Dreadful, human beings are dreadful.

Mid-morning on the first day, I was introduced to a retired Iraqi Army General who spoke English very well and had been designated to be our liaison person. He was quite fatherly and very charming, I got on with him immediately. First cab off the rank this morning though, was to go to the airport and pick up the costumes. I'd worked in Middle Eastern countries for a few years already and knew this could turn out to be quite a day. However, I certainly wasn't prepared for what transpired. The General drove me to the airport and parked the car in a typically dust-covered open-air car park. We went in search of the baggage office, and the fully expected reams of triplicate paperwork. I was armed with the relevant documents and a good book—I know these places too well. From office to office we went, finally tracking down someone willing to help. I saw silver crossing palms on more than one occasion. 'Yes', the trunks have been inspected'. How, I have the keys with me? But, 'No, we don't know where they are'. Office to office to office we went until we were eventually taken through a labyrinth of passages and more offices to the back of the airport.

Finally, we were confronted by an enormous field of three-metre-high pyramids of what looked like junk. This, we were informed, is unclaimed baggage. Unfortunately, our trunks had been designated as such, and we were free to look around. Are you kidding me? There must have been twenty of these mountains, and each one had a little coterie of head-to-toe-black-clad crones diligently digging, prodding and probing around it for commercially viable loot. By this time, it was noon and bloody hot, heat like I'd never encountered. It felt as though my brain was on the boil.

'Okay, let's make a start, General, you take those two mountains, and I'll take these two. We are looking for bright yellow metal trunks, about the size you could stick the average corpse into. Ten in total.' Dig, dig, poke, poke, shuffle, shuffle, pile after pile until the last row was in sight. I was definitely, utterly, positively exhausted and totally deflated. No way are we going to find anything amongst this garbage heap. Then, like Howard Carter peering into King Tut's tomb: 'Gold, gold. Everywhere the glint of gold.'

Well, it wasn't actual gold, but right near ground level of one of the last heaps, I saw sparkling black sequins, the black sequins of the boys' opening jackets. The trunk had burst open on impact with the ground and was slowly but surely about to be engulfed by the world's biggest omelette. The very next unclaimed baggage after ours was obviously a shipment of eggs. These eggs had been dumped onto the pile after our trunks and had slipped and slithered down the sides until the blazing heat started to set them into one gargantuan, congealed egg mass just inches from my precious costumes. The old General must still have carried some weight because he stormed off to the nearest building and came back with an army of workers who waded elbow deep through the mess and retrieved all ten trunks. Only one had come open, and its contents were dusty but whole. Just imagine having to go around the local souks and repurchase my stuff if those old gals had beat me to it. Mission accomplished.

The opening of the hotel, which was to be our opening night, was put off for a week because the hotel was not as near to completion as they'd hoped. Klaus, ever concerned with regards to our wellbeing, sent to Turkey for a swimming pool expert, and flew him in to get the pool up and running for our express comfort. Lazy days by the pool began to be a way of life, and what with having US$100 per day per person allocated on restaurant use, we quickly developed a taste for the good life. Languorously staring up from my poolside lounge one day, I noticed way up on the twentieth floor, a peculiar, and rather fragile-looking protrusion which seemed like a total afterthought. A small, odd, boxy, concrete affair looking feeble and hugely unstable. Then the penny sickeningly dropped, that's our dressing room.

The odd air raid never seemed to bother us. Amazing how quickly you become immune to the sound of air raid sirens, and low-flying fighter jets. In fact, you could tell where the action was, if any, by the sound of the anti-aircraft guns. The News of the World building, third tallest behind us, had anti-aircraft guns mounted on the roof. On one occasion, when they were blazing away at enemy aircraft real or imagined, they managed to blow the top of the Meridian opposite to, and above them. Several days later, while firing again, the guns fell through the roof. Some local engineer hadn't done his homework regarding the ability of the roof to sustain the extra weight of heavy gun emplacements, recoil, ammunition and soldiers.

The Meridian, at the time, was essential to the dancers' sanity. They had a nightclub, ours wasn't open yet. We were granted free entry to this night spot and the dancers were grandly entertained for simply being there and being gorgeous. I don't think they ever paid for a single drink. Apart from freebies from lustful males, there was a deal with the DJ who announced nightly there would be a competition for bottles of champagne. 'And tonight's competition is going to be … high kicks.' Who, I ask you, can kick higher than professional showgirls? The competition was always high kicks, and the dancers always won. For years I had a photo of Giselle and Sally in full swing, or kick, during one of those competitions.

During our stay in Baghdad, our kindly General arranged many social events and sightseeing trips for us. Quite early on, he took us to a traditional feast on the roof/patio of somebody's house. A whole sheep stuffed with rice and heavily aromatic spices was gradually charring on a spit, and an enormous array of Arabic dips and salads filled a groaning sideboard. The smell was headily exotic, and he served us the choicest cuts. Luis and I, being the guests of honour, were befittingly offered the eyes, one each. Oh, dear. I do hate situations like this. With everybody watching there's nothing to do but get on with it. With an appropriately grateful, humble smile, I managed to swallow mine whole without so much as a single chew.

Many places, including the ancient Babylon sites, or what was left of them, were closed for the duration of the war. Still, the General had pull, and took us to every place of historical importance, Babylon being the first must-do on the list. On the way there, the General arranged a picnic in a typical Berber tent in the desert for us. Presumably, this marvellous tent with its floor covered in multiple Persian rugs, was set up just for us. There were no tourists in Iraq at that time nor probably since. One hundred metres in front of this tent was a breathtaking view, the ruins of the great arch of the palace of the Sassanid King Shapur. Built sometime between 242 and 272 BCE the arch has a span of 80 feet, is some 118 feet high and has always been considered one of the most important pieces of Persian history. Sitting on those magnificently woven rugs, eating the heavenly, especially prepared food, I was completely overawed by yet another extraordinary experience that had come my way.

Our first glimpse of Babylon was the impressive blue Ishtar Gate that guards the entrance. Our hotel, the Ishtar Sheraton, was named after these massively imposing gates, and you can imagine my great disappointment to learn these were fake. The General informed us the originals now reside in the Berlin Museum. How many times have I heard similar stories before? Especially in Egypt. I did wonder, given the often-volatile history of these countries, whether it might not be the best thing as far as preservation goes, but it is sad, nonetheless. There was still much to see, and we could follow the plan of the ruined city. Crumbling low relief, moulded, tiles covering walls, and street layouts were still visible. The famous man-and-lion statue was a wonder, and although badly eroded, the outline was still discernible and much smaller than I expected. All the way there and back we passed many rolling army convoys and were told 'no photos'. Of course, we all took photos.

CHAPTER 41

DANCERS AND DESPOTS

When the General offered to take us to Baghdad's oldest building and the spice markets, we jumped at the offer. The spice markets were sensually overpowering. Hundreds of square metres of huge hessian bags, sides rolled down exposing the herbs and spices which gave off pungent, heady and wonderous sensations for the nostrils. The oldest building, however, was probably the biggest disappointment of my life. Always ready to don my amateur archaeologist hat, I was so looking forward to seeing, and touching an ancient Thousand-and-One-Nights construction. For all that, it turned out to be a nondescript, 50s-style edifice currently housing an underpants factory. Poor old Baghdad had been invaded and razed so many times, this miserable building was now the oldest on offer.

Under the circumstances, there was not a great deal to do at night in Baghdad at that time, but we did get ourselves out and about and saw all it was possible to see. One of the things I was keen to take in was the show at Moulin Rouge (nicking the name of the venue already said a lot). A few quick phone calls to the owner and they 'Would be thrilled to have us as guests whenever we cared to go'. A suitable date was made, and we were picked up in the evening and given VIP treatment. Oh, how very pleased I was that we'd never taken up his previous offer of a contract. Not much of a venue and not much of a show. Luis and I decided to walk back to our hotel that evening. On the way, we passed the Ali Baba fountain, a lovely piece with a statue of a woman pouring water into three tiers of pots below her. No water was flowing that night, and the basin designed to hold the water at the base was full of refuse. It was a delightful thing though, and I hope it survived.

With the opening once again postponed, there was still not much to do. One lazy afternoon, I was standing outside my room leaning on the brass railing running around the balcony and checking out the lobby two floors below. A tremendously loud thump overhead brought me out of my reverie. Looking up, I was astonished to see uniformed soldiers sliding across the huge glass panes of the lobby ceiling. This was immediately followed by a great commotion in the lobby itself. Armed troops were pouring in through each and every entrance, and very quickly and efficiently surrounding the entire area. Of course, in Baghdad during a war, the first thing that comes into the mind is invasion. *Holy shit, we are being invaded.* All this takes mere seconds to register, but at the time it seemed to happen very much in slow motion. What is it about impending disaster – real or imagined – that rivets you to the spot?

In this case, nothing as dramatic as an invasion was occurring. It was simply Saddam Hussein, looking every inch as impressive as he did on thousands of posters covering the city, dropping in for an impromptu sticky-beak. His guards were securing the place. I had a ringside seat and was not going to miss this, but I did manage to give a call around to the dancers' rooms and the pool telling everyone to stay right where they were. A bowing and scraping Klaus appeared, and after a quick inspection of the lobby, Saddam was led into one of the waiting lifts which came to a halt only metres from me on the second floor. Klaus had his master keys with him and proceeded to open up any rooms Saddam's aide pointed to, and in they went for a look. Sounds very cool until you remember our entire company was living on that floor. The aide pointed to a room directly opposite across the void, Klaus had the key in the lock immediately. Oh dear, I knew that room was one of ours, and just prayed it was vacant at that moment, no such courtesy as a knock or a yoo-hoo during this inspection.

Klaus stood back to allow Saddam to enter. He was immediately propelled backwards by a whirlwind of blows, shoves and screams by one of our dancers, Jillian. Shower fresh, she did a marvellous job of defending herself and her modesty, swinging slaps with one hand and clutching a towel to her nakedness with the other. Saddam stepped back, overcome by surprise, and Jillian slammed the door shut in his face. Not one guard lifted a finger, they were way too enthralled with the view. Meanwhile, I knew I had turned positively green. I rushed back into our room, yelling to Luis, 'Pack your bags! Call the dancers! We are going to be out of here on the first plane or there'll be a beheading or two!' Imagine what was running through my mind? Firing squads, chains, torture, you name it.

What to do? I called every room advising even more strenuously that they stay put. I went to the pool and rounded up a few strays. There were about four missing, and I thought, well, it's every man for himself. I called Jillian, who was totally unfazed, and thought it was just another Arab pervert. All this took around thirty minutes, then I decided to go calling on each person to make sure they were staying put. Stepping into the passage outside my bedroom, I glanced across to the other side of the void to see at least ten hotel staff, arms laden with flowers, laying them all along the passageway in front of the rooms until it was completely overflowing. Saddam was saying sorry.

A little more here about Jillian. Jillian was one of our topless dancers and was with us for some years. This extraordinarily beautiful woman was our resident Barbie doll. Thick blonde hair, amazing feminine curves, a face with the purest, smoothest, translucent skin like alabaster, and a will of iron. After the dancers had shifted into the villa in Cairo on one of our visits, I once saw a little camel train going past the end of my street. Bobbing and bouncing along on top of each camel was one of our dancers with dance bags slung over their backs, on their way home from a rehearsal. Nothing unusual about that, our girls were into everything. Trailing this little camel caravan however was a sparkling new, exceedingly long Cadillac, driven by, none other than our Jillian. Where the hell had she got it from? No smelly camels for this gal.

The team of people who worked on the opening of the Sheraton Ishtar was full of characters. Maybe these people had seen it all—and nothing, absolutely nothing, fazed them. The Head of Housekeeping, for instance, was a British woman of a certain age, totally worthy of belonging to the cast of any *Carry On* movie. She seemed to be everywhere at once in the hotel, and nothing escaped her scrutiny. Except for the department heads, most of the staff were recruited from the Philippines or Egypt and were undergoing training on the job. I remember walking through the hotel with Mrs Housekeeping, discussing the outfitting of the newly requisitioned dressing rooms, when she spotted a young boy standing a metre or so away from his vacuum cleaner, gazing out of a window totally lost in contemplation. Mrs Housekeeper, without so much as a break in stride, walked between the boy and his appliance, gripped his right hand in her left, vac in her right, joined the two together behind her saying, 'This is your right hand, this is your vacuum cleaner, never should the two be parted.' She was an incredibly dry, funny woman.

Presenting shows on the twentieth-floor restaurant wasn't part of the original plan for the hotel, so no dressing rooms were included. However, Klaus, in his wisdom, wanted shows in the restaurant as there was very little else in the way of entertainment in Bagdad, and this would be a sure-fire money-maker. A big, slightly raised stage was placed in front of the windows across the room directly opposite the lifts and, apart from bringing in ugly temporary screening, there appeared to be no way for our dancers to get changed. Never fear, the ever-resourceful Klaus had thought about this, and converted a cantilevered viewing platform some two metres wide, and probably twelve metres long, with entrances through windows/doors at each end leading directly onto the stage. Clever Klaus. This was the fragile-looking protrusion I had seen from the pool previously while having a swim and tan session.

The afternoon of opening night, rehearsals were under way, and staff were setting up the restaurant, a beautiful room taking up almost the entire twentieth floor, with floor to ceiling windows. It was a picture of perfection with tables in place, new cutlery and flatware gleaming, white plates shining, glassware polished and sparkling, and magnificent flower arrangements placed everywhere possible. Uniformed staff by the dozen buzzing, buzzing, formed a very efficient, well-oiled machine turning the room into opening night splendour. Suddenly a two-metre-long, sharp steel pole crashed through the ceiling, narrowly missing one of the dancers, and embedded itself into the stage. Never a dull moment in Bagdad. Much clutching of pearls, a few words of the *fuck* variety, and not just a little consternation ensued. After an eternity waiting for some sort of panic reaction from the staff and getting none, there was nothing else to do but leave the offending missile exactly where it was and work around it, keeping a wary eye on the ceiling.

We continued with the rehearsal when not long afterwards, it appeared as though an indoor rainstorm had started. Water came flooding through every gypsum joint, every flush-to-ceiling light fitting, every piece of moulded plaster, an inundation running in sheets down every wall. Staff stood and gaped at this deluge, seemingly rendered immobile by what may well have been a re-enactment of the Great Flood. We, on the other hand, had a show to put on, so the dancers grabbed every available ice bucket, vase and anything else that would hold water and began placing them under the worst flows. Mrs Housekeeper was summoned, and without the slightest hint of haste, surprise or concern, this totally unflappable woman's only remark was, 'This will take at least four gins and a lie down.' It appeared that a Nubian gentleman on the roof above had been trying to clear a blocked, right-angled air conditioning pipe and decided giving it a few good slams with a heavy, pointed steel bar was the appropriate way to go about it. He'd used such force that the thing went straight through the pipe, through the roof and ceiling, ending up impaled in the floor. Maintenance staff were obviously not getting paid according to weight of grey matter. Needless to say, the ever-efficient Mrs Housekeeper got everything cleaned up, and opening night was a triumph, none of the guests any the wiser.

Amongst the attendees were Sheraton top brass, the Ambassador and staff of the Australian Embassy, and Saddam Hussein – who loved the show so much he wouldn't let us leave Iraq – more on this later. I had registered our names with the Embassy, as I always did, to be sure they knew we were there, and to not forget us should they have to bury their wherewithal and decamp. Embassy staff have always been good attendees at our shows throughout the world, and there was a bit of social intercourse with this lot as well. Let me tell you, these people live exceedingly well on our taxes. I was told the bill for them that evening was US$13,000—a lot of money in 1982.

The time to leave was rapidly approaching and, as fun as it had been, and as magnificently as we were treated, it really was time to go. Our opening date in Rome was looming. Getting out of Iraq was not as easy as jumping in a cab, getting to the airport and boarding an outward flight. I had only recently learned that we required Exit Visas to leave the country. Exit Visas would be granted only on proof of payment of taxes, and of fulfilment of contractual obligation to the government. Red tape, red tape. There were no problems in that department, so Exit Visas should be automatically granted. Wrong.

Mr Hussein, and the powers that be, so enjoyed the show they'd been to see it several times. As a consequence it was announced we were staying. 'What do you mean we're staying?' Yes, we were granted the great honour of an extended visa and continued work. No way. We open in Rome in one week, and that was that. Tremendously long and exhausting meetings were held with hotel management, visa officials and government representatives. It was finally decided, if I could find a show of equal quality to replace us, we could leave on the due date.

In 1982, communication was not what it is today. Managing these productions while on tour was a full-time occupation. Scouting out further contracts was an absolute trial back then. Letters were written to agents on my trusty hi-tech portable electronic typewriter. My trunk full of photos of dancers and shows was delved into, sorted, and selections stuffed into one of the stacks of manila envelopes I carried around the world. There were post offices to be found, and language barriers dealt with. Wait a week, a month or, however long it took for the missive to arrive at its destination and wait a further interminable time for an answer. There might be a request for more photos, so the delving, stuffing, posting and waiting process would be endured again. Then, if contracts were offered, the process was repeated with the signing, co-signing, sending and waiting. Fortunately, we had good standing with most of the top European agencies so it was possible I might find a way for us to get out of Iraq. I spent long and frustrating days at the keyboard of the hotel telex machine. These machines were slow, and if the person at the other end didn't have one, I would wait for telegrams to be sent and received then telexed on to me. Within the week I'd found a replacement show that satisfied all concerned. Our Exit Visas were granted and issued.

We flew Iraqi Airways via Athens, where a change of planes was necessary.

Some bright spark had not confirmed the Athens Rome leg and our seats had been resold. After a lengthy consultation with the airlines and several nerve-wracking hours in the Athens airport surrounded by all the trunks and baggage, we were given first-class seats, but I paid the difference. Oh, well. It's only money. We must get to Rome. We open tomorrow, and I have never missed an opening night.

A last word on Baghdad. The original name of the hotel was Ishtar Sheraton Hotel & Casino. Although Sheraton managed it under government contract, the building itself was an Iraqi government project. The hotel was popular amongst Western visitors, and as a nightspot for locals. After the 1991 Gulf War, Sheraton broke their management contract and the government continued to use the name without permission for twenty-two years. Who's going to sue? After the 2003 invasion, the hotel remained virtually empty, and being such an inviting target, suffered repeated rocket and mortar attacks. It sustained structural damage from a bomb attack in 2005, and a car bomb killed thirty-seven people in 2010. The poor old Sheraton was renovated in preparation for the Arab Summit in 2011 and renamed the Cristal Grand Ishtar Hotel.

CHAPTER 42

LIONS AND TIGERS AND BARES

On a cold, bright Geneva morning in January 1987, the dancers were packed and ready to set off on the eight-hour bus trip to Lloret de Mar, an hour north of Barcelona. The costume trunks left by truck an hour or so earlier, and each of us had our standard allowance of one suitcase, plus carry-on. The Lloret de Mar contract was for one year. The costumes I had chosen a couple of months earlier on my trip back to Australia were sent by a private shipping company, and all being well, they would arrive a week before we opened. I love touring, but the thought of a whole year in the same venue was feeling marvellous. It was a chance to have a proper apartment and cook and live like ordinary people.

Lloret de Mar is seventy-five kilometres north of Barcelona in Cataluña, on the Costa Brava. The local population was about ten thousand people, which swelled during summer to a fantastic one hundred thousand people, mainly tourists on package tours from the UK, Germany, and Italy but essentially Europeans in general. The great attraction is the extremely long main beach, which is an unbroken 1.7 kilometres of what is supposed to be, white sand. Although Lloret is consistently awarded the coveted Blue Flag for cleanliness, I can tell you; it really isn't that clean. Well, the beach at least. I was at the beach one afternoon waiting for a spot, yes waiting. It's so damned full you must wait for someone to vacate before you can claim a towel's length of sand. After settling in and oiling up, I opened my book ready for a good relaxing read, tan session and swim. I did my front, rolled over, wriggled around to get comfortable, reached for my glasses and book, and only then did I see it.

I wasn't lying on a bed of pristine white sand at all, but on a bed of cigarette butts. Lloret's beach is mechanically combed early each morning. This comb consists of a deep metal rake (pulled by a tractor) lifting the sand, throwing it into a monstrous fan-blown sieve at the back. The concept being, everything except fine sand is caught and the sand drops back onto the beach. All very well in theory except, not only is the sand blown back but the holes are large enough for cigarette butts to pass through, so they get blown out as well. Consequently, the build-up over the summer is massive.

Despite the cigarette butts, the white beach and the non-stop nightlife are great draw cards. Another reason Lloret is so popular – and this is purely my theory – is it is the first town on the railway line where the town and the beach are not divided by the train track. The railway line from Barcelona travels directly along the beachfront, separating the beaches from towns, diverging inland only on reaching Blanes, the town a few kilometres before Lloret.

Until 1805, the town was at Fenals, a little farther down the coast, and inland, centred around the Castle of St Joan. The Third Coalition War that pitted Great Britain against Spain and France, and which concluded at the Battle of Trafalgar, saw the castle bombarded by the British Navy and reduced to rubble. The lonely tower seen by looking from seaward is all that's left. So this sleepy little town we'd arrived in during winter, was to be our home for the following twelve months. There were a few free days during which we had time to find our longed-for apartments before rehearsals began. It was great fun searching for the perfect place to call home, something we hadn't experienced since Korea, two years earlier. Luis and I always wanted to live overlooking the Mediterranean, so we chose an older three-storey apartment block directly off the beach at the very northern end of town. The apartment was on the second floor and offered three bedrooms. It ran back a whole block, with an oversized balcony at the beach end overlooking a vast expanse of the Mediterranean. Plenty of space was required as Dolores, our old sewing lady from Perth, would be joining us to help with fittings, and a few remakes. Not being rude here, Dolores was old. She must have been seventy-five or over by then but she was young at heart, and as fit as a fifty-year-old. We needed spare bedrooms for guests too as Luis's parents were to join us within a week or so.

Gran Palace was a dream to work in. It was not a bar or club, rather a dedicated show room catering to tourists. Set back from the main Lloret/Barcelona road, it had all the creature comforts an artist could want. Private artists' entrance, vast stage, massive lift area centre stage for bringing sets, props and artists up from the basement, mightily high, so tall headdresses were no problem at all, equally tall entrances from the wings and crossover. There were plenty of comfortable dressing rooms, an office for me, showers, enormous wings and an extensive backstage for scenery changes. Truly, this place was ideal. The salon itself was a sloping affair of tiered rows with two to six person tables in a gentle curve around the thrust part of the stage with a seating capacity of probably a thousand patrons. Most people arrived in buses as there was dedicated bus parking out front, tickets for these people were generally included in their holiday package deal.

The producer/agent, Antonio Gallardo, was sent the Sheraton Walker Hill set designs from our Korean show, and these sets were constructed in the same style. We would only be a troupe numbering twelve or fourteen instead of twenty-two, so pretty much a Readers Digest version of the Seoul show. A pair of rolling staircases were constructed with lights installed between stairs for the opening and finale, as well as a styrene Inca temple complete with giant destructive snakes for the Inca routine. It was all looking bloody marvellous. As well as our routines and one or two guest attractions, we would be working in conjunction with a magician. Antonio had spent a great deal of time and much expense to investigate the workings and secrets behind the types of animal disappearing acts he'd seen in Las Vegas. These tricks were built, suitable animals purchased and trained and a magician plus two assistants found to operate it all. The animal menagerie included a lion named Rocky, a tiger named Nadja, two black panthers, two leopards, a camel and half a dozen exotic-looking birds called Grullas Coronadas, African or East African crowned cranes. The animals had two Spanish carers, Perfecto, who our lead lady Donna Hills later married, and Pepe, who everybody else wanted to marry. Sorry girls, that tall, handsome, mammoth of Spanish manhood was gay.

Gran Palace closed for a couple of weeks after New Year's Eve every year. We had those two weeks to get settled, rehearsed, have fittings, make a few new things and open. That's a good long time, and the whole process was smooth and unhurried. Dolores was thrilled to be in Spain; she was half Spanish on her father's side and had the dark or chocolate looks of a southerner. Nata or cream, and chocolate are terms used to help describe someone in Spanish. For instance, you know two people called Pedro, one is light-skinned the other more dusky so, to help separate them, you say Pedro de nata or Pedro de chocolate. It sounds a bit racist but it works.

Dolores travelled with us on and off for ten years or so and was adored by everybody. She'd grown up in the gold mining town of Kalgoorlie, Western Australia, six hundred kilometres east of Perth. As a girl, she learned ballet, and later taught it for a while in Kalgoorlie. She could still drop into the splits, and after a few bevvies, was apt to do so almost anywhere without much prompting. When I'd first met her, she was wardrobe mistress for the West Australian Ballet Company, and there were many, many funny tales about this outrageously wonderful, dippy woman.

One story I can confirm is regarding the time she was on tour with the WA Ballet doing the West Australia–Northern Territory–New Guinea run. Dolores was put in charge of doling out malaria pills to the dancers, management, backstage crew and pilot of the leased plane. On one occasion, having done her pill duty before a performance in a country town, she went off to unpack and do wardrobe-mistress things only to discover, moments before the performance, the entire company spread over the backstage area and dressing rooms sound asleep. Poor darling Dolores had given out her sleeping tablets instead. Luis was Principal Dancer at the time and was one of her victims.

This endearing and sometimes annoying lady went on to sew for us for years to come. On her ninety-something birthday, she took herself off to Kenya on safari. She made herself the full white hunter's costume for the occasion: topee hat, calf-length full khaki skirt with matching safari shirt, calf-length brown boots, leopard print scarf, the works. Arriving at Nairobi's Jomo Kenyatta International Airport, Dolores was unceremoniously taken from the customs line and, non-too politely, informed that her outfit was obnoxious and insulting. She must take her case to an interview room and change into something more appropriate or face having her visa revoked. Dolores went on to live to the ripe old age of a hundred plus.

Antonio called me a week after we settled in, telling me the costumes had arrived at the Port of Barcelona. After discussing what size truck was needed, we arranged a day to go and collect them. The production company office loaned me a car when we arrived, and it was decided I would meet them at the cargo terminal the following Monday. Papers in hand, passport and personal documentation at the ready, I set off on my first solo car trip through Barcelona—in one side, across the city, and out the other. I was a little nervous, but that soon dissipated when I got within the city limits. Barcelona remains in my mind the most car-friendly city in the world. The grid system layout with its two diagonal through-streets, and its traffic lights timed at just under the speed limit, make Barcelona a joy to negotiate. I arrived on time, met Antonio and his assistants, and off we went in search of the trunks.

Having lived in Spain years before under Franco, I knew two things. First, nothing involving paperwork goes smoothly in Spain. Second, corruption. Regarding paperwork, everything is in triplicate, and the corresponding offices for each copy are kilometres apart rather than side by side. Government workers, in fact, all workers, are notoriously slow. There is a saying in Spanish, *Las Cosas del Palacio van despacio*—things in the palace go slowly. Now we'll cover corruption. When the trunks were located, we were informed by Chief Customs Inspector of the cargo section that there was a one million pesetas (about A$10,000) import fee attached to the releasing of the trunks. This was news to all of us. There was absolutely nothing regarding payment in the official letter we received from Customs. 'Oh, that is a mistake, señores. There is indeed a fee if you wish to take them today. Otherwise, they will have to be impounded for thirty days.' The penny dropped, blatant and outrageous corruption. Antonio looked heavenward and dug out his chequebook. After being led into the Chief Inspector's office, the fee was instantly reduced to four hundred thousand pesetas (A$4,000), if a cash cheque could be made out. The trunks were manhandled by cargo workers one by one through the office door, and out the other side to the street. What could you do? Smiles all round, handshakes, '*Gracias y muy Buenos Dias a todos*,' and out we go.

After only a few days rehearsing at Gran Palace, and leaving early evening to go home, I noticed two guard dogs whining and digging frantically at the ground near the entrance where the building met a small garden bed. I didn't take much notice until the following evening when I saw the reason for this frantic behaviour. Just as I stepped out onto the covered portico where taxis could drop their passengers, a tiny, dark, four-legged creature darted out from under a parked car heading for the area that so interested the dogs the previous night. The two dogs were in hot pursuit, and the terrified little animal barely made it to a hole under the building. Hmm, I thought, that's a little kitten. The next day I arrived armed with some tasty meaty bits and a large cardboard box. I settled myself on the raised pedestrian walkway above the hole and dropped a morsel of meat outside it. A patient wait was rewarded by a snuffling, hesitant little nose and gorgeous whiskers. Yes, a wee puss it was indeed. Great. Another little meaty treat, a bit farther away this time, followed by another and another until his entire little body was exposed. Quick as a flash, the box was flung over him. I had myself a little furry friend. I took him/her/it to Luis, we jumped into the car and headed straight off to the vet.

The box on my lap was fairly bouncing with puss's efforts to escape. We got to the vet's just as a few vertical breaches appeared at the top. The veterinarian thought we were certifiable lunatics. 'This kitten is wild,' he said. 'What on earth would you want it for?' We ordered the full range of shots and inoculations, and he called for two assistants, who donned leather gloves then held onto a couple of legs apiece, to keep the little squirming ball steady. Shots done, de-worming done, bill paid, we took our new family member home. We bought some food bowls and a kitty litter tray and deposited the box in the centre of the lounge room, opened it a smidge, and retreated to the kitchen area closing the door behind us. An hour or so later, I investigated. No puss, empty box but no puss. I put out food and water which disappeared every day, and we emptied and cleaned the litter box. We did not sight the cat for at least two weeks. While I was watching TV one afternoon, the strangest-looking creature imaginable crawled out from under the sideboard. It was all wrinkly pink skin with the odd tuft of dirty, scraggly fur. It made its way ever so gingerly to me and jumped into my lap.

That was our gorgeous baby, Kabuki. Gradually, the pink skin became covered in the whitest, softest fur. The dark colour we had seen previously was apparently his little white coat covered in oil and grease from cars he had been hiding up, in and under. This matted, filthy layer had fallen out, and now he was the purest white. Kabuki stayed with us the entire time and would travel with us quite happily in the car to our other casino in Torrequebrada, where we later presented a second show. Sometimes we put the car on the train and took a private compartment so he could play and sleep during the trip. So spoiled, so loved and loving.

Darling Kabuki could not travel to Australia with us. The cost, for three months' quarantine in England, another three in Hawai'i plus two weeks in Australia, with no guarantee he would not be destroyed, was an exorbitant A$8,000—money we simply did not have. Mariana, our Russian lead dancer who married a Spanish man, was staying on in Lloret when our sojourn there ended. She adored Kabuki, so we tearfully and reluctantly left him in her care. Luis visited some years later, and Kabuki was a great, chubby, happy fifteen-year-old puss. He was the most wonderful little companion. I miss him still.

CHAPTER 43

THE RUSSIAN INVASION

Opening night in Gran Palace was upon us before we knew it. Dancers were doing what dancers do before a performance, checking costumes, setting out quick changes, stretching, running through last-minute choreography. Señor Leo, the venue's part-owner and Artistic Director, an unentitled title he had given himself, decided to have a curtain call rehearsal. Well, the time for that was long gone. Besides, a company as well trained as ours simply needs to be talked through such a thing. No, Sr Leo wanted everybody on stage. Why? Who knows? This man and I did not get along. Just one more occasion where this wannabe director managed to show his complete ignorance of all things theatrical. Stand in line, bow, step back, attractions forward, bow again, step back, magicians forward, bow, all in line bow, wait until the curtain comes down. Right, easy peasy, let's go. No. Again ... and again, and again.

By this time, the doors were open, and the audience was filing in. What a sight for them to behold, bits of costume thrown over rehearsal gear, wigs in rollers, no make-up and no lighting. The complete fantasy and mystique of a theatrical event evaporated. Snatching the mike from poor Luis, I told Sr Leo, who was in the soundbox, this should have been done during the past two weeks, now was definitely not the time. I ordered everybody off stage, the curtain down, and stormed off to my office. Sr Leo, or Don Leo as he preferred to be addressed, and I rarely spoke, or even acknowledged each other, from that moment on. Meetings were very strained affairs.

Apart from that little hiccup, the opening night was a spectacular success. The dancers were all in top form and looked superb. Our lead girl, Donna, who was Royal Ballet trained, looked staggeringly beautiful. They danced their hearts out and their entire performance was perfection. The animals disappeared, and appeared on cue, and the attraction acts went smoothly. This standard of performance impressed the venue owners so much that a few months into the contract, they requested us to stay on another year. This went on for five long wonderful years.

A lot was going on with us during those years. Antonio's connections throughout Spain often got us little extra gigs. The official winter close down after New Year's Eve at Gran Palace was for two weeks, and for the rest of wintry January and February audiences were thin on the ground, so we often did only two or three shows per week. The dancers were thrilled because their rate of pay didn't drop. We would be sold on to do galas elsewhere in Sitges or Paris and had lots of TV work. An annual event we looked forward to performing in was the Christmas Special for Cataluña TV. Gran Palace had a little trick up its sleeve. In no time at all, it could be converted into Europe's biggest TV studio. The front seating folded concertina-like and disappeared. The area between the first seats and the stage slid back to reveal railed camera tracking, and on and on. All very clever. We did big fashion parades there, and launched the new European Opel car, where I got to cover a new Opel in mirror, then smash it up turning it into a giant mirror ball to be hit by laser beams…many little side benefits. The Christmas show was great fun. We made and taped a couple of new Christmas routines, including one with the host, and then were paid to do nothing while the rest of the show was recorded over two weeks. For audience reaction, one of our regular shows audiences was taped then cut in where needed, sneaky buggers. A recording schedule was posted backstage; I would come in and sit amongst the crew to watch the taping of any big star I cared to see.

I got to see and work with some marvellous international talent at Gran Palace. Glenn Medeiros, Black, Joe Cocker and Sam Brown (what happened to Sam Brown?), that wonderful reunion with Rocio Jurado. Xavier Cugat, not a name anyone younger than me would remember but, when I was young, he was still way up there with the world's most prominent bandleaders. Cugat was famous, not only for his music and film work in Hollywood but also for his marriages, five or six wives I think, the last being the irrepressible Charo. Maria del Rosario Mercedes Pilar Martinez Molino Baeza, Charo for short, is another Spanish-born artist we happened to run into along the way. This diminutive, little woman – she says 5'4' but more like 5'0' – was so extraordinarily bubbly and her English so mangled, it was hard to get a fix on exactly what came out of her mouth. Charo was famous in the '70s, and '80s for her tits, her hair, her cuchi-cuchi-cuchi, and her English. She did a massive number of live TV appearances, including her own shows as well as touring with Bob Hope, which is what she was doing when Luis was asked to choreograph some moves for her some years previously. Although Charo made a living out of being the dumb Spanish blonde, she was actually a virtuoso classical Spanish guitarist, and one of the most highly recognised twelve-string guitarists in the world. I believe she is still going strong and working a lot on cruise ships. Last I saw of her was as a guest judge on RuPaul's Drag Race, and she looked great. Bless.

We were lucky enough to have Cugat as guest conductor for our New Year's Eve show and party in 1989 at Lloret de Mar. He was still so lively, after the show, we all danced to his music till the wee hours, along with all the guest artists and public. Cugat died the following year at ninety. Bit like elephants going home to die because, although he lived most of his life in Cuba and Hollywood, he was actually born in Girona, near Lloret. What a pleasure to have witnessed firsthand the music and the man.

Another artist who appeared at Gran Palace was Nana Mouskouri. Never in my life have I seen anyone with such a huge head as Nana's. I simply couldn't take my eyes off her. Every time she turned around, she caught me staring from the wings at that head of hers. A woman I adored was Mary Santpere, comedienne extraordinaire. I first saw her in revues in Madrid in the early '70s and, although I didn't speak Spanish then, she was still hilarious. She was so tall. I once saw her in a sketch in a theatre in Madrid, where between lines, she would rest her hand on the box next to and above the stage. She possessed the most expressive face. As I began to understand her, I fell even more in love with this amazing woman. Waiting to cross Gran Via in Madrid once, she was standing next to me. I couldn't wait to get home and tell Luis I'd just seen Mary Santpere. Imagine my delight when I learned this amazing lady was to be a guest artist at Gran Palace. The Gran Palace crowd went crazy because Mary was from Cataluña, and of course, we were in Cataluña. I stood in the wings and was so very pleased to be close to such talent. She possessed a huge body of work: seven LPs, a book, forty films and countless live shows. She won two of Spain's top awards: 1988 – Premio de Honor de la Generalidad de Cataluña; 1991 – Medalla de Oro al Mérito en el Trabajo. Poor darling died in 1992. There is now a theatre-shaped sculpture by Juan Bordes Caballero in Las Ramblas, Barcelona, dedicated to Josep, Rosa y Mary Santpere. I don't know who the others are. Maybe family, maybe other artists. Bless you, Mary Santpere and thank you for so much laughter and joy.

Well, there are people you love, and wish you'd worked with, and there are others you'd happily throw under a bus. One of my 'under the bus' people is a lady called Mari Carmen. This woman, who did only one night with us in Lloret De Mar – one night too many – was a nightmare. Mari is still going, and must be a hundred by now, some people just don't know when to die. She is a ventriloquist, *Mari Carmen y Sus Muñecos* (Mari Carmen and Her Dolls or puppets.) was already getting on a bit when she did her one night with us. She continually smoked backstage, not content to smoke only in her dressing room but, on stage, next to dancers in sheer flammable fabrics. It didn't matter how many times I told her to stop smoking, she took no notice whatsoever until I snatched a cigarette out of her mouth and jumped on it. There was no time for a rehearsal and trying to give her stage direction was a nightmare. She was to go up the backstage stairs where two male dancers would take a hand each and lead her down to present her to the audience. She was to do a ten-minute spot and get off. After thirty minutes of her act, Sr Leo came backstage screaming, 'Get that woman off.' The stage manager was doing the 'PPPPSSSSTTtttt' thing as loud as he could to attract her attention, but no, nobody was gonna get her off. In the end, the curtain was brought down. I'm not sure she stopped even then. Her doll doesn't realise how lucky it is to be made of wood, and not have to look at, or listen to, this nut case.

Lloret was a fun place to live. During the off-season, we got to know the locals very well. Luis and I shifted closer to the heart of town, amazing how even the most spectacular view is taken for granted after a time, to a much smaller place where we stayed for the next four and a half years. Summer was crazy; the streets and beaches were packed, and it was twenty-four-hour party time every day. There were two little gay bars in town, I am not much of a bar person, but I believe they jumped along very nicely. The girls all enjoyed themselves, and there was even a little nude beach where we could swim and avoid tan marks.

Dale, who had stayed on with us after Korea, decided like us to move closer into town, and we helped him shift. Amazing how one suitcase grew, in just a few months, to an entire apartment full of belongings. Dale was in heaven. Way back in Italy, long before there were any plans to go to Spain, Witch Milka from Paradiso in Rome told him, through a card reading: 'to Forget Asia'. Dale, like me, was a big fan of Asia, and spent years in Japan, Korea and Hong Kong. 'Spain is the place for you.' Well, this really did seem to be the case. He took to Spain and speaking Spanish like a duck to water. Most of our girls in Lloret were Australians from previous shows. Annie, who was with us for many years, and being on the shorter side, partnered Luis in South Korea, joined us again. A few years ago, I visited her in Bali where she, and her husband John, have decided to continue their fabulous lives.

The start of the end of our type of entertainment came about because of politics. 'Mr Gorbachev, tear down this wall', a challenge issued by US President Ronald Regan, had a long-reaching, and devastating side effect on showgirls, and tits 'n feather shows, not only in Europe but around the world. Tearing down the wall dividing East and West Berlin, and the beginning of Perestroika for us meant one more thing. Hundreds, no, thousands of incredibly well-trained dancers, living in the Eastern bloc, were now free to go south in search of work. And go they did, in droves. In no time at all, every European venue was employing these talented people but, for half, or less than half, the going rate. These dancers just wanted out. They would go anywhere, do anything, to have work.

It was then that our continuing contracts with both Spanish casinos were offered at much lower rates. Owners, knowing full well Russian dancers could be employed at such cheap rates, lowered their offers accordingly. We could do nothing but comply, and so, bit by bit at first, and then completely, we switched to Russian dancers. The Russian dancers were engaged through an agency, and what percentage of their wages were given over to them in payment, I never found out. Russian dancers are simply amazing; they are superbly well trained, very disciplined, very beautiful and very well-mannered but, they are blocks of ice on stage, impossible to get any emotion from. They perform like robots. They deliver the choreographic goods to perfection, no more, no less, but they are just doing the steps. Smiles are cold, pasted-on affairs without the slightest hint they are enjoying themselves. This lack of emotion communicates itself to the audience as lack of enthusiasm. Quite often, this is the case, but even the most enthusiastic can't cut it.

The other problem was and is, they were brought up under communism. They simply didn't understand they couldn't just take a night off. Girls got their period, of course, and took three days off. They are used to that. The State pays no matter what. So, a whole mindset must be changed, it was a never-ending battle and one I simply didn't care to fight. Another issue that became a problem was that they would do anything not to go back home. A girl, or a guy, meets someone at a disco or the beach, a romance starts, and they are gone. Marrying for a resident visa, or even a new passport, was uppermost in their minds. I can't blame them. Lives of such deprivation, with no chance of change. Who wouldn't grab it? I just didn't want to have to deal with it.

Our lead dancer Donna started dating Perfecto, he of the animal carer's duo and they made a pretty hot-looking couple. Donna is from Ballarat, where I grew up, and it was something of a shock for me to learn I'd attended school with her father. Donna was trained in London at the Royal Ballet School and possessed the most incredible extensions and perfect lines. Long, beautiful legs going on for a mile and an entrancing face and smile. Unfortunately, like so many beautifully trained dancers, she'd grown too tall for classical ballet, so she'd joined the Bluebells touring company. Brigitte Nielsen, Sylvester Stallone's girlfriend in the '80s, had an extraordinary haircut for its day. It was platinum white, and a very short flattop. Donna had her hair cut in this style, and it suited her exceedingly well. So well, we asked her to forego show hats and wigs and show her hair on stage. No girl in our shows ever appeared without wig or hat, so this was very much a first. I agreed to pay the salon costs monthly. I made little glittering pieces of jewellery to hide in her hair which added a touch of bling to her already beautiful face. Donna wore this hairstyle from then on and became quite famous around town. The black and gold Flash Gordon piece now resides in producer extraordinaire Grant Philipo's Showgirl Museum in Las Vegas. None of the other girls could be recognised offstage, but Donna stood out as that girl from the Gran Palace show wherever she went. After two years in Lloret, Donna moved to the south of Spain with our Torrequebrada show and later married Perfecto. They have two daughters.

Jane, from the South Korean days, followed as Lead Dancer after Donna, then our dear Janet, along with her two pet ferrets, joined us replacing Jane. Janet, who started with us at seventeen, had been with us for many years by the time she met her future husband in Italy. Apart from the time they were married, now divorced, she had performed with us pretty much non-stop for the best part of fifteen years. Janet is one of those extraordinary, long-legged creatures just made for this business. Classically trained at the Graduate College of Dance in Perth, Janet simply oozed personality on stage. No way could you take your eyes off her. Janet stayed until the Russian invasion, then joined Moulin Rouge in Paris, ending up as a senior soloist there. Luis and I went to Paris to visit her in her little apartment behind Moulin Rouge in Montmartre. We would sit with Jacki Clérico, owner of Moulin Rouge, and he would say, 'Look, my Janet will be out in a moment', 'Can you see my Janet?' He adored her. Janet always felt she was considered uneducated by others, when she finally gave up show business, she took herself off to university and obtained a host of degrees. You show 'em, gal.

Gallardo and his wife Nadja – yes, the tiger was named after her with good reason – not only owned the Production Company in Barcelona, but they were Spain's top agents as well, supplying showrooms and Spanish TV with a great many artists. In 1989, they brought Bette Davis to Spain where she was honoured at the Donostia–San Sebastián International Film Festival. While she was there, they flogged her around the TV studios doing interviews. Nadja travelled with her during this time, seeing to her travel needs, accommodation, and arranging interviews. When it was all over, and they packed Bette off on her way, with a stopover in Paris because she was too weak to make the trip back direct to the US. Nadja came straight back to Gran Palace and told me all about the stint with Bette, and what a harridan she was. A proper pain in the arse. She said, 'Well, the old bitch has gone, and I hope her fucking plane crashes.' The following morning the news of the day was full of Bette dying in Paris overnight. Nadja was horrified, 'Oh,' she said, 'I didn't mean it. Really, I didn't mean it. Honestly.' I laughed till I almost pissed myself. Darling Nadja.

Once Nadja's young daughter asked if she could have her ears pierced. Nadja's reply was 'No, darling, I think you have enough holes in your body.' She had a tongue on her, she really did. Nadja is an extremely tall German woman. She and Antonio used to have an adagio act together. He was a bodybuilder, training partner of Arnold Schwarzenegger, and was at one time Mr Spain. Antonio met Nadja when she was one of Europe's top-class, highest-paid strippers. She had an act where she sat in a giant Perspex hand, and with her long, long legs, her waist-length blond hair, stunning face, and that six-foot body, she was an instant hit. She would travel from place to place in her famous pink Cadillac, which, by contract, was always parked directly in front of the venue where she was performing. What better advertising could you possibly have? She would arrive nightly clad in her pink, knee-length fur and what appeared to be nothing else, a truly classy and clever act.

After the Russians came, Antonio, who obviously liked his women tall, started an illicit affair with our 6'1' leading lady Katrina. Nadja found out and was furious. I caught her walking the streets of Lloret late one evening. 'Where is he, Tom?' she said. 'I'll kill the bastard.' She opened her handbag extracting an enormous, lethal-looking knife as she said it. I would often have to steer her elsewhere, and console her, calm her down. During one performance,

Katrina came off stage as white as a sheet. 'What's wrong?' I asked her. 'It's Nadja,' she said. 'She's sitting centre front, and every time I look down, she opens her bag and caresses a huge knife.' This little affair ended up in a rather sordid divorce, and Antonio and Katrina eventually married.

CHAPTER 44

THE LIDO, MOULIN ROUGE AND US

Antonio and Nadja were well regarded in Spain and were the country's biggest and most successful agents. During one of the Gran Palace winter close downs when Antonio would sell us on to TV shows and gala performances, we started appearing on *Si Lo Se No Vengo* (If I'd Known I Wouldn't Have Come). This top-rated TV game show and variety program by *Televisión Española* (TVE 1) aired during 1985–88 and was presented by Jordi Hurtado. During the five years we worked at Gran Palace, we often did guest spots on this program, it was hectic but fun. Luis would create a three-minute dance routine relevant to the week's theme. The budget was not enormous and did not include money for designing and making costumes so, generally it meant a trip around the TV costume rental places scavenging for ideas which would meld with the concepts Luis had come up with. Anyone who has been involved with a weekly TV series knows time is of the essence. Starting with learning the routine, rehearsing it, dressing it, and the inevitable alterations always required for hired costumes. Then, there's getting to the TV studio, rehearsing camera angles and lighting, and finally, performing the routine before a live audience. All these components must come together and take place in a really short timeframe. Shorter still if you have regular shows to perform each evening. We did it often enough though, and as well as being exciting work, it was a diversion from the boredom of performing the same show each night for a year's duration.

Other welcome departures from routine diverted us from the daily grind as well. Galas, in European theatre parlance at least, are one-off shows where artists make guest appearances, and can be anything from a fundraiser on a box in the middle of a vineyard to a Royal Command Performance at a State Theatre. Galas were another way to earn a little extra and knock out a bit of fun while staving off the boredom of a long run. It's difficult to remember all the galas we performed unless they were memorable for a particular reason. No doubt such a list would make for dreary reading in any case. How exciting can it be? You choose the parts of the show you want to take; you pack, get on a bus, quick placement rehearsal, perform, pack, get on a bus and go home. There are, however – gratefully not so often – incidents or problems that make some occasions stand out. One such occasion was the gala at the casino of Sitges.

Over the years, Sitges has been called The Saint Tropez of Spain or Little Ibiza, and is known throughout Europe for its casino, its film festival, its carnival, and its seventeen beaches. Sitges developed into a much-loved gay haven as well and is considered one of the most gay-friendly places in the world. So apart from the offer of doing a gala there being a pleasant divertissement, it would be interesting to see what all the fuss was about. Only two routines from the show were requested, the Tropical Finale and the Lions routines. Both were currently performed nightly, so no rehearsal was needed except for placement at the venue in the afternoon. The event was to be part of the famed annual Carnival celebration which has been run between February and March for over a century. It kicks off on *Dijous Gras* or Fat Thursday, with the spectacular arrival of King Carnestoltes, and ends with the symbolic Burial of the Sardine on Ash Wednesday.

The agency laid on buses, and a fairly casual day was planned with plenty of downtime allowing a look-see around. Lloret de Mar is a little over an hour's drive to the Barcelona airport where we were to pick up some other guest artists who were flying in, and then another thirty minutes or so to Sitges, thirty-five kilometres away. The time at the airport dragged on a bit when inbound flights were delayed, and then dragged on even more when one particular VIP decided she was way too exalted to ride in a bus, and a limo had to be found. Oh, save me from these precious, pompous people who, according to them, could well suffer irreversible health problems should they deign to share the same common air as us hoi polloi. Limo arranged—we took off for the last leg to Sitges.

The outdoor stage of the beautiful Sitges Prado Casino was vast and uncomplicated. Plenty of entrances from centre back, and the stairs either side were going to be added value entertainment-wise. We unpacked and proceeded with our rehearsal. Easy peasy, quick sound and light check, then off to lunch which management provided in a nearby restaurant, leaving a bit of time to wander around while the other artists rehearsed. We still had no idea who we would be performing with. The folk who joined us in the bus were unknown to us, and we hadn't glimpsed the Grand Dame who breathed rarefied air. Antonio gave us our performance schedule, and we went our separate ways until the half-hour call. Luis and I returned to the venue to put the finishing touches to the marquee serving as our dressing rooms, it was then we realised just who the mystery woman was.

On stage, doing a lackadaisical run-through, was the person with whom we had the unfortunate experience of working with previously. A grandiloquent Jamaican of a certain reputation, the super brat, Ms Jones. Oh, dear. This could be a long night. The one, and thankfully only, other time we worked together had been on the TV show called *Domenica In* for the television channel RAI 1 in Rome some years before in 1982. This time we hoped there would be no repeat of the last occasion, but should she be running true to reputation, we were prepared for the worst. Come performance time, there was a rather tense argument between Ms Jones, and someone whom we presumed was her manager. Something must have upset her imperiousness, she was threatening loudly, and animatedly, not to go on. When it was explained there would be no payment, Madame threw a piece of sheer, leopard-print chiffon over her head, covering her face, and stalked onto the stage where, presumably, she performed her songs draped in this diaphanous fabric. What the audience thought, or just who indeed they imagined might be under there, we never learned. We were packed, and out of there before the end of her routine, and the subsequent inevitable fireworks.

During the winter break of 1989, we were requested to perform in Paris – a huge deal for an Australian show – there being half a dozen shows already available in Paris. The Grand Hotel on the Place de l'Opera (now the Intercontinental) would be the venue, for a formal dinner for President François Mitterrand. It is the most beautiful venue I've ever worked in. The Grand Hotel was designed by Alfred Armand and was inaugurated on 30 June 1862 by Empress Eugenie, wife of Napoleon III. The hotel has hosted much royalty throughout its long history, including Tsar Nicholas and Tsarina Alexandra, King Edward VII of England, and Queen Rania of Jordan. Victor Hugo hosted parties at Le Grand Hotel, and Émile Zola used the hotel for the setting of the death of his tragic character Nana. The dinner was held in the famous Salon Opera. This room, along with the Café de la Paix on the corner of the Boulevard des Capucines, are National Treasures. The walls are fantastically ornate, and touching is forbidden. Guards dressed in Louis VI powdered wigs and costumes stand around the perimeter. Even the curtains onto the stage were to be pulled aside by guards. Quaint but beautiful. The décor is said to be surpassed only by the Paris Opera house, located opposite.

The Grand treated the show extraordinarily well. We travelled by overnight train from Barcelona, were met by limousines at the Gare de Lyon in Paris, and checked into beautiful rooms at Le Grand. Luis's and my room overlooked the Paris Opera House, it truly was magical. The Office of the President went to great lengths making us feel welcome, even asking the Australian Embassy to get hold of an Americas Cup flag, which Australia had won back in 1983, to hang over the stage. Meals could be taken in any of the hotel restaurants, it was all very glam. A dear friend of ours, Jean Claude, was then Maître de of the Café de la Paix on the ground floor corner. This famous Parisienne meeting spot was the haunt of people such as Sergei Diaghilev and the Prince of Wales, future King Edward VII of the UK, during the Belle Époque. Whenever I stayed at Jean Claude's wacky little garage conversion in St Denis, I always rode his motorcycle, with his dog on board, to pick him up after work. He would invite me inside for a coffee while I waited. Coffee at that exalted watering hole was then US$30, and consisted of full silver service, a bowl of sugars from around the world, and chocolate-covered orange peel. Glad it was free to me. Sit at the Café De La Paix long enough, and you will see every celebrity in the world either dining or going by. After JC finished work, we would go on to Lido or, Moulin Rouge or, any number of famous places for supper. Patrons would be pushed aside, and a space cleared for a table brought in over their heads for Jean Claude, the dog and me. He was famous and such fun to be with. He is gone now, like so many dear friends. Miss you, JC.

The performance was a huge success, and afterwards President Mitterrand's aide came back to congratulate us and enquire 'How much would I charge to do it all again?' He said, 'the President was concerned so many people, hotel staff, and his staff, worked so hard on the evening, and had not seen the show, he would like us to do it again for them.' What can you say after such a question from such an obviously caring man? I consulted the dancers and was happy to tell him it would be our pleasure—at no charge. So, the dancers got back into costume, and did it all over again.

After the second year in Lloret, Antonio Gallardo took over the production of shows in the Casino of Torrequebrada (Broken Tower). It is named after one of two fifteenth-century coastal watchtowers, near Benalmadena on the Costa del Sol in southern Spain. We were offered and accepted the contract. We husbanded a good deal of our money to make the new production for each following year, shows being changed annually. Instead of putting the old show away in mothballs, it could now travel down to the south of Spain for another year's work. This was great for Antonio as well, as he could use the animals, and his expensive magic tricks again. The first year at Torrequebrada, the entire cast decided two years in Lloret was enough and went south with the show.

Benalmadena is beautiful, enjoys good weather and is clean, but has a few too many British ex-pats for my liking. We set Dale up as manager and found him an apartment nearby. I would drive the eight hours from Lloret every few weeks to keep an eye on things. Luis had finally given up dancing and occasionally joined me on these trips, so visits to Dale were sometimes Luis, sometimes me, sometimes both of us, and the cat. The venue was much smaller, so a certain amount of rejigging and rearranging needed to be done, but all is possible, and the show worked well in its new setting. There was no room for big sets or props but, some clever lighting constructions were made, which more than suited our performances. The animals were a big problem as there was absolutely no space, I came to loathe seeing them continually caged. Nadja, the tiger was housed right next to the stage entrance, she became quite listless and flat. The door onto the stage was a strange affair. Great big casino, a large stage with revolve, dressing rooms, star dressing rooms over two floors, and a doorway onto the stage no bigger than a standard house door. What goes through architects' minds when they are drawing up plans? This tiny door forced the girls to huddle up in the three metres between the door, and the actual stage before putting on the enormous hats ready for their entrance.

On opening night, the camel got stuck in the doorway and promptly died. A heart attack was suspected. Here was this poor, dead beast jammed in the doorway. Nobody could get on or off. Stagehands tried to pull the unfortunate animal out to no avail. So heavy was he that in the end, a window next to Nadja's cage was broken, a winch passed through from a tow truck outside, and the hapless dromedary hauled out. Oh, dear, the tears. Showgirls with red, swollen eyes were the order of the day for that disastrous opening.

It was decided for the second Torrequebrada contract to do without the animals, thank all gods, and to put some guest artists into the show. Every few weeks, a big European name was contracted to do thirty minutes or so in the middle of our show. One I didn't want to miss was opera singer Montserrat Caballé. This amazing little lady, who was a great friend of Freddy Mercury, and who received a goodly portion of his estate after his death, put on the most marvellous performance, but I never got to see it. However, one that I simply refused to miss was Barry Humphries as Dame Edna.

Dame Edna Everage. I had always been a great fan but, after Barry's time with us in Torrequebrada, I viewed him in a different light. He was quite tricky with a massive ego, although pleasant, and easy to talk to. Does that sound contradictory? During rehearsal, I worked on getting Barry, and the dancers to try to balance on a small travelling revolving stage starting upstage, revolving 180 degrees then moving downstage. The thing was a bit rocky, so I put a handrail on it for Barry. The dancers were okay, didn't bother them at all, but when the thing first started, there was always a bit of a jerk, and Dame Edna would wobble alarmingly. I kept saying to him 'Barry, you must hold the handrail we installed for you,' but it seemed to go in one ear and out the other. Oh, well, not me who will look silly on the night. I give up. At one point he was giving directions to lighting, and said, 'Now here, I'll walk over to the piano, and say blah blah blah and, when the applause dies down, if it ever does…'. That's confidence plus.

He was between wives at the time and told me he was sleeping rough on a cot under his frocks in his warehouse in London. Poor guy. Opening night was tense because there were maybe twenty minutes to go, and no Barry. He'd got lost looking for a good seafood restaurant. Finally arriving he rushed in, fired questions at me regarding local news, slammed the dressing room door, and emerged minutes later, right on time, in perfect character. The local news snippets popped out of his mouth and were worked beautifully into his routine. What a great memory, such a pro. The one thing that rattled me a little, I must say, was that he refused to come out of his Dame Edna character while in costume. Even backstage after the show when it is all over, he stays in character until he's in his street clothes. Those characters must live in there with him, and I'm sure it's very confusing to be around someone like that all the time. Nonetheless, he was magnificent in a specially made frilled Spanish confection complete with mini-fruit. The laughs came loud, clear, and in all the right places. I must presume there was a largely English-speaking audience, any Spanish-speakers would still be shaking their heads. Barry died in April 2023, at age 89. A State memorial was held in his honour on December 15th.

From a window in an upstairs dressing room, I could see a group of gold domes in distant Marbella, they looked like a carton of gold eggs with one extra-large egg in the centre. Probably a lavish hotel. On a day off, Luis and I drove down to investigate. These domes turned out to be the private estate of Adnan Khashoggi. Khashoggi was the most notorious arms dealer in the world. Born in Mecca and educated in Alexandria, Egypt, he started his career flogging ex-WWII British arms, with British compliance, to the Middle East. Oh, such clean hands the West has. Go back far enough, and you'll find Britain and the US created all of today's problems in that area.

At the height of Khashoggi's career in the '80s, he is reported to have spent a quarter of a million dollars (US) per day maintaining his lifestyle. This then, was one of his houses. The central dome was the main house, surrounded by guest houses, each with its gold dome, and swimming pool. In the marina, we saw his private yacht, a vast affair with multiple staterooms for guests. It was said he was such a wanted man, he rarely appeared in public. According to the Torrequebrada management, there was an exact copy of the casino showroom in Khashoggi's house. Each year, when the show changed, two lots of sets would be built, one for the casino, and one for Khashoggi's place. When he was entertaining his guests, he would have the show bought to his theatre to perform. Outrageous. Probably true, but it certainly never happened in the years we were there.

The second year in Torrequebrada experienced the same fate as Lloret de Mar, in that Russian dancers were employed. Dale was still managing, but after a Spanish classical group was denied entry into Australia at Sydney airport because their visas were incorrect, the Spanish government started making it very difficult for Australians working in Spain. Eventually, no more extensions were allowed, and Dale had to leave. He went to Perth to look after our house there. Having the shows in two different cities, and no manager we could depend on meant things were becoming more and more difficult. Eventually, the contract money on offer was cut to a pathetically small amount. That, and the problem of the Russian dancers made Luis and I decide to call it a day. Enough is enough. We performed our last shows, packed up both productions and the house, stuffed everything into a couple of shipping containers, and in 1992 went home to Australia.

Saying goodbye to friends made over the previous five years was difficult but, for show people, it was nothing new. We were to fly out of Madrid, so we drove our little Ford Fiesta there and gave it to Isabel, Luis's young sister. Pepe, Luis's father, had died after being bedridden for a year or two due to a severe stroke. We stayed with Mama for a few days too, enjoying her epicurean delights before heading home.

CHAPTER 45

QUOKKAS AND CRUISE SHIPS

In the mid 1990's, with the ever-diminishing number of outlets available to perform our genre of entertainment, we jumped at the chance to get onto the burgeoning cruise ship bandwagon and started providing the shows for Star Cruises. A member of Genting Hong Kong Group, the third largest cruise line company in the world, they are credited with single-handedly developing the cruise industry in the Asia–Pacific region.

Once the shows were up and running on the ships, Luis would often go by himself for a few weeks at a time, hopping from ship to ship, checking on the shows, doing a bit of costume maintenance, and changing a bit of choreography here and there where needed. This gave me time to work on the house in Perth, the so-called big house, where I was busy pulling down walls, arches, columns, and generally removing the 'wogginess' from it. During one of these times in 1997, I got a call completely out of the blue from Lawrence Eastwood, renowned TV, stage, and film designer, (now returned to working in architecture, which he studied in London). After a brief introduction, Lawrence explained his involvement with a film being made on Rottnest Island off the coast of Western Australia. Nigel Devenport, art director/artiste extraordinaire, was caught up in Thailand on a film with Marlon Brando, *The Island of Doctor Moreau*. Brando was being difficult, they were filming in the jungle, and rather than be taken to the set by four-wheel drive, Mr Brando's rider (extra conditions) required a white Volvo sedan. This fuss necessitated a road grader going in front of the Volvo each morning to smooth the way. Brando's pretentiousness, amongst other trivialities, put the production behind schedule, stopping Nigel from work on the ill-fated Rottnest film.

The movie I was to work on was called *Under the Lighthouse Dancing*, a film which, with much less public attention than the Titanic, sank just as quickly, and just as surely to depths still unplumbed. So, the question was, could I, would I, take over for Nigel until he could make it back. 'What's the pay like?' was my only question before agreeing. So, I left immediately for Rottnest. I met Lawrence for a very quick briefing before he took off to God-knows-where. The gist of it all was, there was a house being built on a rather desolate promontory. The inside was built around a fake old tree trunk, which was to be painted and given a gleaming coppery gum finish, the entire interior needed a few coats plus an ageing effect added to the raw wood decking and deck furniture, and an old World War II bunker had to be turned into a chapel. I would also be on call for the thousand and one things the director, Graeme Rattigan, might need, such as distressing the odd street sign, denting buckets, muddying up paths, and so on, and so forth. An art department of one. A first surely.

Rottnest Island, known locally as Rotto, is a dreary, sandy, low-slung, barren, limestone rock eighteen kilometres by boat from Perth. Dreariness aside, it is a tremendously popular holiday destination for Perthites who flock to the beautiful beaches in their thousands, particularly over the Christmas break. Why, when coastal Perth, and its surrounding suburban environs, have kilometres of identical beaches, is a mystery to me. This appalling place has holiday-shack-style accommodation, one pub, one general store, no transport other than bicycles, and no natural water supply. The island was visited by Dutch sailors in the seventeenth century, who quickly wrote it off as a rat-infested hole, and the name has stuck. *Rotte Nest* is Dutch for rat's nest but, the rats were, in fact, cute, rat-like marsupials called quokkas, stranded there on their Christmas holidays seven thousand years ago when the land bridge eventually sank. These rare and endangered animals were, for a time, the primary source of amusement for visiting plebs. Games of quokka soccer were played outside the one pub using the quokkas as footballs. This pastime has since been deemed as not endangered-species friendly.

The film tells a story of six friends who, for reasons known only to themselves, decide to spend a weekend on this island paradise, and having absolutely nothing to do, two of them fall in love. It is there the storyline, such as it is, disintegrates, starting its unstoppable, pre-destined slide down one of the island's many steep sand dunes. The cast included Jack Thompson, Jacqueline McKenzie and Naomi Watts. Perhaps they might have preferred me to have excluded their names from this lowlight of their careers. I didn't have much to do with Naomi or Jacqueline except the occasional meal with them and Jack, but they were very pleasant. I had a bit to do with Jack Thompson, so it's integral to the narrative, as they say.

Jack was having a weight problem and seemed to be expanding daily. Maybe it was his way of coping with this disaster. He was given a personal trainer, and I imagine, was on some sort of strict diet. On occasion, he would sneak away from filming on location, and make his way to the house where I was working, on the pretext of a bit of a chat, and stuff his face with food he'd filched from lunch and stuck in his pockets. A strange man, yet obviously a talented, and more than capable actor, being the recipient of numerous acting awards, including being appointed a Member of the Order of Australia in 1986, and named an Australian Living Legend in 2002. Jack will always be remembered for his 1972 Cleo magazine nude male centrefold. A fine figure of Australian manhood, Jack languidly and sensually reclines on a day bed with one hand discreetly placed over the offending appendage. Yes, seems only one hand was needed although two might have been required on a warmer day. The centrefold was outrageous at the time, and a first. His other somewhat scandalous behaviour was his fifteen-year relationship with the Bunkie sisters, cheekily introducing them as Mrs Thompson and Mrs Thompson.

On his visits to me, Jack chatted away in what to me, was a confusing accent. It seemed to vary not only from American (pick a region) to British and back to Australian, not simply on a day-to-day basis but, often sentence to sentence. I never quite knew which Jack I was talking to. I can only assume that after acting such a wide range of parts, some of them appeared to have taken up permanent residence. On one of the rare Sundays off, I decided to take a ferry ride to Perth's port, Fremantle, the obvious choice to stave off total boredom. Perhaps time for a quick lunch at one of the port city's famous seafood places, a stroll amongst Freo's colourful denizens, and back on the last ferry. Jack had the same idea and spent his thirty-minute ferry ride in a determined effort to deplete the on-board snack bar of all its perishables.

Filming took place at several locations around the island and in trying to keep ahead of shooting; I would work at two or three locations per day. This meant I needed some form of transport. The island, because of its fragile, endemic, and endangered fauna and flora, has an A-Class Reserve status, and is administered by the Rottnest Island Authority under a separate Act of Parliament. Consequently, no motorised vehicles are allowed except for those driven by the Island Rangers. The film company was given permission for a bus driven by an island rep to haul the artists and crew around, and somehow I wangled one of the two ranger vehicles, and its driver, to use it to take me from location to location. The reason was twofold, I needed transportation, and one of those overly officious, uniformed rangers was to be on-site with me at all times. This poor bored being's job was to constantly observe my every move in case I spilt a droplet of paint or rested some of my painting equipment against a piece of ancient limestone, causing untold and irreparable environmental damage. The production management and stars were always a bit pissed at me when the set artist, this nobody, in his paint-spattered garb, arrived majestically to a set in his chauffeured 4x4. Weep, babies, weep.

At the house location, a single-storey beach bungalow with a canvas roof was already partially constructed when I got there, and it was ready to be attacked inside, if not out. This construction caused the ranger with me no end of concern. He had already been diligent during the construction stage, making perfectly certain the house rested only on bollards carefully sunken into the sand, and nothing man made went within cooee of nature's natural formations. A fake fireplace of fake bricks needed to look realistic and fire-blackened, and the inside and outside walls had to be painted and weathered, quite a lot for one person. Still, I'm incredibly quick with a brush and have an abhorrence of the spray gun most set decorators prefer. The house was built on a bluff above a relatively long, sandy beach to the right, and a craggy rock drop front and left. To the back were five metres or so of sand before a small rise to a rocky sand-covered ledge. The house was on stilts, approximately a metre high, to bring it level with the rise at the back and there was a wooden walkway suspended between the two. When Jack Thompson was on one of his chatty/feasty visits, I always knew he was coming because his loping bulk on the suspended walkway would send the whole house into spasms. Soon, but not soon enough, my six weeks were up, and it was back to civilisation. Well, Perth anyway. Don't bother looking for the film; it was stillborn and discreetly buried.

Star Cruises had twelve ships in the fleet, each one bearing the name of a sign of the zodiac. At first, we provided shows for the Gemini, and later for Leo and Virgo. Every six months we replaced these existing shows with new shows, the old show moving on to one of the other ships in a rotation system. The worst thing about our time with the ships was foregoing our Australian dancers. Russian doors were now wide open, and slowly we complied with the Entertainment Managers request to cut costs and replace all our artists with the cheaper Russians. The parent company also owned Genting Highlands, hotels and casinos located at the top of Mount Ulu Kali in Genting Sempah, 1,740 feet almost straight up—58 kilometres and forty-five minutes from Kuala Lumpur by car. Our new ship shows were produced there, with plenty of space available for the making of costumes, rehearsals, and the dancers' accommodation.

The four Genting hotels and casino at the peak are the Genting Grand, the Resort Hotel, the Highlands and the First World Hotel. There has been a fifth and sixth added since. All are connected by passageways, bridges, walkways and escalators. The hotels are usually quite full during the week but on weekends or holidays are packed to bursting when people from all over hot, humid Malaysia come to gamble and escape to the relative coolness at that height. We had rooms in one hotel, rehearsed on the main Genting International Showroom stage in another hotel, ate in another, and worked on the costumes in yet another. Getting from one to the other was like salmon swimming upstream. I looked eternally down on a sea of black hair surging around me in every direction.

A trip into KL was organised whenever fabric, trim, feathers, and the myriad other haberdashery needs for costume making required replenishing. The thought of the forty-five-minute taxi ride along that tortuous serpentine road with its hairpin bends, and lunatic drivers consumed me. I'd put it off until it had to be done. Getting back up to the resort was far less harrowing, as the steep roads themselves constrained the speed a driver could reach. The method for going down seemed to be take your foot off the accelerator, and let gravity do its worst. There was a helicopter service from both the airport and KL, which ceased after a crash in 1982 killed all eleven on board.

The ships themselves were a wonderful experience, the ultimate in cruising luxury. I loved every minute onboard. It would take several weeks to mount each show. Luis and I were signed on as Officers and treated accordingly. Of course, being officially crew, we needed to know each ship from bow to stern. We were required to do the fire course, the lifeboat drills, and the dreaded written exam. This process was gone through each time for each ship. When jumping from ship to ship, checking shows, doing a bit of rehearsal and maintenance, the exams became a pain in the butt. Several times we feigned ignorance when one of our officer's duties loomed and were hauled before a senior officer for a 'please explain'. Thankfully the cat o'nine tails was long since done away with. The cabins for us and the dancers, although inside – meaning no windows or balcony – were indeed passenger cabins rather than crew cabins. We had full run of the ship, with meals at the extensive buffet at any time, use of the five-star restaurants twice weekly, or we'd dine at the Officers Mess.

The ships pulled into port every second day or so, and when it was possible, we took the opportunity to go ashore for the eight hours. The only port where we could never get off was Phuket. There being no docking facilities due to depth, lighters were used to ferry passengers to and from the port. Because crew must be the last to leave and be first back on board, it cut the time onshore down dramatically, not really making it worthwhile. I have been to Phuket city since, and I can tell you, we didn't miss a thing. Endless souvenir shops, and vulgar Australian tourists. What's the great attraction? Besides, it's rather lovely to have the ship pretty much to yourself, when most of the three thousand passengers are ashore.

The cruise ship gigs lasted right up until 2003 when the international outbreak of severe acute respiratory syndrome, (SARS, the first covid outbreak) saw all but one of our ships quarantined. That first-identified strain of the coronavirus species very quickly put an end to our cruising days. Eleven of the fleet of twelve ships were quarantined. Only the Super Star Leo escaped. She sailed around the Australian coast out of Perth, with cruises to the East coast, up to Darwin, and day trips to nowhere. Luis and I were on board for a month desperately trying to give the shows some added oomph, some sort of wow factor. We changed costumes, choreography, and themes, trying to encourage passengers onto the trips, but to no avail.

The tolling of the death knell was loud, clear, and heard by all concerned. With an up close and personal view of the death throes, and the imminent end of Star Cruises, we resignedly sailed back to Melbourne and said a fond farewell. The end was nigh.

CHAPTER 46

WET BOTTOMS AND WINDMILLERS

As mentioned, in 1986, while working in Seoul we bought the 'Big house', as we always called it, in Dianella Heights, Perth. It was an enormous mansion of 750 square metres over three floors, with monstrous balconies front and back on two floors, and garaging for five cars. There was a pool, pool house, fernery and fishponds, two dining rooms, two lounge rooms, five bedrooms, three bathrooms, sauna, sewing room, billiard room, service lift, and on, and on. It was of the ghastly Italianate overkill style with columns, arches, and flocked wallpaper in almost every room. A friend of mine described it as Art Dago. In the kitchen alone there were eight columns, and four arches. Over the thirteen years we owned the house, I managed to get rid of every column, most arches, and turned the sixteen medium sized rooms into twelve enormous ones. The dining room was capable of seating twenty-four, and there were many sensational formal parties. My fiftieth birthday party saw two hundred fifty guests, and a string quartet, all comfortably fitting into the top floor lounge, dining room and balcony.

'Why,' you might ask, 'did you need such a large house?' Easy. We turned the entire ground floor billiard room, bar, one-bedroom and three car spaces into costume and trunk storage and a lovely, spacious workroom. We loved it there, but the house was going to need significant work on the roof, as well as a few other places and we could see it being a never-ending money pit. It was time to sell. In 1999 we bought two beautiful three-storey townhouses off the plan of a big complex going up in the city, changed the plans to link the two ground floors into storage and workroom, and waited only six months for completion. In the meantime, we were packing to move to a rental big enough to store all our junk.

At two o'clock one winter's morning, there was a call from Ron Deschamps in Melbourne. 'Do you know of any ice shows that are available immediately?' No, Ron, dear, never had anything to do with ice shows. It turned out Ron's niece Kelli Brett, co-owner of Metropolis Productions in Dubai, along with her husband Jonathan, were badly let down by an English ice show, and needed a replacement ASAP. Always a go-getter, this brave, diminutive woman went to Dubai years ago, long before it was acceptable for single women to be working in very public places in an all-male, very macho Arabic environment. She secured a job in a bar in one of the five-star hotels along the Dubai Creek, and with sheer tenacity, and after taking control of, and running, all the bars in the hotel, left to start Metropolis. This production company was also an agency and supplied a great many of the better upmarket venues with bands, singers, and entertainment.

She'd secured a contract to provide an ice show for the Summer Surprises, an annual event offering winter-style entertainment run by the Dubai Chamber of Commerce in an attempt to keep people from fleeing the country during the scorching heat of summer. This event included ice shows, snow machines in the fifty-degree desert sands, indoor snow skiing, everything wintery imaginable. Metropolis contracted an ice show from England to perform at the Al Nasr Leisureland ice rink/arena for a month. This company reneged on their contract only weeks before the start date, leaving Kelli and Jonathan completely, and utterly up the Dubai Creek with not a paddle in sight. This was not a good thing with a Chamber of Commerce contract and could and would cause massive problems, even to the point of having to wind up and move on.

Ron asked us to call Kelli in Dubai the following day. That phone call somehow led us to say, 'Yes, of course, we can get a fourteen-skater, hour-long, Aladdin on Ice show together.' A little conversation which directed us to one of the most frenzied but delightful times of my life. Firstly, neither Luis nor I had ever had anything to do with ice skating. We possessed nothing in the costume department resembling an Aladdin show, we knew no skaters, nor how to get hold of any, and we were bang in the middle of shifting house. Why do we always do this?

First things first. We need to work out what on earth there was in our stores of existing costuming which might, just might, fit the bill. Secondly, sketch out, and send set and prop designs so Metropolis can get started on building them. Third, find skaters. Where do you find skaters? At the local ice rink, of course. A quick look at opening times, a phone call to enquire when the busiest time was, into the car, and go. Luis' vast experience as a professionally trained dancer and choreographer, not to mention his Spanish Junior Champion roller skater status way back in the day, would surely help us work out who could skate and who couldn't. What a dismal lot those patrons were. After eliminating the soggy-bottomed, the horizontal, the windmillers, and the edge clingers, there were mighty few left who looked like they knew what they were doing. Two in particular stood out, both girls who looked as though they might be instructors and seemed to be in charge of little groups of struggling but determined children. A word with the manager of the rink verified this, and introductions were arranged during their next break.

One of the girls, Ruth, was an Australian who indeed had experience in ice shows. The other one, whose name I have conveniently – and gratefully – forgotten was an American. She also possessed ice show experience and was a former Disney skater. We are positively getting somewhere. This ex-Disney girl was very quick to point out, in her opinion, we hadn't a hope of getting together fourteen professional figure skaters with experience of shows in such a short time. She was a little dismissive of Australian skaters on the whole, saying we'd 'be lucky to find fourteen adequately experienced skaters in all of Australia'. This seemed a little negative, but time was of the essence. A meeting was arranged with her and her American skater husband. The result was, she'd offer telephone numbers, and contacts with Disney in America, in exchange for her becoming a principal skater and assistant choreographer, and hubby a character skater and head of props. All this for an exorbitant amount of dollars. Well, we were in a massive hole, so after much discussion over five minutes, we called her back, and reluctantly agreed.

A start was made. At that point there was a producer/set designer/costume designer (me), a director/choreographer (Luis), an assistant choreographer, prop master and three skaters, Ruth was also recommended and approached, and we were only two days in. Wow, this is moving right along. The telephone number proved to be of Feld Entertainment's Casting Director Judy Thomas. Feld owns the Disney Ice Shows under licence to Disney. Judy turned out to be sympathetic and sweet. She wanted nothing in return for sending us names and contacts of all skaters usually under contract who were currently on a break. Later, when Judy and her husband visited us, she told me she'd done a bit of digging and discovered we were a well-respected, bona fide, international entertainment company. So, we ended up with quite a list of skaters in the US, Canada and England who might be interested. This took at least another four days of constant phone calls at odd hours but for the most part, more than enough skaters were interested whose asking price was not out of the question. We ended up with the eleven more we needed, plus some contingency backups. Furthermore, the skaters who agreed turned out to be mostly Disney soloists, and even a line director. Pick of the bunch, I'd say.

Now the real fun started. Visa information was specific, and applications needed to be made yesterday. Gathering and collating this information from skaters scattered around the world, then passed on by me to Kelli in Dubai, was an extraordinary effort, and an example of dealing with professionals. Kelli and Jonathan appeared to take everything in their stride, and yet in reality as the clock ticked on, they must have been almost at their wits' end. Never once did we see any hint of annoyance or anger at the many delays which are simply a part of this process. Luckily, this was the beginning of the age of the internet and emails. Set dimensions, designs, progress reports, along with my constant requests for more props, were so much easier to deal with in this new age of communication. We might never have made it only a few years earlier in the snail mail era.

The story was progressing, and we were unashamedly cheating like crazy in an effort not to make too many costumes from scratch while we were in Dubai. Luis and I wracked our brains for costumes on hand that might fit in and came up with the idea of Aladdin and Jasmine going on a honeymoon around the world. That way, oh, clever us, we could incorporate things like a trip to Egypt using costumes from our Egyptian number, a trip to South America using our Inca costumes, a trip to Thailand with the Thai costumes, and so it went on. What could we link all this with? Perfect, a magic carpet ride. The only costumes we needed to make in Dubai was peasant stuff, change the existing costumes into Arabian Nights military-style or baggy harem trousers, Arabic-style sleeveless jackets instead of g-strings and bras, and a lot of hats into turbans. We also needed a glittering finale. Using the costly diamante crowns and feathers, with the addition of some fabric and stuffing would turn them, as well, into more turban-like hats. That's still a whole lot of stuff to make. I tell you, once in Dubai there was very, very, little sleep to be had. I well recall, sitting on the floor surrounded by hats in progress, and slumping over them now and again catching forty winks before more, more and even more sewing, prop and set inspections, production meetings, rehearsal attendances, and the bloody never-ending shopping.

We have always been a very hands-on company. Between us, Luis and I were usually able to do, and run everything from producing, directing, choreographing, designing, making and managing. On this occasion, when time was so very short, we took along some extra help. Ron, who acted as chief cook and bottle washer, made sandwiches and hot drinks for the entire company during the night-time rehearsals. The rink was open to the public during the day. Ron cooked all our meals, sewed during the day, ran errands, and made purchases at the various fabric and haberdashery shops. We also had our darling Antonella who, apart from being adorable, and becoming pretty much the company sweetheart, was an extremely experienced costume maker who sewed tirelessly, and endlessly without complaint. Bless your chosen gods for these two marvellous people.

Jonathan supplied me with a rental car the day after arriving, leaving me to learn the city, and the location of the various shops and shopping centres for the buying of fabrics, haberdashery, beads, sequins, and a slew of other things we needed. That took a bit of doing, and apart from missing the last turn off the freeway into Central Mall and ending up twenty-eight kilometres away in the next UAE State of Sharjah a few times, I got the hang of it reasonably quickly.

I also accompanied Jonathan to the airport to assist with customs clearance when the costumes started arriving. Kelli was flat tack with visas, and meeting flights day and night as people arrived in ones and twos. What a lesson in teamwork it was, and what a production we turned out in the end.

A word on skaters. I have spent my whole working life in the presence of dancers. Now, you would imagine these two art forms, skating and dancing, would produce people of much the same nature and temperament. Well, I too thought that would be the case but no, skaters are a breed unto themselves. I find both dancers and skaters to be kind, thoughtful, sophisticated, and professional, but skaters have a different quality as well. Maybe it's because their work is inherently more dangerous. The ice is hard, and unforgiving, they skate on sharp blades, often moving at high speed, and therefore, need an extra sense, an awareness of where everybody else is on the ice. They always reminded me of highly-strung racehorses just waiting to be let loose. On the bus to the venue, loads of joking, and playful banter was the norm, but as we drew closer to the rink, the level of noise and chatter died down until, as the ice itself was approached, there was a deathly silence.

Each and every skater became totally absorbed in the process of fitting their skates, putting little bits of padding here and there, getting the laces to a perfect tension. It constantly amazed me. Luis always allowed ten to fifteen minutes of free time on the ice to warm up. Total quiet, and absorption was the order of the day. Each skater whizzed off in a different direction, jumping, turning, and spinning. They closed in on each other at speed but, always with complete awareness of each other's position, a sort of radar, they would pass through, by and around each other with effortless ease. I would stop doing whatever I was doing just to watch. It never failed to thrill me.

With this dedicated company of people, the show came together in what must be record time for a production of the size, probably a matter of six weeks or so since the original telephone call from Ron. Kelli, Jonathan and the staff at Metropolis had the paperwork and visas under control. The advertising and press releases were done, the set was constructed, painted, and on the ice, and the props finished. Luis and I had the show ready, lighting was plotted, sound recorded, costumes and hats were made, fitted and hanging in the dressing room.

Luis, as always, did a fabulous job with the choreography, it was down, and rehearsed to within an inch of its life. I must admit, the American assistant choreographer did an excellent job of translating Luis's direction into skaters' parlance. One very peculiar difference reared its head very early on. In the dance world during classes, dancers are taught all movements in both right and left directions with equal ease, not so with skaters. Luis would instruct the skaters to spin to the right or left and instantly, there was much confusion. It turns out individual skaters turn either right or left. Never, or rarely, both directions. This caused a halt in proceedings while left and right turners were sorted out. Lefties and righties had to be pretty much grouped from there on in so he wouldn't have to remember just who was comfortable with what.

The last day before opening, a British fireworks company was busy placing fireworks throughout the ice rink, even on the ice itself. There was a certain amount of trepidation regarding fireworks inside a building but, all fears were allayed by the professionals. Kelli and Jonathan were assured all residual smoke from the explosions would be drawn upward towards the ceiling and sucked out by the exhaust fans. Red carpet was laid throughout an entire middle seating section for the royal family, Sheikh Mohammed's aides permanently booked a whole block centre left of the ice. The red carpet was changed daily, I guess Sheiks don't step on anything but new carpet, an Australian company was responsible for its daily removal and re-laying. Nice little lurk, because I'm sure the used stuff wasn't thrown away. The magical time arrived, and if anything was forgotten, it was way too late now.

The stadium sold out, the Sheik his family and entourage seated. The skaters were ready, and anxiously chomping at the bit, lights dimmed, music started, and the cue for the pre-show firework display sent swathes of sparkling, multi-coloured swirls, and bursts of fiery light from the ice to the ceiling. It appeared all was going exactly as planned until the entire venue started filling with eye-watering, lung-choking, thick, grey smoke. Obviously, something was not quite right. I peeked around the set, in time to see the Sheik and his family being hastily bustled to the entrance, followed by several thousand patrons. All ignoring the insistent, soothing voice over the speaker system calling for calm, and to stay seated. The entire audience, with watering eyes but remarkable self-control, slowly but surely exited the stadium. It seems one tiny, but very significant fact was overlooked. The freezing cold of the ice drew the smoke downwards rather than upwards, and the smoke very quickly settled into a ground-hugging smog.

Although the skaters were changing in an area off the ice directly behind the set because of time needs, the actual dressing rooms were stage right downstairs. We herded the artists down to these rooms and closed the doors. One of us kept watch upstairs to check on the slow dispersal of the smoke. It was eventually decided the Army should be called in and they used gigantic fans placed either side of the set in an effort to suck the smoke out through the back loading dock doors. After about half an hour, the smoke cleared enough to see and breathe. Some clever skaters, led by Kho Kho (Michael Kho), took hold of large pieces of cloth and skated around flapping at the smoke to help send it up and out. Eventually, it was deemed safe to continue, and the royal family, and the audience were ushered back to their places. The major problems as far as we were concerned were the two great craters which had formed in front of the fans. The fans, being so incredibly powerful, produced enough friction and energy to melt two-metre-by-two-metres patches of ice down to bare concrete.

Belatedly, and with a certain tension, our show began at last. The music started, and away the skaters went. I was working on costume changes, sets and props, and was lucky enough to be able to hide behind the scenery, and watch a lot of the show through peepholes. It all seemed to go very, very well, the audience soon forgave and forgot, and enjoyed the show. They clapped and cheered the goodies, and appropriately booed the baddies. It was over all too quickly. Kelli arranged for the skaters, cast and crew to come onto the ice to be presented with flowers. Cameras flashed from every corner as the Sheik, and his family strode a hastily carpeted walkway onto the ice for a photo opportunity with the cast. The following day's papers and magazines were full of nothing else.

Ahhh, success. As an opening night party, Kelli arranged a trip down the Dubai Creek – which was actually a good-size river by the way – in a traditional Arabic sailing ship or dhow. Tables positively groaned under the weight of the most mouth-watering food, and with booze laid on, all most definitely had a very pleasant and relaxed time. So relaxed, most of us were unaware that shortly after setting sail, the dhow became stranded on a sand bar, and took three hours to be towed off.

CHAPTER 47

50 DEGREES AND ICE EVERYWHERE

Dubai is truly astonishing. The second largest of the seven states that make up the UAE, it is located on a peninsula of the southeast coast of the Persian Gulf. Surrounded by water, the humidity can reach 50%, and in summer the temperature regularly passes the fifty-degree mark. Public announcements of temperatures higher than 50 degrees are illegal because workers are allowed to stop work on full pay. Dubai, with its twenty-four-hour per day construction boom, is choc-a-block with many thousands of poorly paid migrant workers. Ten minutes outside of Dubai is nothing but oceans of sand. Yet, the city is green and blooming, nurtured by desalinated water.

I loved every minute I spent there during my three visits. Down by the Gold Souk in the old district known as Deira, it is possible to stand on any street corner for several hours people watching. Stand there long enough, and you'll see every form of fantastic ethnic dress go by. Statuesque African women with towering colourful headgear and matching wrapped dresses, exquisite Indian women in finely patterned saris with their multi pleated fronts and colour coordinated blouses, black clad Arab women with fine beaten copper masks covering eyes, nose and mouth. Males are not outdone, with a vast array of ballooned trousered gents with carefully gathered cummerbunds, wearing hats, turbans and head coverings of every description. The covered wood supported Gold Souk itself attracts dowry shopping brides and tourists alike. Many of the quaint shops dealing in gold, platinum, diamonds and silver are up to fifty years old, and specialise in traditional wedding jewellery.

Depending on the depth of your pocket, earrings, bracelets and necklaces extended as far as the waist.

Between 1999 and 2004, we produced three shows in conjunction with Metropolis: two ice shows, the first one being Aladdin on Ice and then Sinbad on Ice, and an open-air panto, Cinderella. During that time, it was already quite staggering to witness the extraordinary growth and speed of development, and the push into the desert. It's incredible to think only sixty or so years ago, armed tribesmen were riding out on horseback from the Al Fahidi Fort in Deira against tribesmen from nearby Sharjah. Today this fort is a museum and disappears amongst kilometre after kilometre of fabulous, and innovative high-rise hotels, office blocks, apartments and shopping centres.

Dubai is what's termed a semi-dry, or semi-wet I guess, State—meaning that alcohol is readily available in venues but can't be obtained by the public in retail outlets. The next wet state, where booze can be bought at bottle shops is Sharjah, but to get there you have to pass through Ajman, which is totally dry. Therefore, people drive to Sharjah, fill their cars with alcohol, and drive back to Dubai. Sometimes the police in Ajman sit near the entrance to the freeway from Sharjah looking for vehicles travelling low at the back—because the boots are full of plonk. They either arrest the occupants, relieve them of their shopping or both. You might think it's only infidels who are drinking in the multitude of bars, clubs and discos, but no. As long as locals are wearing Western dress, they feel they are no longer bound by the laws of Islam. It's 'go for your life'.

Kelli and Jonathan took us all to a bar called Trader Vic's which is done out in pigs-blood-stamped bark walls, or a facsimile thereof, emulating the original Trader Vic's. Super potent cocktails are served in vases, large pots, urns, anything at all, and each is guaranteed to contain no less than a litre of spirits. Multiple metre-long straws are provided for all at the table, and he who sucks hardest gets pissed the quickest.

I loved the Jumeira coastline—that section of Dubai housing many executive ex-pats and their pampered, wealthy, bored wives. These Jumeirah Janes, as they are collectively known, look like cookie-cutter copies of each other, with their perfectly manicured hands, their salon-fresh streaked and bleached hair, their impeccable makeup, and expensive cars—all undoubtedly on the way to yet another boozy lunch or committee meeting.

On one occasion, our entire company took off after a performance, for night-time dune bashing in 4×4s, followed by a desert oasis smorgasbord and belly dance show complete with barrels of booze of every description. Tents were set up in a circle, and straw-filled palliasse style mattresses were at hand to pass out on. There were racks of national dress to don if you cared to, flowing white robes and headdress for the guys, full black burqa for the girls. Might as well go whole hog, some of us certainly got into the spirit. If the film that Kho Kho made of himself, Kevin and the gorgeous Barb Tapia ever got out, we might all have fatwas pronounced against us. Entertainment was supplied by a belly dancer, who was furious when she hauled different cast members to their feet to join her and was out-danced by each and every one.

Our first time in Dubai was fast drawing to a close, and it was hard to say goodbye to our skaters of whom we had become particularly fond. The show was a tremendous success, and Kelli and Jonathan were more than pleased. We threw a farewell party at Planet Hollywood, and some tears flowed along with the booze. It seemed we had been there no time at all and considering what we had all achieved in that short period, I'm amazed we were all still vertical.

Luis and I had searched Dubai for miniature brass Aladdin lamps, and managed to find enough for the entire cast and crew. We had them all individually engraved and gave them out that night. It was a touching moment. Everybody took their separate flights to their various destinations, and we were off back to our rental via Brunei. Another chapter done.

Happily, within two years we found ourselves back in Dubai, and were fortunate enough to get much the same cast, and a lot more time to prepare Sinbad on Ice. How wonderful to see the skaters again and Sinbad was every bit a success as Aladdin. Still, the houses were down owing to Kelli not having control of advertising and PR. That's always a problem. You do a fabulous job and make it look easy, and other people think, 'Oh, we can do that,' and louse it up. The Chamber of Commerce took over the PR side of things, and there wasn't a quarter of the free press we'd had before. Their problem, not ours.

Just a shame. This time, instead of mixed seating, they went all Muslim on us and split the arena into three groups. Married with family, single females and single males. That put a damper on the spontaneity but, once again, not our problem. The costumes were designed and made in Perth, only some hats needed to be made in Dubai.

I designed a huge ship for Sinbad, and Metropolis did a tremendous job of building it. I took great care in designing the dhow, getting the swooping bow and the high stern right, the placement and the angle of the single mast and of the furled lateen rigged sail exactly where they should be. The design of this type of craft is ancient and is still used today having changed little in centuries. Getting it just so was important if it was to be presented to the eyes and scrutiny of the local populace. It was people-powered, 10 skaters were inside, five on each side with no floor, a la Fred Flintstone. These ten skaters pushed the ship around the ice, stopping at an island at the opposite end to pick up passengers, kids from the audience, and take them for a spin. It was hard work, but nobody complained, and the effect was magical.

Dubai had noticeably grown in the years since Aladdin, and some of the charm was slipping away. Traffic was, if possible, even more frenetic. The rule when driving in Dubai is, treat other drivers as though they are out to get you, and get out of the way. A bit like dodgems. Coming back from the venue one night with Luis and Ron on board, I entered a tunnel as a truck overtook me. It cut in too quickly and the truck tray passed over the top of the hood of my car, wiping out my mirror. I tooted, but he sped up, and didn't stop. I sped up as well, following him with my hand on the horn. I wanted to catch him because I was driving a rental car and was in no way inclined to pay for the damage he'd caused. Not far out of the tunnel, we were picked up by a police car that pulled us both over. The truck driver was an Indian and was completely pissed. I could smell the alcohol. I didn't have my licence but we were, by that time, near the hotel, so I rushed in and got it. The last thing I saw was that lunatic being led away.

Due to having a more relaxed pre-production period, we got to see and do a lot more in Dubai. I knew my way around in the car, and it was beginning to feel like home. Again, we no sooner opened than it was all over. Or, it felt that way. Once more, we found ourselves saying emotional goodbyes. I'm happy to say most of the cast members keep in touch. Some, like the delightfully nutty Kho Kho from Toronto, now married with three children and living in Melbourne, and the fabulous Barb Tapia from New Mexico, have become particularly close.

Jump forward yet another two years to 2003, and we found ourselves back in Dubai with Kelli and Jonathan yet again – this time, however, to co-produce a pantomime – Cinderella. Metropolis designed the costumes and sets, and Kelli did a marvellous job writing the dialogue. We found the cast in Australia and were lucky enough to secure the services of well-known comedian Robbie Yule to be one of the Ugly Sisters. We arrived on New Year's Eve, and after settling into our hotel, Kelli had us and the cast picked up in two stretch limos, providing us all with a leisurely one-hour drive around town before heading out to the Jumeirah Beach Hotel. The hotel put on the most lavish beach side buffet dinner imaginable, followed by fireworks up and down the coast. Incredibly considerate. I was later to remind the cast of this extraordinary generosity a short time into the run, when some complained of being asked by Kelli to give up a few hours on a free evening for some publicity.

Luis was to be the other Ugly Sister, and we hoped his Spanish accent could be explained away. I co-produced with Kelli, and she was amazing to work with, her mind never stops. Such a clear idea of where she wanted to go with it all. I had a wonderful time poking around the bazaars and Indian shops for things I wanted to use, such as ugly sister wigs and props. The stage was to be outdoors in Safa Park and demountable dressing rooms were brought in for the cast. Metropolis had put us in an incredibly well-appointed apartment/hotel near the venue, with swimming pool and full gym, rehearsals were held in the ballroom of another hotel nearby.

I took advantage of these facilities and was working out in the gym every day. Kelli thought it might be a good idea to join me. This woman is a Lilliputian who thinks she's 6ft tall. She was at one time a showgirl and always concerned about her lack of height. I've known her since she was a teenager, and she has always worn the highest heels possible to make up for her shortcomings. On the day she decided to make an appearance at the gym, she was wearing, of course, high heels. The gym management told her it was not policy to allow entrance with that footwear; gym shoes would be required. This tenacious bundle of womanhood scoured Dubai and turned up the next day in what might well have been the only high-heel, wedgie gym shoes in existence. They let her in.

Shortly before Cinderella opened, a press conference was arranged with all Dubai newspapers, magazines and TV, and one of the Sheiklings in attendance. Luis was already booked for sound recording on the day, so it was left to me to take his place. Now, this was to be a full cast in full costume affair. I'm always happy to chuck on a frock, but Luis is five inches shorter than my 6 feet. No matter. There was nobody else to do it. So, I squeezed into that red and green crinoline confection, and it came to just below my knees. Well, Ugly Sister, she will be, in every sense. I threw my makeup on and was about to join the rest of the cast for instruction when I was bailed up by Kelli. 'Listen,' she said. 'I know you, and I know you like a giggle, but … on no account are you to go near the Sheik. He's terrified of the mere thought of drag queens.' Kelli and Jonathan had had to get special permission for men to dress as women in Dubai where any hint of homosexuality or sexual perversion was super-illegal. It was even written into the special visas that the guys playing the Ugly Sisters, were, on no account, to appear off stage in women's clothes.

We were led into the conference room to be confronted by a huge gathering of seated press, TV cameras and photographers. The Sheik was seated behind a table covered with a white cloth, floral arrangements either side and a large bowl of expensive-looking chocolates in the centre. We lined up each side of the table, and it was all very proper and staid. Questions flew in a very ordered fashion, and the whole business was exceptionally dull. Well, I thought, this is not very exciting. They'll be bored to sobs. Won't be much good press comes out of this, I decided to liven things up. First on my list was a visit to the Sheik, who visibly reeled slightly backwards. No, you don't Mr Sheik. With that, I lightly slapped his cheek with my fan and parked myself on his lap, the whole time helping myself to his chocolates, stuffing them down my ample bosom for later, yum. I could see Kelli out of the corner of my eye, mentally – if not physically – shrinking into herself. As it turned out, it was a great success. The Sheik got right into the spirit of the occasion; it was all chaotic, screamed questions and replies, and a great deal of fun. The TV and press lapped it up, and we got some fabulous coverage.

Opening night was upon us and, believe it or not, for the first time in forever, it rained in Dubai. Not good for an outdoor venue. Luckily, the stage was covered, but the wind that whipped up was lifting parts of the set, and the heavily weighted red velvet curtains either side of the proscenium were flapping like so much washing. I ended up clinging to one side of the drawn curtains the entire performance. There was just one other little problem occuring. The night before we opened, I'd asked Jonathan to make sure the stage floor was freshly painted. And it was. Unfortunately, some bright spark had used oil-based paint instead of quick-drying acrylic, and the stage was like glue. Each time someone took a step, you could hear the smack of their shoe unsticking from the stage. The poor mice were less fortunate. They had big, false mouse feet over their shoes; these clung to the floor on their first entrance, and they continued, leaving their mouse feet stuck tight on the floor behind them. Some of the cast were still getting used to the idea of being individually miked, and the sound crew were a little unsure just when to turn cast sound off. I did hear, during the opening performance, a very loud and clear, 'Oh, fuck, the doorknob has come off in my hand.'

Such is the business of live shows. As usual, the front seats were permanently reserved for the royal family and, if they were not in attendance, those seats were left empty. Not fun to perform to a row of empty seats. However, when occupied, it made a strange, otherworldly sight to see just one little princess arriving, accompanied by her extensive retinue of carers, which included a couple of nurses, a doctor, several nannies, and others.

Cinderella had a goodish run for the altered times, and this time it was goodbye forever. The September 11 attacks in the US had altered the freedom and friendliness a great deal, and things were never going to be the same. Kelli and Jonathan packed up and shifted to Spain for a couple of years where Kelli started a radio food program, *The Main Ingredient.* She later successfully transplanted that program to Australia, airing on the ABC—a program for which she won the coveted international award the Golden Ladle. They lived in Melbourne for a couple of years where, as well as being head of regional radio ABC, she wrote a cookbook. Kelli is now the co-owner of the New Zealand upbeat food bible, Cuisine Magazine. There is no stopping this fireball.

These productions in Dubai were very important to us, not because they were in Dubai but, because they'd added another string to our bow as producers. We'd proved to ourselves, and the detractors of the 'showgirl genre' that we had what it took to produce entertainment in different fields. Not only had we successfully produced an ice show under extreme circumstances, but had been invited back for a second innings.

CHAPTER FORTY-EIGHT

TOO MUCH OF A GOOD THING WAS WONDERFUL

In 2001, I reconnected with my very dear friend of twenty-two years Stephen Redding in Melbourne. For many years Stephen produced an annual charity show using the many, and varied talents of airline crews. Quite a few of our ex-dancers became flight attendants at the end of their dancing days so Stephen, being crew himself, drew from the huge talent pool at his fingertips for the Flying Bouffants' Reviews. A great deal of money was raised over the years, and charities such as the Burnett Institute were grateful for the substantial sums they received. The various reviews bore airline appropriate names. 'Airline Rivals for the Inflight Idol', 'Plane Madness' and the '2001 Miss Economy Pageant'. The usual venue was the prestigious Comics Lounge in North Melbourne. Stephen had professional choreographers mount spectacular routines with costumes either designed and made for the occasion or rented from various costume shops around Melbourne. He wrote hilarious, timely social commentary sketches, and produced individual drag numbers. It doesn't take a great deal of cajoling to get your average flight attendant to frock up.

I met Stephen in 1979 when, upon answering a knock at the door, I was confronted by a handsome, broad shouldered, six feet two, eighteen-year-old. 'Hello, I'm Stephen,' the still British-laced voice said. 'I hear two gentlemen with a theatrical company live here.' Oh, you hear that do you? More likely living nearby, you saw some glittery things, and a few lengths of feather boa drying on the line, and like a magpie just had to investigate. Polite introductions over, it appeared Stephen – for reasons unknown – was in need of several metres of feather boa. By some extraordinary coincidence we happened to have quite a few metres of assorted boa lying around. 'Would you care to take a look'. And that was it. A deep and lasting friendship started. Stephen, who relocated to Melbourne some decades ago, is still with the airlines, and having him at the other end of the telephone is a great comfort.

In 2001, Stephen wanted to give the latest Bouffants' show a complete Las Vegas look, so he called me in Perth and asked if he could rent some costumes. The outline of the show sounded wonderful, plus I would get to fly over to Melbourne, stay at his lovely house, do fittings, and lend a hand in the prop department. It sounded like a chance for a great mini holiday, I was only too pleased to say 'yes'. With Stephen producing and directing the gig went smoothly, and the cast was a joy to work with. Mind you, there were moments in Stephen's back yard while doing hard labour with spray paint and hot glue on some very important props, I thought I might well starve to death before a sausage would be carelessly slung at me over the first-floor kitchen balcony. Really, I was treated like the help. The show was a sell-out success over the two-week run, and much needed funds were cheerfully handed over to various charities.

During those few weeks in Melbourne, I thoroughly enjoyed being back to my roots after more than thirty years. Although Luis and I produced a huge show for the New Year's Eve 2000 celebrations at the new inner city Melbourne Queensbridge Hotel venue, there was not a spare minute to play tourist, nor for any feelings or yearning. Stephen and I talked about my returning to Melbourne to live. Perth was great, but it was a small city, and so very isolated. The small Perth social scene gets somewhat incestuous, and after giving it much thought I started making plans to return permanently. Stephen said I was like an old elephant going home to die. Charming, and a little too close to the bone. A decision was made and Luis and I made the shift to Melbourne in February 2003.

I've alluded to the disastrous events of the 2003 SARS outbreak—it cost Luis and me greatly. Our lovely inner-city terrace home in Melbourne was mortgaged, and my precious Rolls Royce sold off to enable us to pay everybody out and send them back to Europe. A lifetime's work gone in a moment. Contractually, we were not responsible to do this, act of god, force majeure, whatever, but we have to sleep at night. That really was the coup de grâce as far as we were concerned when it came to show business. Everything went, fittingly, tits up indeed and very speedily—culminating in my diagnosis of stomach cancer shortly after in February 2004.

I was unable to work during over two years of chemo and recuperation and Luis did everything he could for me. Because Luis was unable to handle the colossal mortgage on his own, we sold our wonderful home.

Devastating. When I had substantially recovered, Luis went back to Spain to care for his ageing, recently blind mother, and I took on other financially disastrous business dealings, including, the iconic Melbourne cabaret bar, The Opium Den. It collapsed spectacularly, as did most of the other gay venues around Melbourne over the following year. So, the entrepreneurial side of me went back into its shell. I worked at the State Theatre in Melbourne, mainly with Opera Australia and Australian Ballet until my retirement at 69, when I began writing this cathartic, and significantly healing book.

For two unschooled young guys – I say unschooled rather than uneducated because, although we both had only a basic formal education – we became incredibly knowledgeable in the ways of the world. Imagine daring to dream of taking typical European/Las Vegas style shows from Australia on extended world tours? It was an outrageous, if not laughable concept. But the young know no fear, and we didn't hesitate to take on the European market. The ups and downs, the frustrations and the knockbacks were at times, overwhelming. Possessing nothing else in the way of training or passion to fall back on, neither of us knew anything but what we were doing. That is how we overcame all odds. We presented what we considered to be the cream of entertainment, quality, and value. No expense was spared, and it was class, style, and panache all the way. We never entertained any thoughts of seeking financial backing, either privately or through Government grants. This was the first self-funded international Australian touring shows of any genre.

I have witnessed productions losing all control by going down the outside funding street, and we were never going to give away a single inch of our domain. If a production is presented and results in packed audiences, then that show gets noticed. We hold the record for Australian productions appearing in Europe, and I dare say we will for decades to come.

Retirement for me means it's over, forget it. I know of so many theatre people who simply can't let go. Always contemplating accepting just one more job offer, attending every opening night as though they still belonged, offering a helping hand to amateur groups and being thoroughly disappointed. For me, when something is done, it's done. I turned my back on the theatre and have quite contentedly gone about my still busy life without a second's hesitation.

At 70, I took up archery which is perfect for the perfectionist because it can never be perfected. There is always that stray arrow needing attention. Why did it go off course? Does my release need work? Perhaps the bow needs re-tuning. I can waste an entire day on this minutiae. For five years, I was secretary of our local club, Chewton Archers, and I frustrated the entire committee by taking hours to take minutes. There is always something at the club, or on the grounds needing tinkering with. I also have my own little 50m range at my home in the bush, my many misses give the local choughs and kangaroos something to watch out for.

There is a local animal welfare association, MAAW (Mount Alexander Animal Welfare), where I have spent some time dredging up my old window dressing skills, slapping a coat of paint on here, mending the odd breakage there, chatting to the manager and friend Tania, and the many dedicated volunteers, making a thorough nuisance of myself. If only the Government understood the number of hours put in by volunteers Australia wide. We are not welfare recipients sitting on our arses collecting taxpayer money. We are retirees, the weaver ants of society. We pin together the edges of the unfunded gaps, making them whole, meshing them into the overall tapestry that is humanity.

Luis and I take advantage of today's technology and chat several times a week on the magical WhatsApp. We were born in the first half of last century when only the middle and upper classes possessed telephones. Yet, here we are, having face to face conversations on the opposite sides of the world. What an age. Luis visits when he can, his last visit was on my 70th birthday. I, Scrooge-like, guard my pennies, and visit him when possible. Covid 19 took its toll on our trips but I considered it far enough behind us in 2022 to visit Spain for Luis's 80th birthday. Such an important milestone.

In 2018, I managed a trip to Spain. It was twenty-five years since I last saw Madrid, never my favourite city. I much preferred Barcelona with its harbour, and the great homogenous international population that port cities attract. Madrid was very Spanish which means I would remain a foreigner no matter how long I stayed. Also, during the early days, it was still very much a Franco city. The neglect was getting to the point of beyond salvation. Most buildings long ago lost all but the faintest hint of paintwork, and many were being propped up with great lengths of wood as thick as telegraph poles.

On my last visit, all was fresh paint and lively colours. Many streets were closed to traffic and planted up with magnificent shady trees and banks of flowers. There seemed to be no public rubbish bins, I have no idea what the local populace and the millions of tourists were doing with their trash, but the streets were spotless. Obviously, they were doing as I was, hanging onto it until I got home. Now I always think of Madrid as beautiful.

Luis and I have always had a friendly rivalry concerning weight gain. Weight is very important in the showgirl world as audiences pay good money to see perfection. A kilo here or there either side of the ideal weight written into contracts was frowned upon. On pay nights, I sat with a pair of scales beside me. Each dancer was weighed before signing the pay book. One dollar per kilo per day was the standard fine. The fine money went into a kitty to pay for some sort of fun, maybe Christmas or a special event. Weight, tan marks, even the marks left by the elastic in underwear are all things a cabaret dancer is mindful of. For that very reason, I have always eaten well, exercised daily, and watched my weight. I've managed to stay at 85ks my entire adult life. The idea always was, if I can do it, I can expect others to do it too, a fair thing. However, retirement, especially with the dreaded Covid kilos, puts a certain strain on nature. Indeed, I am now a few kilograms heavier, two-ish to be exact. Gravity has its way, and the altered displacement makes for a drastic change in the silhouette. So, whether I'm visiting Luis or vice versa, the first cab off the rank is a hug. This, I've *missed you so much,* hug is the perfect excuse for a quick, discreet, tactile reconnoitre over familiar territory. This delicate, nimble-fingered manoeuvre must be performed without a word spoken. It decides who gets to occupy the high ground for the duration of the visit.

The days, weeks, and years race by. I thank the gods of the internet for FaceBook, because the idea of being accessible, and up to date with the goings-on of my very dear family of artists scattered around the world is wonderful. I marvel to watch my family of dancers, still in contact with each other, still chatting about their dance careers when those times are well and truly in the past, and longer careers have taken their place. I'm delighted Luis and I have played a part in ensuring so many people have such long-lasting friendships. In many cases, they met their partners overseas, and moved on to foreign countries to live, or stayed exactly where they met. We have ex-AIE artists living in Italy, America, England, the US, Canada, Argentina, Egypt, Spain, Bali and other exotic places. Wonderful to see the husbands, the wives, the children and – this pains me – the grandchildren. I guess this is our legacy. To have provided so many darling people with a means to see the world and develop lifelong friendships. Joy to each and every one of them.

I live alone in the bush at Campbells Creek in the heart of the old gold mining district near Castlemaine, an hour and a half from Melbourne. The mansion has gone, the house full of precious furniture collected from around the world is gone, the paintings and sculptures gone, as well as the Jags and the Rolls. Luis lives in Spain, so he's gone too, I guess. Of my three darling cats, I lost little Rita aged 23, Sheba went aged 25, and Possum, the most incredible friend ever, went in 2018, aged 21. You can't hang onto the three 'Ps'—people, pets and possessions. At seventy-six, I am extremely content. I avoid the word happy as happiness is ephemeral, it comes and goes. Contentedness, however, is achievable.

With the writing of this book, my amazing memories are now forever in print. I don't feel the need or desire to taste anything new, having gorged on lotus for the longest time.

The author with best friend Possum, 2018.

AUTHOR'S NOTE

During the 33 years that Australian International Entertainment (A.I.E.) was active, we toured constantly. There were up to three productions at a time on the road and I, as producer and manager, visited each production. Sometimes I stayed a day, sometimes several months. Therefore, to make the reading of this book more cohesive, I have combined anecdotes and events occurring in a particular country or time together. To the artists, I know there are so very many more stories to be told. Unfortunately, there is a limit to the size of this tome and I think volumes 2, 3 and 4 will remain unwritten.

Tom Robb is an Australian costume and set designer, sculptor, artist, entrepreneur and producer.

This memoir tells his story from a poor childhood in Ballarat to his amazing life from 1970 to 2003 as co-owner (along with his partner Luis Moreno) and producer of Australian International Entertainment (A.I.E.). Together Tom and Luis presented Las Vegas/Moulin Rouge style cabarets in more than sixty cities through twenty-one countries and were dubbed the greatest touring shows in the world. Tom now lives in retirement in Castlemaine Victoria.

ACKNOWLEDGEMENTS

I would sincerely like to thank the following people for their support and generosity during the writing of this book. Without them, I may well have flushed the entire tome down the loo, page by page.

My development editor, the delightful, and at times pushy, Sherri McIver.

Copy editor Kim Bear, whose enthusiasm for this work got me past the post.

The silently suffering Meg Clancy who went patiently through the first draft wearing hobnail boots.

To the magnificent artists who worked for A.I.E.

We, as producers, directors, costume designers, choreographers and managers are wasting our time without artists. Some of you stayed for years, others a single contract, but you were all a joy to work with. You took your work so very seriously. Being away from home for so long with such young people, there could be expected to be major discipline problems. But no, never a hint of misbehaviour or scandal. You made us proud and we counted ourselves lucky indeed.

Thank you all.

Special thanks to Patricia and Fraser for their kindness and generosity.

www.ingramcontent.com/pod-product-compliance
Ingram Content Group UK Ltd.
Pitfield, Milton Keynes, MK11 3LW, UK
UKHW062314290726
14090UKWH00018B/1065